Adobe® Illustrator® CS2

CLASSROOM IN A BOOK®

www.adobepress.com

Adobe

Adobe Press books are published by Peachpit, Berkeley, CA. To report errors, please send a note to errata@peachpit.com.

Printed in the USA

ISBN 0-321-32183-9

9 8 7 6

Adobe

Dear Adobe Illustrator CS2 users,

Welcome to *Adobe Illustrator CS2 Classroom in a Book*, the official training workbook for the drawing program that has long set the standard for creating graphically rich content that can go anywhere— print, the web, motion graphics, and now mobile devices.

With this edition, you're in for a real treat—Illustrator CS2 has some amazing new features to discover. Lesson 1 introduces you to the new context-sensitive Control palette, which gives you access to over 80% of Illustrator's controls from one compact location. Lesson 5 shows you my favorite, Live Trace, a new vector tracing feature that is stunningly easy and fast—a single click lets you turns pixels to vectors in seconds. And in Lesson 5 you'll also see how to use Live Paint to color your designs intuitively, without worrying about how they were built.

Whether you're new to Illustrator or consider yourself a seasoned pro, I'm sure you'll find something new to learn—and love—in this comprehensive guide to Illustrator CS2.

Thanks for believing in Illustrator and the power of vector graphics.

Best regards,

Terry Hemphill
Adobe Illustrator Senior Product Marketing Manager

What's on the CD *

Here is an overview of the contents of the Classroom in a Book CD

Lesson files . . . and so much more

The *Adobe Illustrator CS2 Classroom in a Book* CD includes the lesson files that you'll need to complete the exercises in this book, as well as other content to help you learn more about Adobe Illustrator and use it with greater efficiency and ease. The diagram below represents the contents of the CD, which should help you locate the files you need.

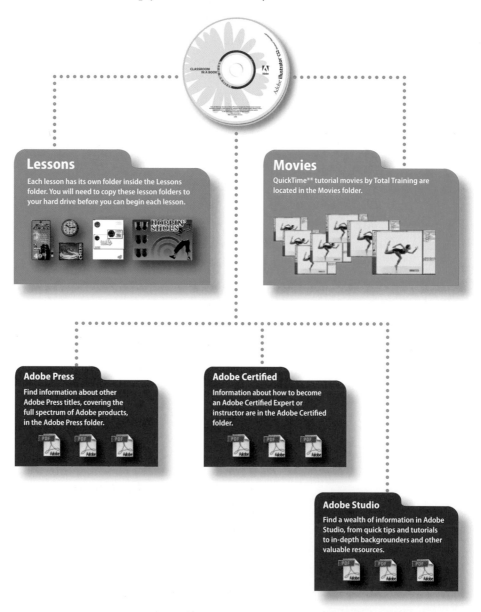

Lessons

Each lesson has its own folder inside the Lessons folder. You will need to copy these lesson folders to your hard drive before you can begin each lesson.

Movies

QuickTime** tutorial movies by Total Training are located in the Movies folder.

Adobe Press

Find information about other Adobe Press titles, covering the full spectrum of Adobe products, in the Adobe Press folder.

Adobe Certified

Information about how to become an Adobe Certified Expert or instructor are in the Adobe Certified folder.

Adobe Studio

Find a wealth of information in Adobe Studio, from quick tips and tutorials to in-depth backgrounders and other valuable resources.

*** The latest version of Apple QuickTime can be downloaded from www.apple.com/support/downloads/quicktime652.html.*

Contents

Lesson 1

Getting to Know the Work Area

Lesson 2

Selections and Shapes

Lesson 3

Transforming Objects

Lesson 4

Drawing with the Pen tool

Lesson 5   **Color and Painting**

Lesson 11

**Applying Appearance Attributes,
Graphic Styles, and Effects**

Lesson 13

**Combining Illustrator CS2 Graphics
with the Creative Suite**

Lesson 14

Printing Artwork and Producing Color Separations

Lesson 15   **Working with Adobe Bridge and Version Cue**

Getting started

Adobe® Illustrator® is the industry-standard illustration program for print, multimedia, and online graphics. Whether you are a designer or a technical illustrator producing artwork for print publishing, an artist producing multimedia graphics, or a creator of web pages or online content, the Adobe Illustrator program offers you the tools you need to get professional-quality results.

About Classroom in a Book

Adobe Illustrator CS2 Classroom in a Book® is part of the official training series for Adobe graphics and publishing software from Adobe Systems, Inc.

The lessons are designed so that you can learn at your own pace. If you're new to Adobe Illustrator, you'll learn the fundamentals you need to master to put the program to work. If you are an experienced user, you'll find that *Classroom in a Book* teaches many advanced features, including tips and techniques for using the latest version of Adobe Illustrator.

Although each lesson provides step-by-step instructions for creating a specific project, there's room for exploration and experimentation. You can follow the book from start to finish, or do only the lessons that correspond to your interests and needs. Each lesson concludes with a review section summarizing what you've covered.

Prerequisites

Before beginning to use *Adobe Illustrator CS2 Classroom in a Book*, you should have a working knowledge of your computer and its operating system. Make sure you know how to use the mouse and standard menus and commands, and also how to open, save, and close files. If you need to review these techniques, see the printed or online documentation included with your Windows or Mac OS documentation.

Note: When instructions differ by platform, Windows commands appear first, and then the Mac OS command, with the platform noted in parentheses. For example, "press Alt (Windows) or Option (Mac OS) and click away from the artwork." Common commands may be further abbreviated with the Windows command first, followed by a slash and the Mac OS commands, without any parenthetical reference. For example, "press Alt/Option" or "Ctrl/Command+click."

Installing the program

Before you begin using *Adobe Illustrator CS2 Classroom in a Book*, make sure that your system is set up correctly and that you've installed the required software and hardware.

You must purchase the Adobe Illustrator CS2 software separately. For complete instructions on installing the software, see the "How to Install" file on the application CD.

Installing the Classroom in a Book fonts

The Classroom in a Book lesson files use the fonts that installed with Adobe Illustrator CS2. If it is necessary to reinstall these font files, you can perform a custom installation from your Adobe Illustrator software CD to reinstall only the fonts. See the "How to Install" file on the application CD.

Copying the Classroom in a Book files

The Classroom in a Book CD includes folders containing all the electronic files for the lessons. Each lesson has its own folder. You must install these folders on your hard disk to use the files for the lessons. To save room on your hard disk, you can install the folders for each lesson as you need them.

To install the Classroom in a Book files

1   Insert the *Adobe Illustrator CS2 Classroom in a Book* CD into your CD-ROM drive.

2   Create a folder on your hard disk and name it AICIB.

3   Do one of the following:

- Copy the Lessons folder into the AICIB folder.

- Copy only the single lesson folder you need.

Restoring default preferences

The preferences file controls how palettes and command settings appear on your screen when you open the Adobe Illustrator program. Each time you quit Adobe Illustrator, the position of the palettes and certain command settings are recorded in the preferences file. If you want to restore the tools and palettes to their original default settings, you can delete the current Adobe Illustrator CS2 preferences file. Adobe Illustrator creates a preferences file, if one doesn't already exist, the next time you start the program and save a file.

You must restore the default preferences for Illustrator before you begin each lesson. This ensures that the tools and palettes function as described in this book. When you have finished the book, you can restore your saved settings.

To save your current Illustrator preferences

1   Exit Adobe Illustrator CS2.

2   Locate the AIPrefs (Windows) or Adobe Illustrator Preferences (Mac OS), as follows.

• In Windows, the AIPrefs is located in the Document and Settings\username\ Application Data\Adobe\Adobe Illustrator CS2 Settings folder.

Note: You may have to choose Folder Options from the Control panel to show hidden files to locate this preference, from the Folder Options window, click on Views. Check the radio button to the left of Show Hidden Files or Folders.

• In Mac OS X, it is located in the Mac OS X\Users\Home\Library\Preferences\Adobe Illustrator CS2 Settings folder.

Note: If you cannot locate the preferences file, use your operating system's Find command, and search for AIPrefs (Windows) or Adobe Illustrator Preferences (Mac OS).

If you can't find the file, either you haven't started Adobe Illustrator CS2 yet or you have moved the preferences file. The preferences file is created after you quit the program the first time, and is updated thereafter.

3   Rename the AIPrefs file (Windows) or Adobe Illustrator Prefs file (Mac OS), if you want to save them, otherwise, delete the file.

4   Start Adobe Illustrator CS2.

Note: To locate and delete the Adobe Illustrator preferences file quickly each time you begin a new lesson, create a shortcut (Windows) or an alias (Mac OS) for the Illustrator CS2 Settings folder.

To restore your saved settings after completing the lessons

1   Exit Adobe Illustrator CS2.

2   In the Adobe Illustrator CS2 Settings folder delete the current AIPrefs (Windows) file or Adobe Illustrator Prefs file (Mac OS) and return the original file to it's original name.

Note: You can relocate the original preferences file rather than renaming it.

Additional resources

Adobe Illustrator CS2 Classroom in a Book is not meant to replace documentation that comes with the program. Only the commands and options used in the lessons are explained in this book. For comprehensive information about program features, refer to these resources:

•   Illustrator Help, which you can view by choosing Help > Illustrator Help. (For more information, see Lesson 1, "Getting to Know the Work Area.") If you have installed the entire Creative Suite, you can also access Help for all applications from the Adobe Bridge application.

•   Training and support resources on the Adobe Web site, Adobe.com, which you can view by choosing Help > Online Support if you have a connection to the Internet.

Adobe Certification

The Adobe Training and Certification Programs are designed to help Adobe customers improve and promote their product-proficiency skills. The Adobe Certified Expert (ACE) program is designed to recognize the high-level skills of expert users. Adobe Certified Training Providers (ACTP) use only Adobe Certified Experts to teach Adobe software classes. Available in either ACTP classrooms or on site, the ACE program is the best way to master Adobe products. For Adobe Certified Training Programs information, visit the Partnering with Adobe Web site at partners.Adobe.com.

What's New in Adobe Illustrator CS2

Illustrator CS2 is packed with new and innovative features to help you produce artwork more efficiently, whether that be for print, web, or wireless publication. Here we've included a brief explanation of many new features, and included references to particular lessons where you can learn more about them.

Control palette

Using the new contextually sensitive Control palette, you can streamline your workflow and find many of the attributes you need quickly and easily, without accessing multiple palettes. Using text fields, you can enter numerical values for items such as strokes and opacity, or click to be linked to the appropriate palette, such as Fill, and Opacity. The Control palette is referenced thoughout many of the lessons.

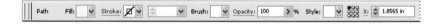

Workspaces

Adobe Illustrator CS2 now allows you to organize palettes for your workflow and save the workspace (visible palettes and their location on screen) to a named file. You are also able to load any given Workspaces file, and select from a default list of available pre-configured options. Dual display setups are also supported. Read more about Workspaces in Lesson 1, "Getting to Know the Work Area."

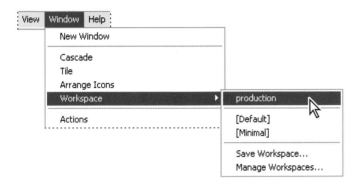

Live Trace

Converting Raster images to vector is easy with Live Trace. The Live Trace feature allows you to take raster images, and to trace-convert them into vector art.

Adobe Illustrator CS2 smartly traces raster images, using the least amount of points, and produces artwork that looks as close to the original as you like. Using the Live Trace options, you can choose to use a particular palette of colors for the image, or extract a palette from the raster artwork.

In addition, with Live Trace you can change the trace settings as many times as you like, to create the effect you are looking for. You can even edit the original image and Illustrator automatically updates the traced raster image. Read more about Live Trace in "A Quick Tour of Adobe Illustrator CS2" and Lesson 5, "Color and Painting."

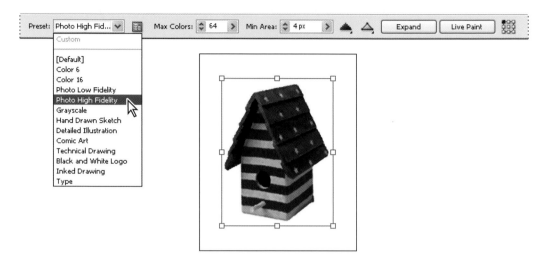

Live Paint

With Live Paint, gain a paint-like experience in the vector world, with all the benefits and intuitiveness of paint, and the power of vector.

The Live Paint Bucket tool (⬧) automatically detects regions composed of independent intersecting paths and fills them accordingly. The paint within a given region remains live, and flows automatically, even if any of the paths are moved. The Live Paint Bucket also paints strokes (if enabled in the Live Paint Bucket options), detecting stroke segment regions resulting from independent intersecting paths. As with fills, the color of a stroke flows as the intersecting regions are changed.

A companion feature to the Live Paint Bucket is support for Gap Detection. With this feature, Illustrator is able to automatically and dynamically detect, and close, small/undesired gaps that may be part of the artwork. Users have a choice in determining whether they actually want paint to flow across region gap boundaries. Read more about Live Paint and Gap Detection in Lesson 5, "Color and Painting."

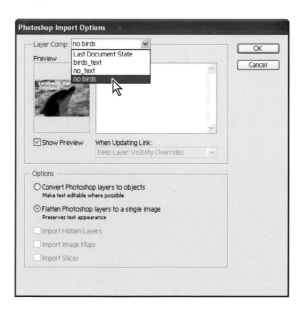

Photoshop import enhancements

You can now specify in Illustrator's Place dialog window which Layer Comps you want to import. Simply save a Photoshop file with a number of saved Layer Comps; upon placing the file, the import window automatically appears. Read more about importing images in "A Quick Tour of Adobe Illustrator CS2."

Spot-color rasters

In Illustrator CS2, you have the ability to preserve spot color rasters in live effects including: Rasterize, Feather, Inner/Outer Glow, Gaussian blur, and Radial blur in both CMYK and RGB document color spaces

You also have the ability to colorize an embedded grayscale image with one spot or process color, in either CMYK or RGB document color spaces. Read more about spot color in Lesson 14, "Printing Artwork and Producing Color Separations," learn about Effects in Lesson 11, "Applying Appearance Attributes, Graphic Styles, and Effects."

SVG 1.1 support

Illustrator CS2 has the ability to import and export to SVG 1.1 format, and includes support for profiles such as Tiny, Basic, and Full.

In addition, Illustrator CS2 includes features that produce cleaner SVG output, and enhanced maintenance of elements and attributes.

Offset paths

Illustrator CS2 provides the ability to offset stroke alignment around a path. It is now possible to offset the path to either be completely inside a path, or completely outside, with the default still the center of the stroke. Find these new options in the Stroke palette. Learn more about Strokes in Lesson 5, "Color and Painting."

Underline text and strikethrough

Those of you who have been working in Illustrator for many versions will be happy to discover that Illustrator CS2 allows you to underline, and strikethrough text. Read more about text features in Lesson 6, "Working with Type."

While this list is by no means an exhaustive description of the new features of Illustrator CS2, it exemplifies Adobe's commitment to providing the best tools possible for your publishing needs. We hope you enjoy working with Illustrator CS2 as much as we do.

—**The Adobe Illustrator CS2 Classroom in a Book Team**

This interactive demonstration of Adobe Illustrator CS2 is designed to give an overview of new and exciting features in the program. You will discover new features like Live Trace and Live Paint, and learn key fundamentals of the program.

A Quick Tour of Adobe Illustrator CS2

This interactive demonstration of Adobe Illustrator CS2 is designed to give an overview of the program and some of the exciting new features in about an hour.

Getting started

You will work with one file during this tour. All art files are located on the *Adobe Classroom in a Book* CD that is located on the inside back cover of this book. Make sure that you copy the AICIB folder from the CD to your hard drive before starting this exercise. Before you begin, you need to restore the default preferences for Adobe Illustrator CS2. Then you'll open the finished art file for this lesson to see what you will create on your own.

Note: If you are new to Adobe Illustrator or to vector-drawing applications, you might want to begin with Lesson 1, "Getting to Know the Work Area."

1 To ensure that the tools and palettes function exactly as described in this tour, delete or deactivate (by renaming) the Adobe Illustrator CS2 preferences file. See "Restoring default preferences" on page 3.

2 Start Adobe Illustrator CS2. When the Welcome Screen appears, choose Open Document, or select File > Open.

3 Open the tour_done.ai file in the Lesson00 folder located inside the Lessons folder within the AICIB folder on your hard drive. If a Missing Profile warning appears, click OK.

Note: The tour file uses an OpenType font named Chaparral Pro. Illustrator CS2 comes with many OpenType fonts for you to use. OpenType is an exciting advancement in font technology. Read more about OpenType in Lesson 6, "Working with Type."

Zoom Out to make the finished artwork smaller, and leave it on your screen as you work. Use the Hand tool (✋) to reposition the artwork to the upper left of the window, then drag the lower right corner of the document window to make the window smaller. If you don't want to leave the image open as you work, choose File > Close.

The completed Tour illustration.

1   For the tour file, you will start with a blank document. Create a new document in Adobe Illustrator by choosing File > New or by using the keyboard shortcut Ctrl+N (Windows) or Command+N (Mac OS).

2   When the New Document window appears, leave the defaults settings unchanged and click OK. A new blank document window appears.

3   Choose View > Show Rulers, or use the keyboard shortcut Ctrl+R (Windows) or Command+R (Mac OS) to show rulers on the top and left part of your artboard.

4   Select the Rectangle tool (▭) and click once on the artboard; do not click and drag. The Rectangle window appears.

5   Enter the Width value **600 pt**, and the Height **50 pt**, then click OK. A rectangle appears on the page. You will reposition it on your page in the next step.

With any shape tool, you can click once on the artboard to enter exact values for the shape.

*Note: If your document is not measuring in increments of points, you can still enter "pt"
after the value to create the rectangle in points.*

6   Choose Window > Transform to view the Transform palette. The Transform palette
allows you to enter exact coordinates for vertical and horizontal placement as well as
other transformations. This palette is discussed in Lesson 3, "Transforming Objects."

Using the Selection tool (➤), click and drag the rectangle to the upper part of the page.
Use the Transform palette to enter an exact location. Click once in the upper left corner
of the Point of reference indicator (▦), then type in an x coordinate of **6 pt** and a y
coordinate of **675 pt**. Press Enter.

*Enter Coordinates in the
Transform palette.*

7   Choose File > Save. In the Save As window, enter the name **hopping.ai**. Leave the
file format set to Adobe Illustrator, and click Save. In the Illustrator Options window,
leave the options at their defaults and click OK.

Setting up the blend

Create a duplicate, or clone, of your rectangle, so that you have a shape to start and
finish the gradient blend.

1   Click once on the rectangle with the Selection tool (➤), then hold down the Alt
(Windows) or Option (Mac OS) key. Click on the rectangle and drag it toward the
bottom of the page. Notice that the cursor changes to a double cursor (➤➤). Release the
mouse first, then the Alt/Option key. A copy appears, leaving the original intact.

2   Using the Transform palette, make sure the reference point is still in the upper left corner and type in the x coordinate text box **6 pt**, and the y coordinate **275 pt** for the bottom rectangle; press Enter.

Note: As a default, the zero point of the ruler is in the lower left corner. This value is based upon basic PostScript principles. Remember, the higher the y value, the further up the object is positioned on the page.

3   If the Swatches palette is not visible, choose Window > Swatches.

4   With the Selection tool, click once on the topmost rectangle to select it. Notice at the bottom of the toolbox that there are controls for the fill and the stroke. The stroke is essentially a border, the fill is the interior of a shape. When the fill is forward, any selected color will become assigned to the interior of the selected object. Activate the fill by clicking the solid swatch. Read more about strokes and fills in Lesson 5, "Color and Painting."

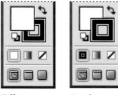

Fill is   Stroke is
forward.   forward.

For this example, you will assign colors using the Selection tool and the Swatches palette. Before you get started, notice that when you move the cursor over the swatches on the Swatches palette, a tooltip appears, providing you with the name of the color. Keep this in mind, as you will need to reference certain colors in the next few steps.

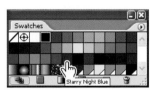

Move the cursor over the swatches
in the Swatches palette to see color names.

5   Make sure the topmost rectangle is still selected and choose the Fill swatch at the bottom of the toolbox. This brings the fill forward. Then choose Starry Night Blue from the Swatches palette; the rectangle now has a dark blue fill.

6   Now select the bottom rectangle and assign the fill color Pure Cyan.

Note: *If you inadvertently apply a color to the stroke, remove it by clicking on the None icon (☑) when the Stroke is forward.*

7   Choose Select > All, Ctrl+A (Windows) or use Command+A (Mac OS) to select both rectangles. Select Stroke from the bottom of the toolbox to bring it forward, and click on None. This removes any default stroke that is applied to your rectangles.

Remove stroke
by choosing
None.

8   Now you are ready to create the blend. With both rectangles still selected, select the Blend tool (🔖), then click once on the top rectangle, and again on the bottom rectangle. You are instructing Illustrator to create a blend (like morphing) from the top rectangle to the bottom rectangle. A gradual blend from one color of blue to another appears. Blends are discussed in more detail in Lesson 8, "Blending Shapes and Colors."

9　To avoid moving this blend as you build the rest of this file, choose Object > Lock > Selection, or use the keyboard shortcut Ctrl+2 (Windows) or Command+2 (Mac OS).

10　Choose File > Save, keep the file open.

Placing Photoshop images in Illustrator CS2

Placing a native Photoshop file into Illustrator is not a new feature, but in Illustrator CS2 you can assign Layer Comps before you place the image on the artboard. Layer Comps are a Photoshop feature that allow you to save combinations of layers, using the Layer Comp palette. Layer Comps can be based upon visibility, position, and Layer appearance. Get more details about Layer Comps in Lesson 13, "Combining Illustrator CS2 Graphics with the Creative Suite."

1　Choose File > Place.

2　When the Place window appears, check the Link checkbox in the lower left corner and navigate to your AICIB folder to Lesson00, and select the file shoes_color.psd. Click Place.

Illustrator recognizes when a file has been saved with Layer Comps, and opens a Photoshop Import Options window. The file in this example has been saved with three different Layer Comps.

3　In the Photoshop Import Options window, check the Show Preview checkbox and use the Layer Comp drop-down menu to select the comp named green_sneakers, and click OK. If you receive a color warning, disregard it for this example and click OK. The image of green sneakers is placed on the page.

4   Choose Select > Deselect to deselect the placed image.

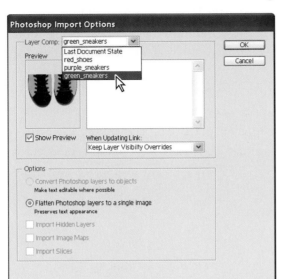

Illustrator recognizes Layer Comps saved in Photoshop files.

5   Repeat step 2-4 two more times, importing the two remaining Layer Comps. Choose the purple_sneakers and the red_sneakers Layer Comps. You should have three different pairs of colored sneakers, stacked on top of each other, on the artboard. Each is generated from the same Photoshop file.

6   Choose File > Save.

Aligning the shoes

In this next step, the exact position of the shoe images is not important, but you will use the Align palette to align them to each other. Before starting this part of the lesson, use the Selection tool (➤) to reposition the placed shoe images so they are not stacked on top of each other.

1   Continuing to use the Selection tool, select the green sneaker image and drag it to the upper left corner of the blended rectangle, leaving about a half inch from the edges. Then select the purple sneaker image and position in the middle left side of the blended rectangle. Lastly, select the red sneaker image and drag it to the lower left side of the blended rectangle.

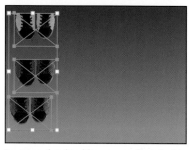

Position the shoe images on the left side of the blended square.

2   Choose Select > Deselect. With the Selection tool, click to select the green sneaker image, hold down the Shift key and click on the purple sneaker image, and then the red sneaker image. By holding down the Shift key, you can select multiple objects.

3   Choose Window > Align to show the Align palette. The Align palette can be used to align objects to the artboard or to other objects.

4   With the images still selected, choose the Horizontal Align Left button on the Align palette.

5   Then, choose the Vertical Distribute Center button. The images are aligned on the left and are distributed evenly from each other.

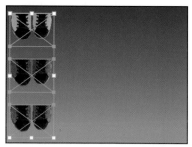

Choose Horizontal Align Left and then Vertical Distribute Center.

Result.

6   Choose File > Save.

Using the Live Trace tool

Live Trace is a new feature in Adobe Illustrator CS2 that provides incredible tracing options. Use it to trace logos, artwork, or even create vector color images from photographs. In this example, you will trace a color photograph to create a piece of black and white line art.

1   Choose File > Place. If you are not already in the Lesson00 folder, navigate to it and select the image named dancing.psd. Click Place.
Using the Selection tool (➤), position the image so that it is on the right side of the blended square. Exact position is not important.

2   With the image selected, click and hold the Tracing presets and options button to the right of Live Trace in the Control palette.
If your Control Palette is not visible, choose Window > Control Palette.

Notice all the presets tracing options available. For this example, scroll to the bottom and release on Tracing Options.

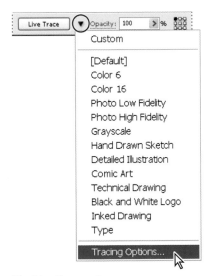

The Live Trace options.

When the Tracing Options windows appears, check the Preview box (on the right). For this example, leave the preset at the default.

As you see, the color image is converted to a black and white image. Click on the arrow (⊠) in the Threshold drop-down menu on the left side of the dialog box. A slider appears. Use this slider to adjust what Illustrator automatically chooses to be white or black. This can be helpful when working with images with fine lines that might get lost in the translation. Click the Trace button. The Live Trace feature is discussed in more detail in Lesson 5, "Color and Painting."

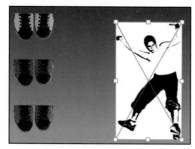

The new Live Trace feature can convert pixels to vector art.

Note: *Live Trace lives up to its name. If you were to edit the live trace image in Photoshop, the file would update the Live Trace image in Illustrator.*

3   With the traced object still selected, choose the Expand button on the Control palette. This breaks down the traced image into individual components.

4   Choose Select > Deselect and then, using the Direct Selection tool (▷), click on the white background behind the traced image. This activates only the white area surrounding the image. This is a bounding box that we want to remove.

5   Choose Select > Same > Fill Color. This automatically selects any other object with a white fill.

6   Press the Delete or Backspace key to remove the white objects, such as the background, but keep the traced image intact.

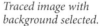

Traced image with background selected.

Traced image with background removed.

7   Choose File > Save. Keep the file open.

Using the Control palette for typesetting

Now you will have the opportunity to use the new Control palette in Illustrator CS2 for typesetting. Before getting started, make sure that you choose Window > Workspace > [Default]. This ensures that the Control Palette is at the top of your document window.

Choose Window > Workspace > [Minimal] if you are working on a tablet. This closes many of the palettes, which you can now access from the Control palette, and positions the Control palette at the bottom of the workspace.

1   Select the Type tool (T), and click once on the artboard. Don't worry about location, the text will be repositioned later in the lesson.

Note: *Make sure that you click and release on the artboard where there are no other objects. Also, do not click and drag, this creates a small, limited text area. More on type is discussed in Lesson 6, "Working with Type."*

2   Type the word **HOPPIN'**. While still on the Type tool, choose Select > All, or use Ctrl+A (Windows) or Command+A (Mac OS).

3   Using the Font Size textbox in the Control palette, change the selected text to **85 pts**. Press Enter, after typing the new size.

4 Make sure the text is still selected and then do the following:

• Click and drag over the Font Name in the Font text field on the Control palette.

Select the font name in the Control palette.

• Press the Up (↑) or Down (↓) arrow key on your keyboard. This navigates up and down through your font list, in alphabetical order. Using this method, change to the font named Chaparral Pro, an OpenType font. If you are at the default font of Myriad, you will need to press the up arrow many times, or you can also use the shortcut to get directly to Chaparral Pro by typing **chap** while the font name is selected.

5 In the Font Style drop-down menu, select Bold.

Change the font dynamically by selecting the font name in the Control palette and using the Up and Down arrow keys.

💡 *Would you rather see the entire Character palette? Simply click on the underlined word Character in the Control palette. You can also use the Control palette to access the Stroke, Paragraph, and Transparency palettes.*

6   Switch to the Selection tool (⬆). The text area becomes active. If the Transform palette is not visible, choose Window > Transform and type in the x coordinate of **200 pt** and the y coordinate of **675 pt**. Press Enter.

Position the text area using the Transform palette.   *Result.*

Creating outlines of text

In the next part of this exercise, you will convert the text from font to outlines. An outline of a font is a vector shape of the font. It no longer is editable text but can be used in a variety of ways.

1   Select the text area with the Selection tool (⬆).

2   Choose Type > Create Outlines. The text is converted into vector shapes.

3   The outlined text is grouped together as a default. Before accessing individual letters and attributes, choose Object > Ungroup, or use Shift+Ctrl+G (Windows) or Shift+Command+G (Mac OS).

4   While the letters are still selected, choose Select > Save Selection. When the Save Selection window appears, name the selection **hoppin'** and click OK. This makes it easier to reselect the text later in the exercise.

5   Choose File > Save.

Using the Appearance palette

1   If the Appearance palette is not open, choose Window > Appearance. The Appearance palette is an incredibly powerful palette that allows you to specifically control an object's attributes such as stroke, fills and other effects. Discover more about Effects in Lesson 11, "Applying Appearance Attributes, Graphic Styles, and Effects."

2   If the text is no longer selected, choose Select > hoppin' to reactivate the outlined text. If you do not have a saved selection, you can also select the first outlined letter H then hold down the Shift key and click on each outlined letter. This adds them to the selection.

Note in the Appearance palette that the selection is listed as a Compound Path and that both a stroke and fill are listed as attributes.

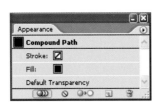

The Appearance palette can be used for simple fills and strokes, as well as complex objects attributes that include multiple strokes and fills.

3   If the Swatches palette is not visible, choose Window > Swatches. Select the word Stroke on the Appearance palette and then click on the White swatch on the Swatches palette. The stroke becomes white.

4   Choose Fill in the Appearance palette and click on the Red swatch.
Your text now has a White stroke and a Red fill.

Applying Effects

Now comes the fun part, using the Appearance palette to create some simple effects that might be difficult to create otherwise.

1   If the HOPPIN' text outline is no longer selected, choose Select > hoppin' to reactivate the selection.

2   Choose Stroke in the Appearance palette.

3 Choose Effect > Path > Offset Path. When the Offset Path window appears, enter the amount of offset as **2 pt**. Click OK. The stroke on the text has now been offset by 2 pt, but the fill remains unchanged.

Choose Stroke.   *Then the Offset Path Effect.*   *Result.*

4 With the HOPPIN' text still selected, select Fill on the Appearance palette.

5 Click on Opacity on the Control palette to view the Transparency palette.

6 Change the Blending mode to Hue, by holding down on Normal and scrolling to the Hue mode. The Hue blending mode will be more apparent later in the lesson when text is overlapped.

Access the Transparency palette from the Control palette.

Saving the Appearance as a Graphic Style

Perhaps you like the combination of attributes you have applied to an object and want to store them for later use. This can easily be done by saving a Graphic Style.

1 If the Text outline HOPPIN' is not selected, choose Select > hoppin'.

2 If the Graphic Styles palette is not visible, choose Window > Graphic Styles. The Graphic Styles palette can be used to store combinations of attributes applied to objects. This is discussed more in Lesson 11, "Applying Appearance Attributes, Graphics Styles, and Effects."

3   With the HOPPIN' text outline still selected, choose New Graphic Style from the Graphic Styles palette menu. When the Graphic Styles Options window appears, type **offset-stroke** in the Style Name text box; click OK. The Graphic Style you just created appears as the last thumbnail on the palette.

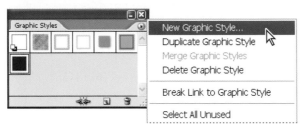

Save combinations of object attributes as a style in the Graphic Styles palette.

4   Choose Select > Deselect and choose the Type tool (T). Type the word **SHOES** anywhere on the artboard, but off your existing artwork. Make sure that the text attributes are still set as Chaparral Pro, Bold, 85 pt. If not, enter those values using the Control palette.

5   Choose the Selection tool (🔺), and select the Shoes text area. Using the Transform palette (make sure the point of reference indicator is still in the upper left corner), position the word SHOES at the x coordinate of **200 pt** and the y coordinate of **625 pt**. Press Enter after typing these values in the Transform palette.

6   With the SHOES text area still selected, click on the thumbnail of the Graphic Style you saved in the Graphic Style palette. Your saved attributes are applied to the text.

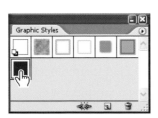

The SHOES text overlaps HOPPIN', and has the same Graphic Style applied.

7   Choose File > Save. Leave this file open for the rest of the tour exercise.

Using the Live Paint feature

You can now automatically fill paint regions in Illustrator CS2. You explore this feature in the tour, but get more details in Lesson 5, "Color and Painting."

1   With your hopping.ai file still open, choose File > Open and locate the image named target.ai in the Lesson00 folder.

2   Choose Select > All, or Ctrl+A (Windows)/Command+A (Mac OS).

3   Choose Edit > Copy, or Ctrl+C (Windows)/Command+C (Mac OS).

4   Choose File > Close, and return to the hopping.ai document.

5   Choose Edit > Paste, or Ctrl+V (Windows)/Command+V (Mac OS). The target art appears on the artboard.

6   With the target artwork still selected, choose Select > Save Selection just in case you need to reference it again in the future. In the Save Selection dialog window, name the selection **target**. Click OK. Leave the target selected. At this point it does not matter where the target is positioned.

7   Choose Object > Live Paint > Make to create this as a Live Paint group.

8   Choose the Live Paint Bucket tool (🪣) and cross it over the target shape (don't click!). Even though this shape is created from many circles, Live Paint recognizes the visual shapes and highlights them as you cross over them.

9   Choose red from the Swatches palette, cross over the outside ring, until the ring is highlighted, then click. The red is applied to the outside ring. Apply the Live Paint (red) fill to every other ring toward the middle of the circles.

The Live Paint feature paints automatically detects paint regions.

10 Now choose the None swatch (⊘) from the Swatches palette. Using the Live Paint Bucket tool, apply the None fill to every other ring, creating an alternating pattern.

11 Choose File > Save.

Applying a blending method

Next you will apply a blending mode to the target. A blending mode determines how the object and its colors interact with the underlying objects.

1 If the Transparency palette is not visible, choose Window > Transparency.

2 Using the Selection tool (▶), select the target and choose Overlay from the Blend drop-down menu.

Changing the Blending method of an object changes the way it interacts with objects below.

Result.

3 Choose the Selection tool and click and drag the Live Paint target object to a position so that it appears as though the dancer's foot is kicking the inside circle. This will position the target off the blended background.

Creating a clipping mask

The image is almost finished! Just a little clean-up work around the edges, and it will be complete. To clean up the edges, you will create a clipping mask. A clipping mask essentially blocks or covers the object area not included in the object defined as the mask. This can be adjusted, of course. Details relating to this are found in Lesson 7, "Working with Layers."

1   Click and hold down on the Rectangle tool (▣) to select the Rounded Rectangle tool (▣).

2   Click once on the artboard. This opens the Rounded Rectangle options window.

3   Enter a Width of **585 pt** and a Height of **400 pt**, leave the Corner Radius set for the default of **12 pt**. Then press the OK button. The rounded rectangle appears on the page. It does not matter what color the fill or stroke are for this object.

4   Choose the Selection tool (▸), click on the stroke, and drag the rounded rectangle to position it so that it is encompassing the existing artwork. This may exclude some of the target, as well as the blend.

5   Choose Object > Unlock all, this will unlock the blend you created earlier.

6   Choose Select > All.

The rounded rectangle is positioned over the artwork.

7   Choose Object > Clipping Mask > Make.

8   Choose Select > Deselect. Congratulations, your artwork is completed, and you have completed the tour of Adobe Illustrator CS2.

9   Choose File > Save and File > Close.

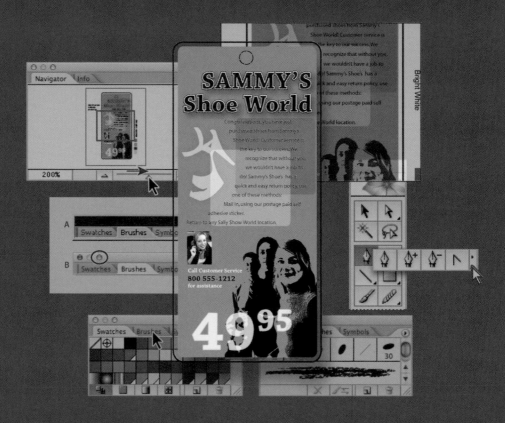

To the make best use of the extensive drawing, painting, and editing capabilities in Adobe Illustrator CS2, it's important to learn how to navigate the work area. The work area consists of the artboard, the scratch area, the toolbox, and the default set of palettes.

1 | Getting to Know the Work Area

In this introduction to the work area, you'll learn how to do the following:

- Use the Welcome Screen.
- Open an Adobe Illustrator CS2 file.
- Select tools from the toolbox.
- Use viewing options to enlarge and reduce the display of a document.
- Work with palettes, including the new Control palette.
- Use Illustrator Help.

Getting started

You'll be working in one art file during this lesson, but before you begin, restore the default preferences for Adobe Illustrator CS2. Then, open the finished art file for this lesson to see an illustration.

1 To ensure that the tools and palettes function exactly as described in this lesson, delete or deactivate (by renaming) the Adobe Illustrator CS2 preferences file. See "Restoring default preferences" on page 3.

Note: Due to the differences in Color Settings from one system to another, you may receive Missing Profile alert messages as you open various exercise files. Click OK when you see this message. Color Settings are discussed in Lesson 14, "Printing Artwork and Producing Color Separations."

2   Double-click the Adobe Illustrator icon to start the Adobe Illustrator program. When started, Adobe Illustrator displays a Welcome Screen with hyperlinked options.

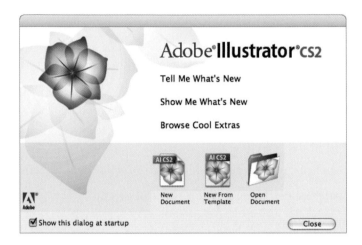

Use the Welcome Screen to find out what's new in Illustrator CS2, and gain access to tutorials and Cool extras. Cool extras include fonts and sample files. The Welcome Screen also offers the option to create a new document from scratch, or from a template, or to open an existing document. For this lesson you'll open an existing document.

Note: If you prefer not to have the Welcome Screen appear at startup, uncheck the Show this dialog at startup checkbox. You can open the Welcome Screen at any time by selecting Welcome Screen from the Help menu.

3   Click on the Open Document button in the lower right of the Welcome Screen, or choose File > Open, and open the L1strt.ai file in the Lesson01 folder, located within the AICIB folder on your hard drive.

The work file is a tag prepared for print.

When the file is opened, and Illustrator CS2 is fully launched, the menu bar, the toolbox, and five palette groups appear on the screen. The Transparency/Stroke/Gradient palette group is docked with the Color/Attributes palette group. Notice the new Control palette across the top of the work area. Illustrator CS2 consolidates many of your most frequently accessed palette items into the Control palette. This lets you operate with fewer visible palettes.

You will use the L1strt.ai file to practice navigating, zooming, and investigating an Adobe Illustrator CS2 document and work area.

4   Choose File > Save As, name the file **Shoeworld.ai**, and select the Lesson01 folder in the Save As menu. Leave the type of file format set to Adobe Illustrator Document, and click Save. If a warning message appears referencing spot colors and transparency, click Continue. The Illustrator Options window appears; leave the options at the default and click OK.

About the artboard

The artboard represents the entire region that can contain printable artwork. However, the artboard's dimensions do not necessarily match the current page size. For example, your artboard may be 10 x 20 inches while your print settings specify 8.5 x 11 inch paper. You can view the page boundaries in relation to the artboard by showing page tiling (View > Show Page Tiling). When page tiling is on, the printable and nonprintable areas are represented by a series of solid and dotted lines between the outermost edge of the window and the printable area of the page.

*A. Printable area. **B**. Nonprintable area.*
*C. Edge of the page. **D**. Artboard. **E**. Scratch area.*

Printable area is bounded by the innermost dotted lines and represents the portion of the page on which the selected printer can print. Many printers cannot print to the edge of the paper. Don't get confused by what is considered nonprintable.

Nonprintable area is between the two sets of dotted lines representing any nonprintable margin of the page. This example shows the nonprintable area of an 8.5″ x 11″ page for a standard laser printer.

The printable and nonprintable area is determined by the printer selected in the Print Options dialog box. (See Lesson 14, "Printing Artwork and Producing Color Separations" for more information about assigning a printer.) If you are saving an Illustrator document to be placed in a layout program, such as InDesign, the printable and nonprintable areas are irrelevant; the artwork outside the bounds will still appear.

Edge of the page is indicated by the outermost set of dotted lines.

Artboard is bounded by solid lines and represents the entire region that can contain printable artwork. By default, the artboard is the same size as the page, but it can be enlarged or reduced. The U.S. default artboard is 8.5″ x 11″, but it can be set as large as 227″ x 227″.

Scratch area is the area outside the artboard that extends to the edge of the 227″ square window. The scratch area represents a space on which you can create, edit, and store elements of artwork before moving them onto the artboard. Objects placed onto the scratch area are visible on-screen, but they do not print.

—From Illustrator Help

Viewing artwork

When you open a file, it is displayed in Preview view, which displays artwork the way it will print. When you're working with large or complex illustrations, you may want to view only the outlines, or wireframes, of objects in your artwork, so that the screen doesn't have to redraw the artwork each time you make a change.

1   Choose View > Outline. Only the outlines of the objects are displayed. Use this view to find objects that might not be visible in Preview.

2   Choose View > Preview to see all the attributes of the artwork. If you prefer keyboard shortcuts, Ctrl+Y (Windows) or Command+Y (Mac OS) toggles between these two modes.

3   Choose View > Pixel Closeup (at the bottom of the menu) to zoom in to a preset area of the image. This custom view was added to the document.

Note: To save time when working with large or complex documents, you can create your own custom views within a document to quickly jump to specific areas and zoom levels. You set up the view that you want to save, and then choose View > New View. Name the view; it is saved with the document.

4   Choose View > Overprint Preview to view any lines or shapes that are set to overprint. This view is helpful for those in the print industry who need to see how inks interact when set to overprint. See Lesson 14, "Printing Artwork and Producing Color Separations" for more information on overprinting.

5   Choose View > Pixel Preview to view how the artwork will look when it is rasterized and viewed on-screen in a Web browser.

Outline view.   *Preview view.*   *Overprint preview.*   *Pixel preview.*

About page tiling

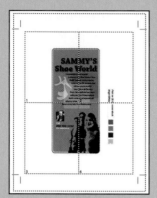

*Artboard divided into multiple
page tiles.*

Illustrator is generally not meant to create multi-page documents. That would be more a function
of a page layout program such as InDesign. Illustrator can tile multiple pages for the purposes of
accommodating artwork that is too large for an output device.

What is Tiling?

By default, Illustrator prints your artwork on a single sheet of paper. However, if the artwork is larger
than the page sizes available on your printer, you can print onto multiple sheets of paper.
Dividing the artboard to fit a printer's available page sizes is called tiling. You can choose a tiling
option in the Setup section of the Print dialog box. To view the page tiling boundaries on the artboard,
choose View > Show Page Tiling.

When you divide the artboard into multiple page tiles, the pages are numbered from left to right and
from top to bottom, starting with page 1. These page numbers appear on-screen for your reference
only; they do not print. The numbers enable you to print all the pages in the file or specify particular
pages to print.

—From Illustrator Help

Using the Illustrator tools

The Illustrator toolbox contains selection tools, drawing and painting tools, editing tools, viewing tools, and the Fill and Stroke color selection boxes. As you work through the lessons, you'll learn about each tool's specific function.

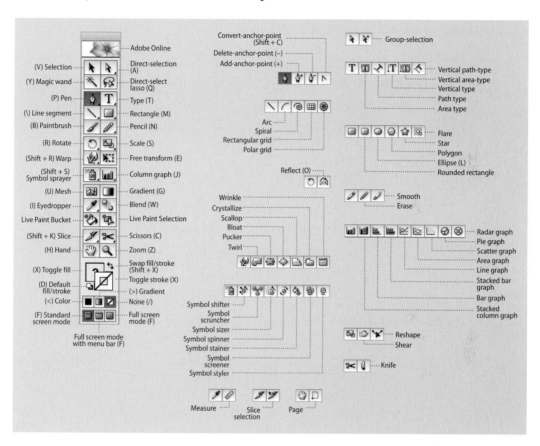

1 To select a tool, either click the tool in the toolbox or press the tool's keyboard shortcut. For example, you can press **M** to select the Rectangle tool (▢) from the keyboard. Selected tools remain active until you click a different tool.

2   If you don't know the keyboard shortcut for a tool, position the pointer over the tool to display the tool's name and shortcut. All keyboard shortcuts are also listed in the Keyboard Shortcuts section in Illustrator Help. You'll learn to use Illustrator Help later in the lesson.

Some of the tools in the toolbox display a small triangle at the bottom right corner, indicating the presence of additional hidden tools.

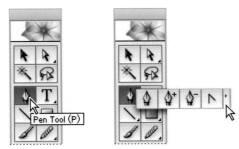

Name and shortcut.   *Hidden tools.*

3   Select hidden tools using the following methods:

• Click and hold the mouse button on a tool that has additional hidden tools. Then drag to the desired tool, and release the mouse button.

• Hold down Alt (Windows) or Option (Mac OS), and click the tool in the toolbox. Each click selects the next hidden tool in the hidden tool sequence.

• Click and drag to the right of the hidden tools and release on the arrow. This tears off the tools from the toolbox so that you can access them at all times.

Changing the view of artwork

You can reduce or enlarge the view of artwork at any magnification level from 3.13% to 6400%. Adobe Illustrator displays the percentage of the artwork's actual size in the title bar, next to the filename, and at the lower left corner of the Adobe Illustrator document window. Using any of the viewing tools and commands affects only the display of the artwork in Illustrator, not the actual size of the artwork.

Using the view commands

To enlarge or reduce the view of artwork using the View menu, do one of the following:

- Choose View > Zoom In to enlarge the display of the Shoeworld.ai artwork.

- Choose View > Zoom Out to reduce the view of the Shoeworld.ai artwork.

Each time you choose a Zoom command, the view of the artwork is resized to the nearest by 50%. The preset zoom levels appear at the lower left corner of the window in a menu, indicated by a down arrow next to the percentage.

You can also use the View menu to fit the artwork to your screen, or to view it at actual size.

1 Choose View > Fit in Window. A reduced view of the entire document is displayed in the window. A helpful keyboard command for this view is Ctrl+0 (zero) (Windows) or Command+0 (Mac OS).

Note: With a Scratch area that extends to the 227" area, you can easily lose sight of your illustration. By using View > Fit in Window, or the keyboard shortcuts, or Ctrl+0 (Windows) or Command+0 (Mac OS), artwork is centered in the viewing area.

2 To display artwork at actual size, choose View > Actual Size. The artwork is displayed at 100%. The actual size of your artwork determines how much of it can be viewed on-screen at 100%.

3 Choose View > Fit in Window before continuing to the next section.

Using the Zoom tool

In addition to the View commands, you can use the Zoom tool to magnify and reduce the view of artwork. Use the View menu to select predefined magnification levels or to fit your artwork inside the document window.

1   Click the Zoom tool (🔍) in the toolbox to select the tool, and move the cursor into the document window. Notice that a plus sign (+) appears at the center of the Zoom tool.

2   Position the Zoom tool in the upper left corner of the customer service representative image and click once. The artwork is displayed at a higher magnification.

3   Click two more times over the customer service representative image. The view is increased again, and you'll notice that the area you clicked is magnified. Next you'll reduce the view of the artwork.

4   With the Zoom tool still selected, position the pointer over the customer service representative image and hold down Alt (Windows) or Option (Mac OS). A minus sign (-) appears at the center of the Zoom tool.

5   With the Alt/Option key still depressed, click in the artwork twice. The view of the artwork is reduced.

A much more controlled and effective zoom is achieved by dragging a marquee to magnify a specific area of your artwork.

6   With the Zoom tool still selected, hold down the mouse button and drag over the area of the illustration you want to magnify; watch as a marquee appears around the area you are dragging, then release the mouse button. The area that was included in the marqueed area is now enlarged to fit the size of the document window.

7 Drag a marquee around the lower customer service representative image.

The percentage at which the area is magnified is determined by the size of the marquee you draw with the Zoom tool–the smaller the marquee, the larger the level of magnification.

Area selected.   *Resulting view.*

Note: *Although you can draw a marquee with the Zoom tool to enlarge the view of artwork, it is not efficient to draw a marquee when reducing the view of artwork.*

You can also use the Zoom tool to return to a 100% view of your artwork, regardless of the current magnification level.

8 Double-click the Zoom tool in the toolbox to return to a 100% view.

Because the Zoom tool is used frequently during the editing process to enlarge and reduce the view of artwork, you can select it from the keyboard at any time without deselecting any other tool you may be using.

9 Before selecting the Zoom tool from the keyboard, click any other tool in the toolbox and move it into the document window.

10 Now hold down Ctrl+spacebar (Windows) or Command+spacebar (Mac OS) to use the Zoom tool without actually choosing that tool. Click or drag to zoom in on any area of the artwork, and then release the keys.

11 To zoom out using the keyboard, hold down Ctrl+Alt+spacebar (Windows) or Command+Option+spacebar (Mac OS). Click the desired area to reduce the view of the artwork, and then release the keys.

12 Double-click the Zoom tool in the toolbox to return to a 100% view of your artwork.

Scrolling through a document

You use the Hand tool to scroll to different areas of a document. Using the Hand tool allows you to push the document around much like you would a piece of paper on your desk.

1   Click the Hand tool (✋) in the toolbox.

2   Drag downward in the document window. As you drag, the artwork moves with the hand.

As with the Zoom tool (🔍), you can select the Hand tool from the keyboard without deselecting the active tool.

3   Before selecting the Hand tool from the keyboard, click any other tool except the Type tool (T) in the toolbox and move the pointer into the document window.

4   Hold down the spacebar to select the Hand tool from the keyboard, and then drag to bring the artwork back into view.

You can also use the Hand tool as a shortcut to fit all the artwork in the window.

5   Double-click the Hand tool to fit the document in the window.

Note: The spacebar shortcut will not work when the Type tool is active and your cursor is within a text area.

Using the Navigator palette

The Navigator palette lets you scroll through a document. This is useful when you need to see the entire illustration in one window and edit it in a zoomed-in view.

1   Make sure that the Navigator palette is at the front of its palette group. If necessary, click the Navigator palette tab, or choose Window > Navigator.

2   In the Navigator palette, drag the slider to the right to approximately 200% to magnify the view of the price tag. As you drag the slider to increase the level of magnification, the red outline in the Navigator window becomes smaller, showing the area of the document that is being magnified.

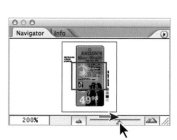

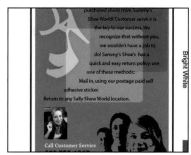

Dragging slider to 200%.   *200% view of image.*

3   Position the pointer inside the Navigator window. The pointer becomes a hand.

4   Drag the hand in the Proxy Preview Area of the Navigator palette to scroll to different parts of the artwork.

5   With the pointer still positioned in the Navigator palette, hold down on the Ctrl (Windows) or Command (Mac OS) key. When the hand changes to a magnifier, drag a marquee over an area of the artwork. The smaller the marquee you draw, the greater the magnification level in the document window.

Working with palettes

Palettes make modifying artwork easier by providing you access to many of Illustrator's functions. By default, they appear in stacked groups. To show or hide a palette as you work, choose the appropriate Window command. Selecting a Window command, displays the selected palette at the front of its group; deselecting a Window command conceals the entire palette group.

You can reorganize your work space in various ways. Try these techniques:

• To hide or display all open palettes and the toolbox, press Tab. To hide or display the palettes only, press Shift+Tab.

• To make a palette appear at the front of its group, click the palette's tab.

• To access additional options, use palette menus that are available on some palettes.

A. Title bar. B. Tab. C. Palette menu.

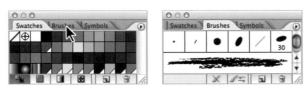

Click the Brushes tab to move that palette to the front.

• To move an entire palette group, drag its title bar.

• To rearrange or separate a palette group, drag a palette's tab. Dragging a palette outside an existing group removes it from the group.

Palettes are grouped.   *Drag a palette by its tab to separate the palette from its group.*

• To move a palette to another group, drag the palette's tab to that group.

• To display a palette menu, position the pointer on the triangle in the upper right corner of the palette, and hold down the mouse button.

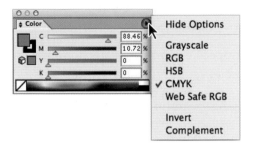

• If a palette has the option to change the height, you can drag its lower right corner. Some palettes cannot be resized.

• To collapse a group to palette title bars only, click the minimize/maximize box (Windows) or the resize box (Mac OS); click the box again to expand the palette group.

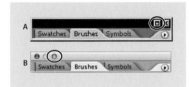

Click to collapse or expand palette.
A. *Windows.* **B.** *Mac OS.*

• To cycle through the available sizes for a palette, double-click the palette's tab. Some palettes also display arrows to the left of the palette name. With these palettes, you can single click the arrow icons to expand or reduce the size of the palette.

About the Control palette

The Control palette offers quick access to options that pertain to the objects you select. By default, the Control palette is docked to the top of the work area. For example, when you select a text object, the Control palette displays text-formatting options in addition to options for changing the color, placement, and dimensions of the object.

If you use a tablet, choose Window > Workspace > Minimal to position the Control palette at the bottom of the Illustrator work area.

Control palette with shape selected.

Control palette with text selected.

When text in the Control palette is blue and underlined, you can click the text to display a related palette. For example, click the word Stroke to display the Stroke palette.

Use the text field beside an option, such as Fill to quickly assign a color, or opacity by entering a value.

Using and saving Workspaces

New in Illustrator CS2, you can revert back at any time to the default locations of the palettes, or even create your own custom configuration of palettes and save it as a workspace.

1   Close several palettes and arrange two or three open palettes where you find them to be convenient.

2   Choose Window > Workspace > Save Workspace…

Note: *When you see ellipses (…) after a palette menu item, expect to see an additional Options window.*

3   In the Save Workspace dialog window, name your workspace **production**, and click OK.

4   Return to the default workspace (as it appeared upon initial launch), by choosing Window > Workspace > [Default].

5   Now try your saved workspace. Choose Window > Workspace > production. Your palettes return to the location and visibility that you determined.

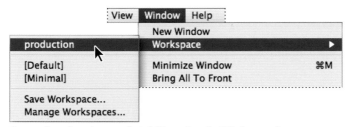

Save palette locations and visibility using the Workspace feature.

Using context menus

In addition to the menus at the top of your screen, context-sensitive menus display commands relevant to the active tool, selection, or palette.

To display context-sensitive menus, position the pointer over the artwork, palette list, scrollbar, or Document magnification level. Then click with the right mouse button (Windows) or press Ctrl and hold down the mouse button (Mac OS).

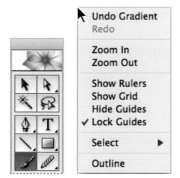

Options for the Brush tool,
displayed in its context-sensitive menu.

Using Illustrator Help

For complete information about using palettes and tools, you can use Illustrator Help. Illustrator Help includes keyboard shortcuts and additional information.

Illustrator Help is easy to use because you can look for topics in these different ways:

• Scanning a table of contents.

• Searching for keywords or phrases.

• Using an index.

• Jumping from topic to topic using related topic links.

Displaying the Help contents

First you'll look for a topic using the Contents screen.

1   To display the Help Contents menu, choose Help > Illustrator Help, or press F1 (Windows).

2   Drag the scroll bar, or click the arrows, to navigate through the contents. The contents are organized in a hierarchy of topics, much like the chapters of a book.

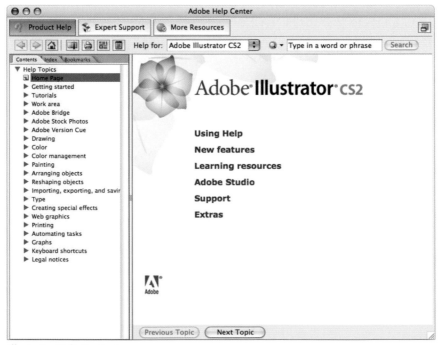

Illustrator Help Contents screen.

3   If the Contents tab on the left is not forward, click on it, and select Work area. The arrow turns down, revealing topics to the Adobe Illustrator CS2 work area.

4   Click on the topic of "Palettes, tools, and menus". A sub-menu appears.

5   Locate the topic About the toolbox and click to display it. An illustration of the toolbox appears along with tooltip information.

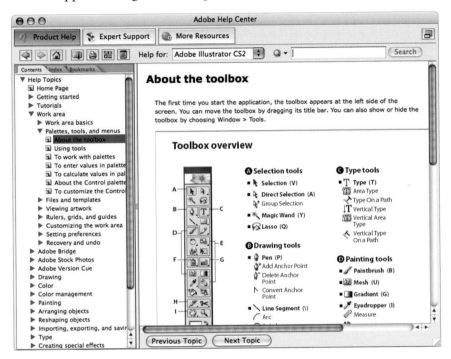

Using keywords, links, and the index

If you can't find the topic you want to review by viewing the Contents page, you can try searching using Search. You can search using keywords or phrases.

1   In the Search textbox, type **Brushes**. Click the Search button to go to that topic. A list appears of the items containing information about brushes.

2   Click "To create brushes" to learn about creating brushes. Notice, under See also, that there are several subtopics available for further research.

3   Click Calligraphic brush options to read about the options available when using a calligraphic brush.

Locating a topic using the index

1   Click on the Index tab in the left column to go to an alphabetical listing of topics. You will see an alphabet.

2   Click the letter H to get a listing of all the topics starting with H.

3   Click on "hanging punctuation" to see how to create this text formatting attribute.

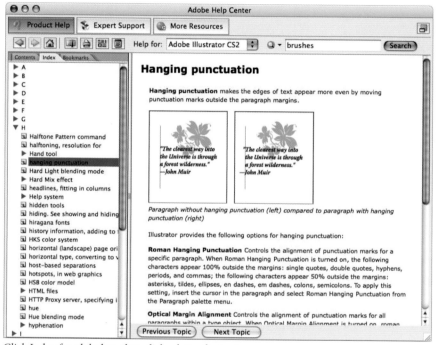

Click Index for alphabet, then click a letter for topics.

4   When you are finished investigating Illustrator Help, close the window and return to your Illustrator document window.

Using Adobe online services

Another way to get information about Adobe Illustrator CS2 or related Adobe products is to use the Adobe online services. Selecting the Illustrator artwork at the top of the toolbox takes you directly to the product page on Adobe.com that lists the latest information for Illustrator.

For online information click on the toolbox artwork.

Visiting the Adobe web site

If you have an Internet connection and a web browser installed on your system, you can access the U.S. Adobe Systems web site (at Adobe.com) for information on services, products, tutorials, tips, and community events on Illustrator.

1   If you have an Internet connection, click the flower image on the top of the toolbox.

2   When you have finished browsing the Adobe page, close and exit the browser.

Exploring on your own

Open a sample file from Adobe Illustrator CS2 to investigate and use some of the navigational and organization features learned in this lesson.

1   Open the file named Yellowstone Map.ai in the Lesson01 folder.

2   Perform the following on this artwork:

•   Practice zooming in and out. Notice that at the smaller zoom levels the text is "greeked," appearing as though it is a solid gray bar. As you zoom in closer the text can be viewed more accurately.

•   Save zoomed in views using View > New View for different areas such as; Mammoth Springs, Tower-Roosevelt and Canyon Village.

• Create a zoomed in view of Madison in the Outline View. Create a Preview view of the entire map.

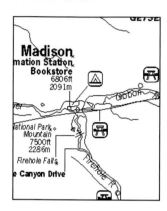 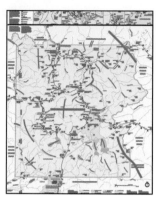

• Enlarge the Navigator palette and use it to scroll around the document and to zoom in and out.

• Create a Saved workspace that shows only the toolbox, Control palette and Layers palette. Save it as map tools.

• Use the Control palette to change the font and size of various text areas.

Review

▶ **Review questions**

1 Describe two ways to change your view of a document.

2 How do you select tools in Illustrator?

3 Describe three ways to change the palette display.

4 Describe how to get more information about the Illustrator program.

5 How do you save palette locations and visibility preferences?

▶ **Review answers**

1 You can select commands from the View menu to zoom in or out of a document, or fit it to your screen; you can also use the Zoom tool in the toolbox, and click or drag over a document to enlarge or reduce the view. In addition, you can use keyboard shortcuts to magnify or reduce the display of artwork. You can also use the Navigator palette to scroll artwork or change its magnification without using the document window.

2 To select a tool, you can either click the tool in the toolbox or press the tool's keyboard shortcut. For example, you can press **V** to choose the Selection tool from the keyboard. Selected tools remain active until you click a different tool.

3 You can click a palette's tab or choose Window > Palette Name to make the palette appear. You can drag a palette's tab to separate the palette from its group and create a new group, or drag the palette into another group. You can drag a palette group's title bar to move the entire group. Double-click a palette's tab to cycle through a palette's various sizes. You can also press Shift+Tab to hide or display all palettes.

4 Adobe Illustrator contains Help, plus keyboard shortcuts and some additional information and full-color illustrations. Illustrator also has context-sensitive help about tools and commands, and online services, including a link to the Adobe Systems web site (Adobe.com), for additional information on services, products, and Illustrator tips.

5 New in Adobe Illustrator CS2, you can choose Window > Workspace > Save Workspace to create custom work areas and make it easier to find the controls you need.

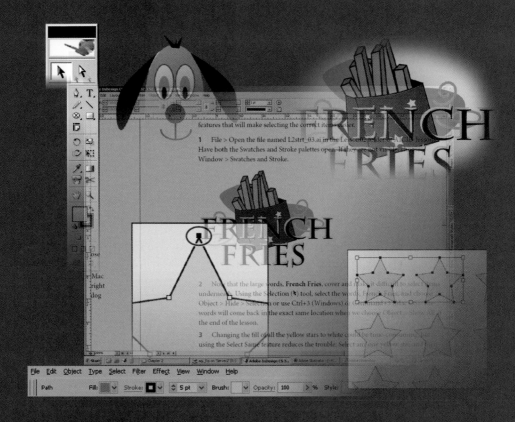

In this lesson, you will learn how to correctly locate and select objects using the Selection tools, as well as protect others by hiding and locking them.

You will also learn how to use basic shapes to create a logo.

2 Selections and Shapes

In this lesson, you'll learn how to do the following:

- Differentiate between the various selection tools.
- Group and ungroup items.
- Clone items with the Selection tool.
- Lock and hide items for organizational purposes.
- Save selections for future use.
- Use tools and commands to create basic shapes.
- Copy and combine objects to create new shapes.
- Use rulers, guides, and grids as drawing aids.
- Use selection tools to select and change parts of objects.

Getting started

When changing colors, size, adding effects or any number of attributes, you must first select the object to which you are applying the changes. Consider this lesson a primer in the fundamentals of the Selection tools. More advanced selection techniques using layers are available, and are discussed in Lesson 7, "Working with Layers."

Before you begin, you'll need to restore the default preferences for Adobe Illustrator CS2. Then you will open the art file that you will be working with.

1   To ensure that the tools and palettes function exactly as described in this lesson, delete or deactivate (by renaming) the Adobe Illustrator CS2 preferences file. See "Restoring default preferences" on page 3.

2   Start Adobe Illustrator CS2.

3   Choose File > Open, and open the L2strt_01.ai file in the Lesson02 folder, located inside the Lessons folder within the AICIB folder on your hard drive.

Using the Selection tool

1   Choose the Selection tool (⬈). Position the mouse over the different star shapes without clicking. Note the icon that appears as you pass over objects (⬈▪), indicating that there is an object that can be selected under the pointer. Click on the yellow star in the upper left corner. A bounding box with eight handles appears.

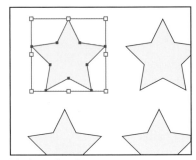

The bounding box.

The bounding box is used for transformations such as resizing and rotating; it also indicates that this item is selected and ready to be edited. This could mean changing its size, color, position, or any number of other things.

2   Using the Selection tool, click on the star to the right and notice that the first star is now deselected and only the second star is selected.

3   Add another star to the selection by holding down the Shift key and clicking on the first star. Both stars are now selected.

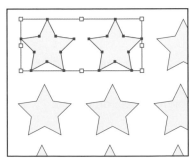

Add other items to a selection by holding down the Shift key.

4 Reposition the stars anywhere on the document by clicking in the center of either selected star and dragging. Since both are selected, they travel together.

Note: If selecting an item without a fill, you must click on the stroke (border).

5 Deselect the stars by clicking on the artboard where there are no objects. If you prefer, choose Select > Deselect.

6 Revert to the last saved version of the document by pressing the F12 key or choose File > Revert. In the Revert dialog box, click Revert.

Using the Direct Selection tool

1 With the same file open, L2strt_01.ai switch to the Direct Selection tool (↖). Again, don't click, but move the mouse over the different points on the stars with the Direct Selection tool. When the Direct Selection tool is over an anchor point of an unselected or selected path or object, it has a hollow square next to it. Click on the top point of the first star and drag the anchor point. Note that only the point you dragged is solid, representing that it is selected, while the other points in the star are hollow and not selected.

Only the point that is selected is solid.

2 With the Direct Selection tool still active, click and drag down the individual point. This allows you to edit the shape of an object. Try clicking on other points, and notice that the initial point is then deselected and you can edit other points individually.

3 Revert to Saved by choosing the F12 key or File > Revert. In the Revert dialog box, click Revert.

Note: Using the Shift key, you can select multiple points to move them together.

Creating selections with a marquee

Some selections may be easier to make by creating a marquee around the objects that you want to select.

1 With the same file open, L2start_01.ai, switch to the Selection tool (➤). Instead of Shift+clicking to select the first two stars, position the mouse above the upper left star and then click and drag downward and to the right to create a marquee that overlaps just two points of the stars.

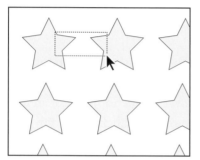 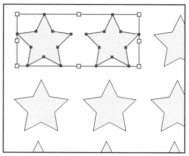

When dragging with the Selection tool, you only need to encompass a small part of an object to include it in the selection.

2 Try dragging a marquee starting outside the stars and crossing over all three points in the top row. All stars become active.

3 Select > Deselect or click where there are no objects.

4 Using the same method, but with the Direct Selection tool (➤), click outside the first star and drag to select the top points of each of the stars in the top row.

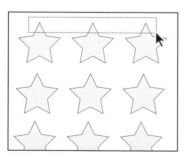 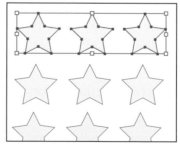

Click and drag across the top points.

Only the top points become selected. Click on one of the anchor points and drag to see how they reposition together. Use this method when selecting a single point. That way, you don't have to click exactly on the anchor point that is to be edited.

5   Revert to the last saved version of the file by pressing the F12 key or choose File > Revert. In the Revert dialog box, click Revert.

Grouping items

You can combine several objects into a group so that the objects are treated as a single unit. This way, you can move or transform a number of objects without affecting their attributes or relative positions.

1   With the same file open, L2start_01.ai, switch to the Selection tool (↖). Click outside the top left of the first star and drag a marquee that touches each star on the first row to select all three.

2   Choose Object > Group, then choose Select > Deselect.

3   With the Selection tool, click on the first star. Notice that since it is grouped with the other two stars, all three become selected.

Adding to a group

Groups can also be nested; that is, they can be grouped within other objects or groups to form larger groups.

1   With the top group of three stars still selected, Shift+click on the first star in the second row. With this added to the selection, choose Object > Group. The bounding box is expanded to include this new selection, but only the left star has anchor points activated.

2   Shift+click on the middle star in the second row and also choose Object > Group. Repeat this for the third star in the second row.

3   Choose Select > Deselect when finished.

You have created a nested group. You may think of them as groups within groups. This is a common technique used when designing artwork.

4   Choose the Selection tool (↖) and click on any one of the grouped stars. They all become selected.

5   Click off the stars to a blank area on the artboard to deselect them.

6   Hold down on the Direct Selection tool (↖) in the toolbox, and drag to the right to access the Group Selection tool (↖⁺).

7 Click once on the first star. Only the star becomes active. Click again and the initial group of three stars becomes active. As you continue to click, each individual group you created becomes selected.

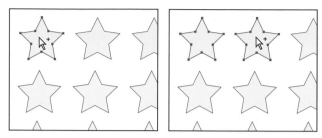

The Group Selection tool allows you to add selections within groups.

8 Ungroup the items by choosing Object > Ungroup. Note that you will have to repeat this action for each of the groups created. In other words, to get these back to individual stars, you would have to choose Object > Ungroup four times.

9 Choose File > Close, do not save the file.

Applying the selection techniques

In this next lesson, you will use some of the techniques discussed previously in this lesson, as well as other selection options.

1 Choose File > Open, and open the L2strt_02.ai file in the Lesson02 folder, located inside the Lessons folder within the AICIB folder on your hard drive.

2 Make sure that the entire artboard is visible by choosing View > Fit in Window. On the right you see the completed project; on the left are the objects needed to create the finished dog.

3   Start this lesson by hiding the palettes; you won't need them for this lesson. Press Shift+Tab to hide the palettes, or hide palettes individually, or by groups, using the Window menu.

4   With the Selection tool (➤), select the brownish-red circle. To avoid grabbing a bounding box handle and accidently resizing the circle, click and drag the center of the circle to slide it to its new location as the nose of the dog.

5   Using the Selection tool, drag both ears, the tuft of hair, and the mouth into position.

Note: Be careful with the mouth. It contains two objects, so, using the Selection tool, Shift+click to select the top and bottom objects and move them together.

Use the selection tools to move parts into place.

6   Select the dog's head (the light brown shape) and choose Object > Lock > Selection to keep it in position. You will not be able to select it until you choose Object > Unlock All. Leave it locked for now.

7 Using the Direct Selection tool, click on the anchor point in the first peak, or tuft, of hair. When the individual point is selected it appears as a solid point (active), whereas the other anchor points are hollow (inactive). Click and drag the individual anchor point to change its position.

If you are having difficulty accessing only one anchor point, remain on the Direct Selection tool and choose Select > Deselect. Then click and drag a marquee around the point, encompassing it with your selection marquee.

Using the Direct Selection tool, click and drag individual anchor points.

8 Individually select other anchor points in the hair shape and position them in different directions. You are giving a ruffled look to the dog's hair.

9 Choose the Selection tool. The eye is made of several parts. Use either the marquee selection technique or the Shift key to select all three parts of the eye. Choose Object > Group. Drag the eye into position on the face to create a left eye.

10 While still using the Selection tool, press and hold the Alt (Windows) or Option key (Mac OS) and drag the selected eye to the right to clone the left eye. Position the cloned object as the right eye. Make sure that you release the mouse before releasing the Alt/Option key. The dog now has two eyes.

Note: If you also hold down the Shift key when cloning, the newly cloned object is constrained and snaps to a straight 45°, 90°, or 180° angle.

11 Choose File > Save and close the file. Press OK in the Options dialog box.

Hiding selections

As you create more complex artwork, existing objects may get in the way and make it difficult to activate selections. A common technique is to hide selected artwork. Do this by choosing Object > Hide > Selection, or Ctrl+3 (Windows)/Command+3 (Mac OS). A hidden object cannot be moved or selected; it is essentially an object that no longer exists on the active artboard. Bring all hidden objects back at the same time by choosing Object > Show All, or use Ctrl+Alt+3 (Windows)/ Command+Option+3 (Mac OS).

Advanced selection techniques

When working on complex artwork, selections may become more difficult to control. In this section, we combine some of the techniques you've already learned with some additional features that make selecting objects easier.

1   Choose File > Open. Open the file named L2strt_03.ai in the Lesson02 folder of AICIB lessons. Open both the Swatches and Stroke palettes. If they are not visible, choose Window > Swatches and Window > Stroke.

2   Note that the large words make it difficult to select items underneath. Using the Selection tool (✎), select the words, French Fries, and choose Object > Hide > Selection or use Ctrl+3 (Windows) or Command+3 (Mac OS). The words will come back in the exact same location when you choose Object > Show All at the end of the lesson.

3   Select any yellow star and choose Select > Same > Fill and Stroke. All the other yellow stars become selected. Make sure that the fill box is forward in the toolbox and select white from the Swatches palette. The stars all change to white.

4   Select one of the shapes creating the french fries and then choose Select > Same > Stroke Weight. The french fry shape had a 3 pt stroke, so all strokes that are 3 pt are now activated. Using the Control Palette, type **5** into the stroke weight textbox and press the Enter key to increase the weight to 5 pt. Keep these items selected.

5   With your previous selection still active, choose Select > Save Selection. Name the selection **5 pt stroke**. Click OK. This allows you to reactivate this selection at a later time.

6   Choose Select > Deselect to deselect the objects. Choose Select > 5 pt stroke from the bottom of the Select menu to make the selection active.

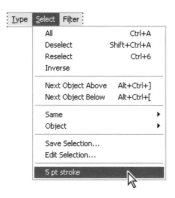 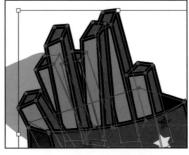

7   Choose Object > Show All to bring back the words French Fries.

8   Choose File > Save and File > Close to close the file.

Creating basic shapes

You'll begin this exercise creating a new document and setting the ruler units to inches, displaying a grid to use as a guideline for drawing, and closing the palettes that you won't use.

1   Choose File > New to open a new, untitled document. Leave the Color Mode and Artboard Size at the default settings, and click OK.

2   Choose File > Save As, name the file **Pencil.ai**, and save in the Lesson02 folder. Leave the Type of File Format option set to Adobe Illustrator Document, and click Save. In the Illustrator Options, leave the default settings unchanged and click OK.

3   If they are not already closed, close all the palettes by clicking their Close boxes or by holding down Shift and pressing Tab once. You won't need to use them in this section.

4   Choose View > Show Grid to display a grid that's useful for measuring, drawing, and aligning shapes. This grid won't print with the artwork.

5   Choose View > Show Rulers, or use Ctrl+R (Windows) or Command+R (Mac OS) to display rulers along the top and left side of the window. The ruler units are set by default to points.

You can change the ruler units of measure used for all documents or for only the current document. The ruler unit of measure applies to measuring objects, moving and transforming objects, setting grid and guide spacing, and creating ellipses and rectangles. It does not affect the units in the Character, Paragraph, and Stroke palettes. These are controlled by the options in the Units & Undo Preferences dialog box.

6   Choose File > Document Setup to change the ruler units for only this document. In the Document Setup dialog box, for Units choose Inches, leave the other settings unchanged, and click OK.

You can change the units of measure for rulers by right-clicking (Windows) or Ctrl-clicking (Mac OS) on a ruler in your active document. Choose the unit of measure from the context menu that appears.

Using basic shape tools

In this lesson, you'll create a simple logo using the basic shape tools. The shape tools are organized under the Rectangle tool. You can tear this group off the toolbox to display its own toolbar.

1   Hold down the mouse button on the Rectangle tool (▣) until a group of tools appears, and then drag to the tear-off triangle at the end and release the mouse button.

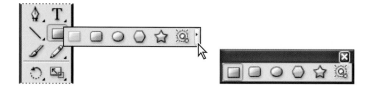

Tearing off the Rectangle tool group.

2   Move the Rectangle tool group away from the toolbox.

Drawing the pencil shape

In Adobe Illustrator CS2, you control the thickness and color of lines that you draw by setting stroke attributes. A stroke is the paint characteristic of a line, or the outline of an object. A fill is the paint characteristic of the inside of an object. The default settings let you see the objects you draw with a white fill and a black outline.

First you'll draw a series of rectangles and triangles that make up the pencil. You'll display Smart Guides to align your drawing.

1   Select the Zoom tool (🔍) in the toolbox, and click in the middle of the window once or twice until you are zoomed in to 150%. Notice that 150% is displayed in the bottom left corner of the window.

2   Choose View > Smart Guides to turn them on. Smart Guides automatically snap the edges of objects to nearby objects or their intersecting points as you move them.

Smart Guides also show Text Label Hints that display information on the position the pointer is currently snapped to (such as "center") as you manipulate the pointer.

About Smart Guides

When Smart Guides are turned on and you move the cursor over your artwork, the cursor looks for objects, page boundaries, and intersections of construction guides to snap to that area within the tolerance range set in Smart Guides Preferences.

Smart Guides are temporary snap-to guides that help you create, align, edit, and transform objects relative to other objects. To activate Smart Guides, choose View > Smart Guides.

You can use Smart Guides in the following ways when you create, move, and transform objects:

• When you create an object with the pen or shape tools, use the Smart Guides to position the new object's anchor points relative to the other object.

• When you move an object, use the Smart Guides to align to the point on the object that you have selected. You can align to the anchor point at the corner of a selected object near the bounding box. To do so, select the object just inside the bounding box handle. If the tolerance is 5 points or greater, you can snap to the corner point from 5 points away.

• When the Transform tools option is selected in Smart Guides Preferences and you transform an object, Smart Guides appear to assist the transformation.

Note: When Snap to Grid is turned on, you cannot use Smart Guides (even if the menu command is selected).

—From Illustrator Help

3   Choose Window > Transform to display the Transform palette. Then choose Window > Info.

4   Select the Rectangle tool (▢), and drag it to draw a rectangle that's approximately 0.75 inch wide and 1 inch tall. Use the rulers and the grid as guides. This will be the body of the pencil. You can also use the Info palette to help determine the size.

When you release the mouse button, the rectangle is automatically selected and its center point appears. All objects created with the shape tools have a center point that you can drag to align the object with other elements in your artwork. You can make the center point visible or invisible using the Attributes palette, but you cannot delete it.

5 In the Transform palette, note the rectangle's width and height. If necessary, enter **.75 inch** in the width text field and **1 inch** in the height text field.

The Transform palette displays rectangle's width and height.

You'll draw another rectangle centered inside the first one to represent the two vertical lines on the pencil.

6 With the Rectangle tool still selected, position the pointer over the center point of the rectangle, hold down Alt (Windows) or Option (Mac OS), and drag out from the center point to draw a rectangle that's centered inside the other. Release the mouse button and then the Alt/Option key when the rectangle is the same height as the first rectangle (1 inch).

Holding down Alt/Option as you drag the Rectangle tool draws the rectangle from its center point rather than from its top left corner. Smart Guides indicate when you've snapped to the first rectangle's edge, by displaying the text label hint "path."

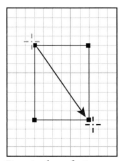 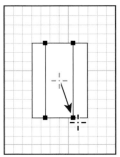

Drag to draw first   *Alt/Option+drag to draw*
rectangle.   *second rectangle.*

Besides dragging a tool to draw a shape, you can click with the tool to open a dialog box of options. Now you'll create a rounded rectangle for the eraser by setting options in a dialog box.

7   Select the Rounded Rectangle tool (▣), and click once in the artwork to open the Rounded Rectangle dialog box. Type **0.75** in the Width text field, press Tab, and type **0.75** in the Height text field. Then press Tab again, and type **0.20** in the Corner Radius text box (the radius is the amount of the curve on the corners). Click OK.

💡 *To automatically enter identical Width and Height values in the Ellipse or Rectangle dialog box, enter a Width or Height value, and then click the name of the other value to enter the same amount.*

You'll use Smart Guides to help you align the eraser to the top of the pencil body.

8   Choose View > Hide Bounding Box to hide the bounding boxes of selected objects. This will prevent you from accidentally distorting the eraser shape when you move and align it.

The bounding box appears as a temporary boundary around selected objects. With the bounding box, you can move, rotate, duplicate, and scale objects easily by dragging the selection or a handle (one of the hollow squares surrounding the selected objects).

9   With the Rounded Rectangle tool still selected, hold down Ctrl (Windows) or Command (Mac OS) to access the Selection tool (▸) temporarily. Select the right edge of the eraser without releasing the mouse button, and then drag the eraser to the right side of the pencil body. (Smart Guides indicate the path of the right side.) Release the mouse button to drop the eraser on top of the pencil body.

10   Press and hold Ctrl (Windows) or Command (Mac OS), select the bottom edge of the eraser, and drag it up to the intersect point at the top of the pencil body. Release the mouse button.

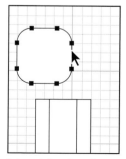 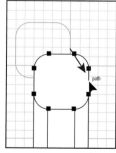 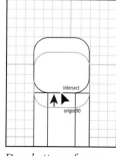 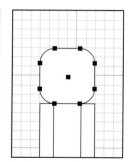

Select right edge of eraser shape.　*Drag eraser to path on pencil body.*　*Drag bottom of eraser to top of pencil body.*　*Result.*

Next you'll create two shapes to represent the metal bands connecting the eraser to the pencil.

11 To create the first band, click once anywhere in the artwork to open the Rounded Rectangle dialog box again. Type **0.85** in the Width text box, **0.10** in the Height text box, and **0.05** in the Corner Radius text box. Click OK.

12 Click the Selection tool to select the band, select the bottom left anchor point, and move the band to the top of the pencil body. Release the mouse button. (Smart Guides snap the anchor point to the top corner of the pencil body.)

13 With the band still selected, hold down Alt (Windows) or Option (Mac OS), select the anchor point again, drag straight up to make a copy, and move it above the original band. Release the mouse button. (Smart Guides snap the anchor point of the new copy to the top of the original band.)

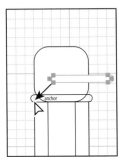  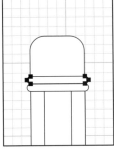

Move first metal band between eraser and pencil body.   *Alt/Option+drag a copy above first metal band.*   *Smart Guides snap objects into position.*

You've been working in Preview view. This default view of a document lets you see how objects are painted (in this case, with a white fill and black stroke). If paint attributes seem distracting, you can work with just the wireframe view of an object.

Now you'll draw two triangles to represent the pencil tip and its lead, using Outline view.

14 Choose View > Outline to switch from Preview view to Outline view.

Illustrator lets you control the shape of polygons, stars, and ellipses by pressing certain keys as you draw. You'll draw a polygon and change it to a triangle.

15   Select the Polygon tool (⬡), and position the pointer over the center point of the two rectangles.

16   Drag to begin drawing a polygon, but don't release the mouse button. Press the Down Arrow key three times to reduce the number of sides on the polygon to a triangle, and move the mouse in an arc to rotate one side of the triangle to the top. Before you release the mouse button, hold down the spacebar and drag the triangle down to position it below the pencil body. Release the mouse button when the triangle is positioned.

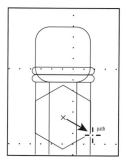
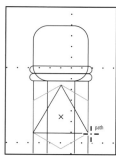
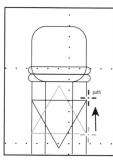
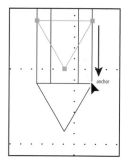

Drag to draw polygon; don't release mouse button.

Press Down Arrow key three times.

Drag to rotate triangle.

Hold down spacebar and move triangle.

Now you'll create the second triangle for the pencil's lead tip using the Scale tool.

17   With the triangle still selected, select the Scale tool (▱) in the toolbox and then Alt+click (Windows) or Option+click (Mac OS) the bottom corner point of the triangle.

Clicking the corner point of the triangle sets the reference point from which the new triangle will scale. Pressing Alt/Option as you click displays the Scale dialog box.

18 In the Scale dialog box, type **30%** in the Scale text box and click Copy. (Don't click OK.)

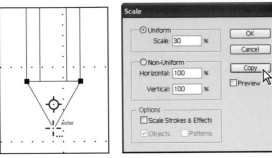 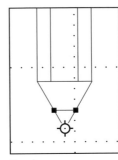

Alt/Option+click to set   Set scale value.   Result.
scaling reference point.

Next you will use the Line Segment tool to quickly draw a horizontal line segment near the top of the pencil.

19 Select the Line Segment tool (╲), and position the pointer over the left side of the pencil near the top. Click where you want the line to begin, and drag to where you want the line to end. As you drag, hold down the Shift key to constrain the line horizontally.

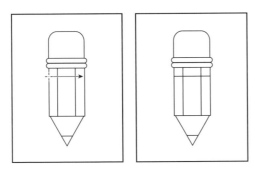

Note: The Line and Arc Segment tool Options dialog boxes display the values of the last segment created. Display the Options dialog box by selecting the Line or Arc tool and clicking once on the artboard. You can then reset the default values by pressing Alt (Windows) or Option (Mac OS) and clicking Reset.

20 Choose View > Preview, and then choose File > Save to save your work.

Tips for drawing polygons, spirals, and stars

You can control the shapes of polygons, spirals, and stars by pressing certain keys as you draw the shapes. As you drag the Polygon, Spiral, or Star tool, choose any of the following options to control the shape:

• To add or subtract sides on a polygon, points on a star, or number of segments on a spiral, press the Up Arrow key or the Down Arrow key while creating the shape. This will not work if you have already released the mouse. The tool remains set to the last value you specified.

• To rotate the shape, move the mouse in an arc.

• To keep a side or point at the top, hold down Shift.

• To keep the inner radius constant, start creating a shape and then hold down Ctrl (Windows) or Command (Mac OS).

• To move a shape as you draw it, hold down the spacebar. This also works for rectangles and ellipses.

• To create multiple copies of a shape, hold down the ~ (tilde) key as you draw.

Exploring on your own

Experiment with shapes by creating a shape such as a circle, star or rectangle. Clone it several times using the Alt/Option key. Apply different colors and strokes to the shapes and reselect them using the Select Same menu item. Try to clone while using the Shift key to constrain the angle of the newly created object. Try cloning multiple items at the same time.

Review

▶ **Review questions**

1   Why might an object that has no fill not become selected when you click on it?

2   How can you select one item in a group?

3   How do you edit the shape of an object?

4   What should be done after spending a lot of time creating a selection that is going to be used repeatedly?

5   If something is blocking your view of a selection, what can you do?

6   What are the basic shape tools? Describe how to tear or separate a group of shape tools away from the toolbox.

7   How do you draw a square?

8   How do you draw a triangle?

9   Describe three ways to specify the size of a shape.

▶ **Review answers**

1   Items that have no fill must be selected by clicking on the stroke.

2   Using the Group Selection tool, you can click once for an individual item within a group. Continue to click to add the next grouped items to the selection. Read Lesson 7, "Working with Layers," to see how you can use layers to make complex selections.

3   Using the Direct Selection tool, you can select one or more individual anchor points and make changes to the shape of an object.

4   For any selection that you will need to use again, choose Select > Save Selection. Name the selection and reselect it at any time from the Select menu.

5   If something is blocking your access to a selection, you can choose Object > Hide > Selection. The object is not deleted, just hidden in the same position until you choose Object > Show All.

6   There are five basic shape tools: Ellipse, Polygon, Star, Rectangle, and Rounded Rectangle. To separate a group of tools from the toolbox, hold the pointer over the tool that appears in the toolbox and press the mouse button until the group of tools appears. Without releasing the mouse button, drag to the triangle at the end of the group, and then release the mouse button to tear off the group.

7   To draw a square, select the Rectangle tool in the toolbox. Hold down Shift, and drag to draw the square, or click to enter equal dimensions for the width and height in the Rectangle dialog box.

8   To draw a triangle, select the Polygon tool in the toolbox, start dragging to draw the shape, and press the Down Arrow key to reduce the number of sides to three. Or click to enter the radius and number of sides in the Polygon dialog box.

9   To specify the size of a shape, you can do any of the following:

• Select the shape and specify new dimensions in the W (width) and H (height) text boxes in the Transform palette.

• Select the shape and then select the Scale tool in the toolbox. Alt/Option+click to set the point of origin and specify the dimensions in the Scale dialog box (click Copy to make a scaled copy of the selected object).

• Select the shape, and drag a side or corner handle of the shape's bounding box to resize its width, height, or both. (Shift+drag a corner handle to resize the selection proportionally.)

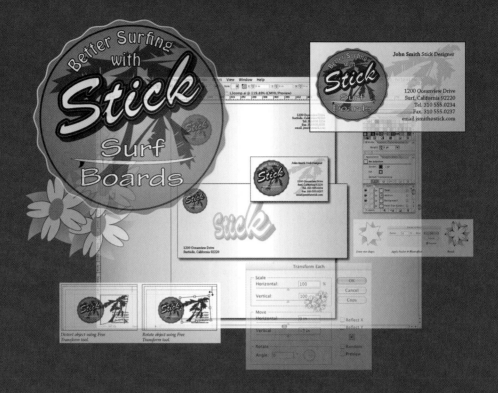

You can modify objects in many ways as you create your artwork— including quickly and precisely controlling their size, shape, and orientation. In this lesson, you'll explore the various transform tools, commands, and palettes as you create three pieces of artwork.

3 | Transforming Objects

In this lesson, you'll learn how to do the following:

- Select individual objects, objects in a group, and parts of an object.

- Move, scale, and rotate objects using a variety of methods.

- Reflect, shear, and distort objects.

- Adjust the perspective of an object.

- Apply a distortion filter.

- Position objects precisely.

- Repeat transformations quickly and easily.

- Experiment using variables to create different versions of a design.

Getting started

In this lesson, you'll create a logo using partially completed files to use in three pieces of artwork to create a letterhead design, an envelope, and a business card template. Before you begin, you'll restore the default preferences for Adobe Illustrator CS2; then you'll open a file containing a composite of the finished artwork to see what you'll create.

1   To ensure that the tools and palettes function exactly as described in this lesson, delete or deactivate (by renaming) the Adobe Illustrator CS2 preferences file. See "Restoring default preferences" on page 3.

2   Start Adobe Illustrator CS2.

3   Choose File > Open, and open the L3comp.ai file in the Lesson03 folder, located inside the Lessons folder within the AICIB folder on your hard drive.

This file contains a composite of the three pieces of finished artwork. The Stick Surf Boards logo in the top left corner of the letterhead is the basis for all the modified objects. The logo has been resized for the letterhead, envelope, and business card.

Note: You can also view the individual pieces of finished artwork by opening the files L3end1.ai, L3end2.ai, and L3end3.ai in the Lesson03 folder.

4   Choose View > Zoom Out to reduce the view of the finished artwork, adjust the window size, and leave it on your screen as you work. (Use the Hand tool (☝) to move the artwork where you want it in the window.) If you don't want to leave the image open, choose File > Close.

To begin working, you'll open an existing art file set up for the letterhead artwork.

5   Choose File > Open to open the L3start1.ai file in the Lesson03 folder, located within the AICIB folder on your hard drive.

This start file has been saved with the rulers showing, custom swatches added to the Swatches palette, and blue guidelines for scaling objects used to create the logo.

6   Choose File > Save As, name the file **Letterhead.ai**, and select the Lesson03 folder in the Save in Menu. Leave the format set to Adobe Illustrator Document, and click Save. In the Illustrator Options dialog box, accept the default settings by clicking OK.

Scaling objects

You scale objects by enlarging or reducing them horizontally (along the x axis) and vertically (along the y axis) relative to a fixed point of origin that you designate. If you don't designate an origin, the objects are scaled from their center points. You'll use three methods to scale the objects that will make up the complete logo.

First you'll set the preference to scale strokes and effects, then you'll scale the logo background by dragging its bounding box and align it to the blue guides provided.

1   Choose Edit > Preferences > General (Windows) or Illustrator > Preferences > General (Mac OS), and check Scale Strokes & Effects. This will scale the stroke width of any object scaled in this lesson. Click OK.

2   Using the Selection tool (◥) in the toolbox, click the stroke of the circle to select the group of objects that make up the logo's background.

3   While holding down the Shift key, click and drag the top right corner of the object's bounding box up to the blue horizontal guide. If you do not see the bounding box choose View > Show Bounding Box.

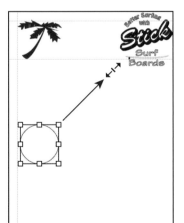 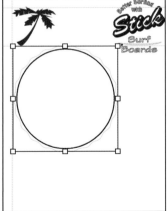

Note: *Holding down the Shift key constrains the object proportionally.*

You'll use the Control palette link to the Swatches palette to paint the logo background with a radial gradient. To learn how to create your own custom gradients, see Lesson 8, "Blending Shapes and Colors."

If the Control palette is not visible, choose View > Workspace > Default.

4 Select the Fill box in the Control palette to link to the Swatches palette. With the logo background selected, move the cursor over the swatches in the Swatches palette until you see their names. Then click the Logo background swatch to paint the object with a gradient. Scroll to the bottom of the Swatches palette list if the swatch is not visible.

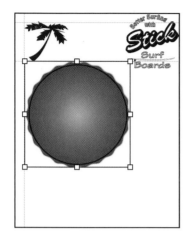

5 With the logo background object still selected, choose Object > Lock > Selection to lock the object and deselect it. Locking the background object makes it easier to select other objects you'll add to the artwork. Once objects are locked, they cannot be selected or edited.

Next you'll use guides on another layer to position the group of outlined text objects. Then you'll use the Transform palette to scale up the logo text by entering new dimensions and designating the point of origin from which the text will scale.

6 If the Layers palette is not visible, Choose Window > Layers to display the Layers palette.

7   Click on the box to the far left of the Text Guides layer to display the layer containing the guides. Scroll to the bottom of the list if the layer is not visible.

8   Choose the Selection tool in the toolbox, and click the outlined text in the upper right of the page to select the group of outlined text objects.

9   Drag the grouped text objects over the logo background, and align the bottom left of the letter B in the word Boards to the intersection of the guides.

10   Choose Window > Transform to display the Transform palette.

The Transform palette contains a small square indicating the reference point of a selected object.

11 Click the in the bottom left corner reference point to set the point of origin from which the objects will scale. Click the Chain Link icon on the right side of the palette to turn on Constrain width and height proportions and Type **290** in the W text field, and then press Enter or Return to increase up the size of the text.

Next you'll use guides on another layer to position the palm tree and then use the Scale tool to resize the palm tree and set a fixed point for the scaling.

12 Click on the eye icon (👁) to the left of the Text layer to turn off the visibility of the text. Turning off the visibility of the text layer will allow for easier scaling of the palm tree object.

13 Click on the eye icon to the left of the Text Guides layer to turn off the visibility of the layer containing the guides used to align the text.

14 Click on the box to the far left of the Palm Tree Guides layer to display the guides.

15 Choose the Selection tool in the toolbox, and click the palm tree to select it. Drag the palm tree and align the left side and bottom of the trunk of the tree with the guides.

16 Select the Scale tool (🔲) in the toolbox, hold down Alt (Windows) or Option (Mac OS), and click the intersection of the Palm Tree Guides.

Clicking the intersection point of the guides sets the point of origin from which the palm tree will scale. Holding down Alt/Option as you click displays the Scale dialog box.

17 In the Scale dialog box, type **175%** in the Scale text field and click OK to make the palm tree 1.75 times larger. It is OK if the tree is positioned off the artwork at this point.

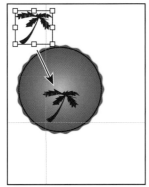
Move palm tree.

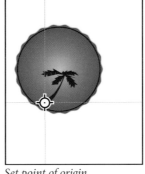
Set point of origin.

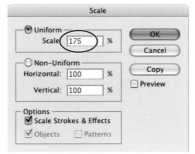
Scale dialog box.

Rotating objects

Objects are rotated by turning them around a designated point of origin. You can rotate objects by displaying their bounding boxes and moving the cursor to an outside corner. Once the rotate cursor appears, click to rotate the object around its center point. You can also rotate objects using the Transform palette to set a point of origin and a rotation angle.

You'll rotate the palm tree 20° around a selected reference point using the Rotate tool.

1 With the palm tree selected, select the Rotate tool (○) in the toolbox.

Notice that the palm tree's point of origin is still at the intersection of the Palm Tree Guides.

2 Begin dragging the selected palm tree. Notice how the movement is constrained to a circle rotating around the point of origin. Continue dragging until the palm tree is in its original position on the logo background, and then release the mouse button. You can also choose Edit > Undo Rotate.

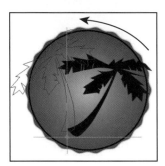

3 Now, with the palm tree still selected, hold down Alt (Windows) or Option (Mac OS), and click the intersection of the palm tree guides.

4 In the Rotate dialog box, check Preview, and type **20** in the Angle text field, then click OK to rotate the palm tree 20° around the selected point of origin.

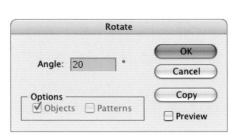

Note: When an object is selected and you double-click the Rotate tool in the toolbox, the object is rotated exactly from the center of the object.

5 Choose File > Save.

Reflecting objects

Objects are reflected by flipping them across an invisible vertical or horizontal axis. Copying objects while reflecting creates a mirror image of the objects. Similar to scaling and rotating, in reflecting you either designate the point of origin from which an object will reflect or use the object's center point by default.

Now you'll use the Reflect tool to flip and copy the palm tree object 90° across the vertical axis and then scale and rotate the copy into position.

1   Choose the Selection tool (▸) to select the palm tree.

2   Select the Reflect tool (⬚) nested with the Rotate tool (◌) in the toolbox, then hold down Alt (Windows) or Option (Mac OS), and click on the tip of the right-most palm frond of the palm tree.

3   In the Reflect dialog box, make sure that the Vertical option is selected and **90°** is entered in the Angle text field. Then click Copy (not OK).

4   Double-click the Scale tool in the toolbox and Enter **70** in the Uniform Scale text field and click OK.

5   Double-click the Rotate tool (⟳) nested with the Reflect tool (◪) in the toolbox. In the Rotate dialog box enter **-45°** in the Angle text field and click OK.

Note: You can also use the Transform palette to reflect selected objects by choosing Flip Horizontal or Flip Vertical from the palette menu.

6   Choose the Selection tool in the toolbox, click and drag the reduced palm tree, aligning the bottom of the trunk to the right-side bottom of the larger palm tree's trunk.

7   Choose File > Save.

8   Click on the eye icon (👁) next to the Palm Tree Guides layer to turn the visibility off, and then turn on the visibility of the Text layer.

9   Choose Object > Unlock All to unlock the logo's background.

10   Choose Select > All to select all the objects of the completed logo.

11   Choose Object > Group to group the selected objects of the logo.

12   Double-click the Scale tool (⊡) in the toolbox, and in the Scale dialog box enter **30** in the Uniform Scale text field. Press OK.

13   Choose the Selection tool from the toolbox, and drag the logo, aligning it to the upper left blue guides.

14   Click on the eye icon next to the Address layer to turn the visibility on for this layer.

15   Choose File > Save.

Distorting objects

Various tools and filters let you distort the original shapes of objects in different ways. For example, the wavy yellow circle around the logo's background object on the letterhead was created by applying the Zig Zag distort filter to the smooth edge.

Now you'll create a flower, first using the Twist distort filter to twirl the shape of a star, and then applying the Pucker & Bloat distort filter to transform another star in front of it.

To begin, you'll draw a star for part of the flower and use the Twist filter and Info palette to distort it.

1 Select the Star tool (★) from the same group as the Rectangle tool (▣) in the toolbox, and position the cursor in the artwork in the lower right corner of the letterhead. Drag the tool to draw a five-pointed star that's about 150 pt wide.

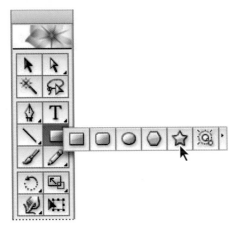

Note: Choose > Window > Info to display the Info palette to use as a guide for sizing the star.

The star is painted with the paint attributes of the last selected object (in this case, the logo's background).

2 With the star still selected, select the Fill box in the Control palette and choose the gradient swatch named Flower gradient. Leave the stroke set to None.

Now you'll distort the star using the Twist distort filter. This filter twists objects around their centers.

Twist distortion can be applied to objects two ways: Applying it as a Filter permanently distorts the object; applying it as an Effect maintains the original shape and lets you remove or edit the effect at any time using the Appearance palette. You will be using both methods in the following exercise. Read more about using effects in Lesson 11, "Applying Appearance Attributes, Graphic Styles, and Effects."

3 Choose Filter > Distort > Twist. Type in the value of **45°** in the Twist dialog box and click OK.

Now you'll draw another star that's centered on top of the first star.

4   With the star selected, choose Window > Attributes to display the Attributes palette. Then click the Show Center button (▣) to display the star's center point.

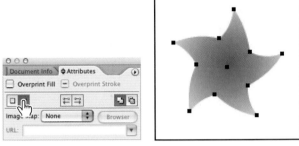

Display center point of star.

5   Select the Star tool again, and drag from the center point to draw another star, about the same size, over the center of the first one. Before you release the mouse button, drag the star in an arc to rotate it so the points appear between the points of the star behind it. Keep the star selected.

6   In the Attributes palette, click the Show Center button (▣) to display the second star's center point.

7   Shift+click on the Fill box in the Control palette to link to the Color palette. Click the White color box at the right end of the color bar to paint the star's fill white.

By Shift+clicking on the Fill box, in the Control palette, you can choose the Color palette instead of the default link to the Swatches palette.

8   Click the Fill box to hide the Color palette and click back on the Fill box to link to the Swatches palette. Then select the Stroke box, and click a color in the Swatches palette to paint the star's stroke. (We selected the Crimson color swatch.)

Now you'll distort the frontmost star using the Pucker & Bloat effect. This effect distorts objects inward and outward from their anchor points.

9   With the white star selected, choose Effect > Distort & Transform > Pucker & Bloat. Applying it as an effect maintains the original shape and lets you remove or edit the effect at any time.

10 In the Pucker & Bloat dialog box, select the Preview option, and drag the slider to the right to distort the star (we selected 50%). Click OK.

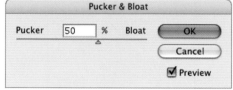

Draw star shape.   *Apply Pucker & Bloat effect.*   *Result.*

11 Keep the artwork selected, and choose File > Save.

Shearing objects

Now you'll complete the flower with an orange center, scale it, and shear it. Shearing an object slants, or skews, the sides of the object along the axis you specify, keeping opposite sides parallel and making the object nonsymmetrical.

1 Select the Ellipse tool (○) from the same group as the Star tool (★) in the toolbox.

2 With the stars still selected and their center points visible, press Alt (Windows) or Option (Mac OS), position the Ellipse tool's crosshairs over the stars' center points, and drag to draw an oval from the center.

3 Click the Fill box in the toolbox to select the object's fill. In the Swatches palette, click the Orange swatch to paint the oval an orange color.

4 In the Color palette, select Show Options, and drag the None icon (☑) and drop it on the Stroke box in the Color palette to remove the stroke.

Draw oval shape and paint fill.   *Drag and drop None button over Stroke box.*

Now, you'll group and then shear the flower.

5   Choose the Selection tool (➤), Shift+click to select the three parts of the flower, and choose Object > Group to group them together.

6   In the Transform palette, type **10°** in the Shear text field, and press Enter or Return to apply the shearing effect on the flower.

Enter 10° shear angle.   Result.

7   Type **0.75 in** in the W text field to scale the flower down to three-quarters of an inch.

Although the default unit of measure is set to points, when you type inches (or in) in the text fields, Illustrator calculates the equivalent measurement in points.

💡 *You can have Illustrator convert unit values and perform mathematical operations in any text box that accepts numeric values. To automatically multiply or divide the size of an object by a number you specify, enter, respectively, an asterisk (*) or a slash (/) respectively, and a number after the value in either the W or the H text box, or in both text boxes, and press Enter or Return to scale the object. For example, enter /2 after the values in the W and H text boxes to scale the object by 50%.*

8 Use the Selection tool to drag the flower to the bottom right corner of the page. Then Alt (Windows) or Option (Mac OS) click, and drag the flower two times to make a cluster of flowers in the corner.

9 Choose Select > Deselect to deselect the artwork.

10 Choose View > Guides > Hide Guides to hide guides, and then choose File > Save.

You've completed the letterhead artwork. Keep the file open so that you can use its artwork later in the lesson.

Positioning objects precisely

You can use the Transform palette to move objects to exact coordinates on the x and y axes of the page and to control the position of objects in relation to the trim edge.

To learn how to produce crop marks for the trim edge, see "To add printer's marks" in Illustrator Help.

You'll create the envelope by first pasting a copy of the logo into the envelope artwork, and then specifying its exact coordinates on the envelope.

1 Double-click the Hand tool (✋) in the toolbox to fit the artwork in the window.

2 Using the Selection tool (▴), click on the logo to select it.

3 Choose Edit > Copy to copy the logo to the Clipboard.

Now you'll open the start file for the envelope artwork.

4 Choose File > Open to open the L3start2.ai file in the Lesson03 folder, located inside the Lessons folder within the AICIB folder on your hard drive.

5 Choose File > Save As, name the file **Envelope.ai**, and select the Lesson03 folder. Leave the type of file format set to Adobe Illustrator Document, and click Save. In the Illustrator Options dialog box, accept the default settings by clicking OK.

6 Choose Edit > Paste.

You'll move the pasted logo to within 1/4-inch of the top left corner of the envelope by specifying the x and y coordinates in relation to the ruler origin. The ruler origin is the point where 0 appears on each ruler. We changed the ruler origin in this file to begin at the top left corner of the envelope, and the ruler units to inches.

[?] For more information, see "To work with rulers" in Illustrator Help.

7 In the Transform palette, click the top left reference point and then type **0.25 in** (18 pt) in the X text field and **–0.25 in** (a negative coordinate) in the Y text field. Press Enter or Return to apply the setting you typed.

Copy the logo from the letterhead.   *Paste into the envelope.*   *Select top left reference point and enter x and y coordinates.*

8   With the logo still selected, hold the Shift key and drag the bottom right corner of the bounding box to scale the logo and make it fit within the blue square guideline.

9   Click away from the artwork to deselect it, and then choose File > Save.

Changing the perspective

Now you'll use the Free Transform tool to change the perspective of the company name.

1   Select the Group Selection tool (⇗) in the toolbox, and click on the company name two times to select the group.

2   Hold down the Option/Alt key, then click and drag slightly down and to the right to copy the selected text.

3   Select the Scale tool (⬛) from the toolbox, then Alt (Windows) or Option (Mac OS) click the left side of the text to set the scaling reference point, and to open the scale dialog box. Enter **300** in the Uniform Scale text field. Click OK.

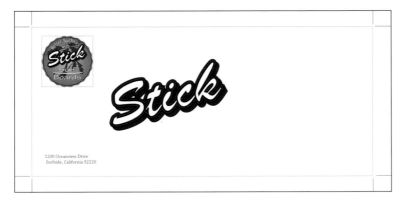

4   With the text selected, select the Free Transform tool (⬛) in the toolbox.

5   Position the double-headed cursor (↔) over the bottom right corner of the object's bounding box. The next step will require a little coordination, so follow directions closely. Click and drag the bottom right corner handle, while dragging press Shift+Alt+Ctrl (Windows) or Shift+Option+Command (Mac OS), slowly drag downward to change the perspective of the object.

Note: If you were to use the modifier keys at the same time as clicking to select, the perspective feature would not work.

Holding down the Shift key as you drag scales an object proportionally. Holding down Alt/Option scales an object from its center point. Finally, holding down Ctrl/Command as you drag distorts an object from the anchor point or bounding box handle that you're dragging.

6   Choose Window > Transparency to open the Transparency palette and enter **20** in the opacity textbox to fade the text into the background.

Change perspective.   *Change transparency.*

7   Choose Select > Deselect.

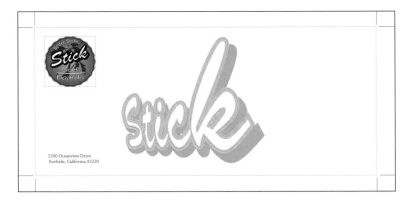

8   Choose File > Save. You can either minimize the file and leave it open on your desktop, or close the file.

Using the Free Transform tool

The Free Transform tool is a multipurpose tool that, besides letting you change the perspective of an object, combines the functions of scaling, shearing, reflecting, and rotating.

Now you'll use the Free Transform tool to transform objects that you copy from the logo into a business card.

1   Choose File > Open, and open the L3start3.ai file in the Lesson03 folder, located inside the Lessons folder within the AICIB folder on your hard drive.

2   Choose File > Save As, name the file **Buscards.ai**, and save it inside the Lesson03 folder. Leave the type of file format set to Adobe Illustrator Document, and click Save. In the Illustrator Options dialog box, accept the default settings by clicking OK.

3   Choose Window > Navigator to display it. In the Navigator palette, click the Zoom In button (⌂) a few times to zoom to 200%, and then move the red view box over the top left corner of the artwork.

 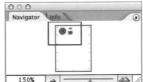

4   Choose the Selection tool (▶), and click to select the palm trees in the logo. Then, Alt+drag (Windows) or Option+drag (Mac OS) to make a copy of the object. Position the new palm trees to the right of the logo.

Now you'll use the Free Transform tool to scale, distort, and rotate the palm trees, then apply a lighter color.

5 With the palm tree still selected, select the Free Transform tool (⊞) in the toolbox. Holding down Shift+Alt (Windows) or Shift+Option (Mac OS), drag the bottom right corner down to scale the object from its center and make the palm trees bigger.

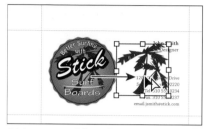 

Make a copy of the palm tree. *Use Free Transform tool to scale object.*

Although you can scale objects using the Selection tool, scaling with the Free Transform tool lets you perform other transformations without switching tools.

6 To distort the palm trees using the Free Transform tool, select the bottom right corner of the object's bounding box, but don't release the mouse button. Begin dragging, and then hold down Ctrl (Windows) or Command (Mac OS) and slowly drag toward the opposite corner of the object.

7 To slightly rotate the palm trees, position the Free Transform tool just outside the bottom right corner of the object's bounding box, until you see the rotate cursor, and then drag to rotate the object.

Distort object using Free Transform tool. *Rotate object using Free Transform tool.*

8 Choose the Selection tool, and click on the palm trees to select. Then choose Object > Arrange > Send to Back, and move the palm trees underneath the text.

9 Select the Tan swatch for the fill color to fade the trees into the background.

Now you'll explore a slightly different way of distorting objects. Free Distort lets you distort a selection by moving any of its four corner points. It can be used either as a filter to apply a permanent change or as an effect to apply a change that can be removed.

10   With the palm trees still selected, choose Filter > Distort > Free Distort.

Note: Choose the top Filter > Distort command. The bottom Filter > Distort commands work only on bitmap images.

11   Drag one or more of the handles to distort the selection. Click OK. We dragged the right handles up.

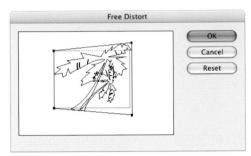
Previewing a free distortion.

Result.

12   Click outside the artwork to deselect it, and choose File > Save.

Making multiple transformations

Now you'll create multiple copies of the business card, and replicate the symbol instances in a few easy steps.

1   Double-click the Hand tool (🖑) in the toolbox to zoom out and fit the artwork in the window.

2   Choose Select > All to select all the objects on the business card.

3   Choose Object > Transform > Transform Each.

The Move options in the Transform Each dialog box let you move objects in a specified or random direction. Now you'll move a copy of the selected objects down 2 inches from the original objects.

4 In the Transform Each dialog box, enter **–2 in** in the Move Vertical text field, leave the other settings as they are, and click Copy (don't click OK).

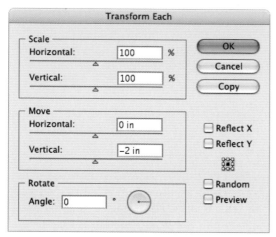

Move object down 2 inches and copy it.

5 Choose Object > Transform > Transform Again to create a third copy. Now you'll use the keyboard shortcut to repeat the transformations.

6 Press Ctrl+D (Windows) or Command+D (Mac OS) twice to transform two additional times, creating a total of five cards in the column.

> *You can also apply multiple transformations as an effect, including scaling, moving, rotating, and reflecting an object. After selecting the objects, choose Effect > Distort & Transform > Transform. The dialog box looks the same as the Transform Each dialog box. Transforming as an effect has the advantage of letting you change or remove the transformation at any time.*

Next you'll use some shortcuts to make a copy of the column.

7 Press Ctrl+A (Windows) or Command+A (Mac OS) to select everything on the five business cards, and right-click (Windows) or Ctrl+click (Mac OS) in the window to display a shortcut menu. Choose Transform > Transform Each from the shortcut menu.

8 This time in the Transform Each dialog box, enter **3.5 in** in the Move Horizontal text field and **0 in** in the Move Vertical text field. Leave the other settings as they are, and click Copy (don't click OK).

9   To clear the window so that you can view the finished artwork, press Ctrl (Windows) or Command (Mac OS) and click outside the artwork to deselect it. Then choose View > Guides > Hide Guides to hide the blue guidelines, and press Tab to close the toolbox and palettes.

Pressing Tab toggles between hiding and showing the toolbox and all the palettes. Pressing Shift+Tab alternately hides or shows only the palettes.

10   Choose File > Save and then choose File > Close.

Converting straight lines to zigzags

The Zig Zag filter adds anchor points to an existing line and then moves some of the points to the left of (or upward from) the line, and some to the right of (or downward from) the line. You can specify the number of anchor points to create and the distance to move them. You can also choose whether to create smooth anchor points for a wavy-line effect or corner anchor points for a jagged-line effect.

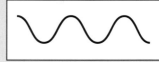

Original line.   *Line with four corner ridges applied.*   *Line with four smooth ridges applied.*

To convert straight lines to zigzags

1 *Do one of the following:*

• *To apply the distortion permanently, use any selection tool to select the line you want to convert. Then choose Filter > Distort > Zig Zag.*

• *To apply the distortion as an effect that can be removed, select an object or group, or target a group or layer in the Layers palette. (For more on targeting, see Lesson 7, "Working with Layers.") Then choose Effect > Distort & Transform > Zig Zag.*

2 *Select how you wish to move points: either Relative by a percentage of the object's size, or Absolute by a specific amount.*

3 *For Size, enter the distance you want to move points on the line, or drag the slider.*

4 *For Ridges per Segment, enter the number of ridges per line segment you want, or drag the slider.*

5 *Select the type of line to create: Smooth to create smooth points for a wavy line, or Corner to create corner points for a jagged line.*

6 *Click Preview to preview the line.*

7 *Click OK.*

Exploring on your own

You can update text, graph data, linked files, or graphics dynamically, and change them in your artwork using certain variables. For example, you can create a series of business cards in which individual names and titles change, but all other information remains constant.

The Variables feature lets designers create highly formatted graphics as templates (called data-driven graphics), and then collaborate with developers to control the links between a template and its content. For more complex applications, you could, for example, produce 500 different Web banners based on the same template. In the past, you had to manually fill in the template with data (images, text, and so on). With data-driven graphics, however, you can use a script referencing a database to speedily generate the Web banners for you.

In Illustrator, you can turn any piece of artwork into a template for data-driven graphics. All you need to do is define which objects on the artboard are dynamic (changeable) using variables. In addition, you can create different sets of variable data to easily view what your template will look like when it is rendered.

If you're a developer, you can code variables and data sets directly into an XML document, then import the variables and data sets into the Illustrator file to create a design based on your specifications.

Making text dynamic

To get an idea of the power and usefulness of the Variables feature, you can try out this procedure using the business card artwork in the lesson.

1 Choose File > Open, and open the L3start3.ai file in the Lesson03 folder, located inside the Lessons folder within the AICIB folder on your hard drive.

2 Choose File > Save As, name the file **Buscard2.ai**, and save it in the Lesson03 folder. Leave the type of file format set to Adobe Illustrator Document, and click Save. In the Illustrator Options dialog box, accept the default settings by clicking OK.

3 Using the Zoom tool (⌕), zoom in on the business card artwork in the upper left corner.

4   Choose Window > Variables to display the Variables palette.

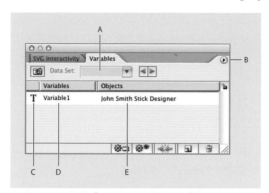

*A. Data set. **B.** Palette menu. **C.** Variable type.*
*D. Variable name. **E.** Name of bound object.*

You'll create some text variables so that you can change the name and title on the business cards. This technique lets you create a series of business cards with a name and title that you can easily modify for other employees. You could also create variables for the address, for example, so that you can change the address for different branch offices.

5   Using the Selection tool (*****), in the artwork select the name and title "John Smith, Stick Designer."

6   At the bottom of the Variables palette, click the Make Text Dynamic button. A new variable, named Variable1, appears in the palette.

The (T) icon appears to the left of the variable, indicating that it's a text string. The Objects column lists the object to which the variable is bounded—in this case, the text you selected in step 5.

7   Double-click the variable (Variable1), and in the Variable Options dialog box, enter **name_title**. The type already is set to Text String. Click OK.

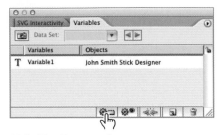 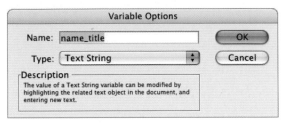

Make Text Dynamic button.   *Variable Options dialog box.*

You can create four types of variables in Illustrator: Graph Data, Linked File, Text String, and Visibility. A variable's type indicates which object attributes are changeable. For example, you can use a Visibility variable to show or hide any object in your template. The Graph Data, Linked File, and Text String variables make those respective objects dynamic.

8   In your artwork, make sure that the text "John Smith, Stick Designer" is still selected.

9   In the Variables palette, click the Capture Data Set button in the upper left of the palette to capture the information. Data Set 1 appears in the Data Set drop-down menu as your first variable.

Capture Data Set button and Data Set 1 in Variables palette.

A data set is a collection of variables and associated data. When you create a data set, you capture a snapshot of the dynamic data that is currently displayed on the artboard. You can switch between data sets to upload different data into your template.

Now you'll revise the text and create another data set.

10 Select the Type tool (T) in the toolbox. In the artwork, drag to select the text "John Smith," and type **Maggie Riley.** Then select "Stick Designer," and type **Sales** to replace the two lines of text using the existing text attributes.

11 Notice that the Data Set 1 variable now appears in italics in the Variables palette. The italics indicate that the variable has been edited. You can modify a data set after you create it, as you'll do now.

12 In the Variables palette, click the Capture Data Set button in the upper left of the palette to capture the information. Data Set 2 appears in the drop-down menu as the current variable.

Creating variables is a two-step process. First you define the variable, and then you bind it to an object attribute to make the object variable. The type of object and type of variable determine what attributes of the object can change. You can bind a Visibility variable to any object to make the object's state of visibility dynamic. If the object is text, a linked image, or a graph, you can also make the object's content dynamic.

13 To create another variable for the address, click in a blank area of the Variables palette to deselect the variable you just created. If you want to create a new variable that matches the type of the selected object, make sure that no variable is selected in the Variables palette.

14 Use the Selection tool to select the address text.

15 Click the Make Text Dynamic button at the bottom of the Variables palette. Variable1 appears, a text string variable with the first line of the address as the object appears in the palette. You can double-click the variable and rename it. (We renamed it **address**.) Then click OK.

16 Using the Type tool, revise the telephone number and e-mail address on the card. We used **310 555.5678** and **mriley@stick.com**.

17 Click the Capture Data Set button at the top left of the Variables palette to capture this information. You've created Data Set 3.

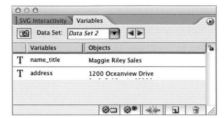

Data Set 3.

18 To view the variables you just created, click the Next Data Set button (▶) to the right of the Data Set menu to scroll through the variables.

Notice that Data Set 2 lists the wrong telephone number and e-mail address for Maggie Riley. You can easily delete data sets.

19 With Data Set 2 selected in the Variables palette, choose Delete Data Set from the Variables palette menu, and click Yes at the alert message.

You could create a series of data sets for business card information, and then use a batch process to update all or part of the information—such as the names and titles, branch office addresses, and telephone numbers.

20 Choose File > Save.

Importing data and batch processing

In addition to being able to change data variables on an individual basis, you can import data files from outside sources and batch process your information to create multiple documents.

In this section, you will import additional names and addresses from an XML document, create an action to save the files as EPS documents and then batch process the data to create one EPS document for each of the names in your database.

1   With Buscards2.ai still open, select Load Variable Library from the Variables
palette menu. Select data.xml from the Lesson03 folder of the AICIB folder on
your hard drive and select Yes to overwrite the current variables and data sets.

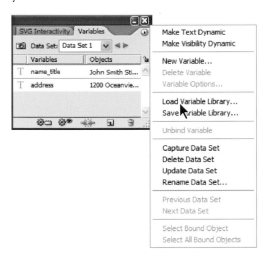

2   Click on the drop-down menu to the right of Data Set in the Variables
palette. A list of seven Data Sets appears. Select each Data Set and notice that the
name and address on the business card changes for each set.

Now you will create an action to save each one of the business cards as a separate
.EPS document. (For more information on working with Actions see "To use the
Actions palette" in Illustrator Help)

3   Choose Window > Actions to display the Actions palette.

4 Select New Action from the Actions palette menu. In the Name field type **Save as EPS**, leave the other fields at their defaults and click Record.

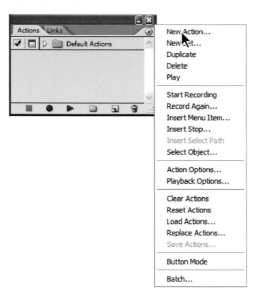

5 Choose File > Save As. Name the file **buscards2.eps**, choose Illustrator EPS as the type and save in the Lesson03 folder. Click Save. In the EPS Options dialog box, accept the default settings by clicking OK.

6 Click on the Stop Recording icon (■) in the Actions Palette. You have just created the Action that will save each file as an .EPS.

You will now create a batch to process the Save as EPS action for each of the individual data sets. (For more information on Batch Processing, see "To play an action on batches of files" in Illustrator Help.)

7   Select Batch from the Actions palette menu to display the Batch Dialog Box. Choose the Default Actions Set and Save as EPS Action. Choose Data Sets as the source. In the Destination choose None. Check Override Action "Save" Commands and then choose the Lesson03 folder in the AICIB folder on your hard drive. For the File Name, select File + Data Set Name. Click OK.

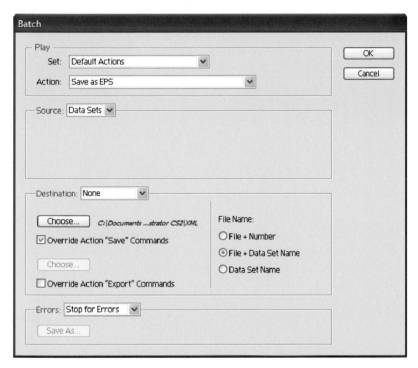

8   To view the files that Illustrator created, Choose File > Open and select any one of the files named buscard_name.eps in the Lesson03 folder.

Review

▶ **Review questions**

1   How can you select and manipulate individual objects in a group?

2   How do you resize an object? Explain how you determine the point from which the object resizes. How do you resize a group of objects proportionally?

3   What transformations can you make using the Transform palette?

4   What does the square diagram indicate in the Transform palette, and how will it affect your transformations?

5   What's an easy way to change perspective? List three other types of transformations you can perform with the Free Transform tool.

6   How do you create a variable? What are some uses for variables in your artwork?

▶ **Review answers**

1   You can use the Group Selection tool to select individual objects or subgroups of objects within a group and change them without affecting the rest of the group.

2   You can resize an object several ways: by selecting it and dragging handles on its bounding box, or by using the Scale tool, the Transform palette, or Object > Transform > Scale to specify exact dimensions. You can also scale by choosing Effect > Distort & Transform > Transform.

To determine the point of origin from which an object scales, select a reference point in the Transform palette or in the Transform Effect or Transform Each dialog box, or click in the artwork with the Scale tool. Holding down Alt (Windows) or Option (Mac OS) and dragging the bounding box or double-clicking the Scale tool will resize a selected object from its center point.

Shift+dragging a corner handle on the bounding box scales an object proportionally, as does specifying either a uniform scale value in the Scale dialog box or multiples of the dimensions in the Width and Height text fields in the Transform palette.

3   You use the Transform palette for making the following transformations:

- Moving or strategically placing objects in your artwork (by specifying the x and y coordinates and the point of origin).

- Scaling (by specifying the width and height of selected objects).

- Rotating (by specifying the angle of rotation).

- Shearing (by specifying the angle of distortion).

- Reflecting (by flipping selected objects vertically or horizontally).

4   The square diagram in the Transform palette indicates the bounding box of the selected objects. Select a reference point in the square to indicate the point of origin from which the objects as a group will move, scale, rotate, shear, or reflect.

5   An easy way to change the perspective of selected objects is to select the Free Transform tool, hold down Shift+Alt+Ctrl (Windows) or Shift+Option+ Command (Mac OS), and drag a corner handle on the bounding box.

Other types of transformations you can perform with the Free Transform tool are distorting, scaling, shearing, rotating, and reflecting.

6   To create a variable, you make a selection in your artwork, and then bind a variable to the object. The type of object and type of variable determine what attributes of the object can change. You can bind a Visibility variable to any object to make the object's visibility dynamic, or changeable. If the object is text, a linked image, or a graph, you can also make the object's content dynamic.

Using variables is a quick way to make artwork versions for a client that shows different iterations of the same design. You can also use variables to automate tedious design tasks, such as designing and updating business cards for hundreds of employees. You can use variables to update text, graph data, linked files, or graphics, and change them dynamically in your artwork.

The Pen tool is a powerful tool for drawing straight lines, Bézier curves, and complex shapes. While the Pencil tool is easier for drawing and editing free form lines, the Pen tool is easier for drawing more precisely. You'll practice using the Pen tool on a blank artboard and then use the Pen tool to create an illustration of a pear.

4 | Drawing with the Pen tool

In this lesson, you'll learn how to do the following:

- Draw straight lines.
- Use Template layers.
- End path segments and split lines.
- Draw curved lines.
- Select and adjust curve segments.

Getting started

The first part of this lesson involves manipulating the Pen tool on a blank artboard.

1 To ensure that the tools and palettes function exactly as described in this lesson, delete or deactivate (by renaming) the Adobe Illustrator CS2 preferences file. See "Restoring default preferences" on page 3.

2 Open the file named L4strt_01.ai from the Lesson04 folder, located inside the Lessons folder within the AICIB folder on your hard drive. The top portion of the artboard shows the path that you will create. Use the bottom half of the page for this exercise.

3 Choose File > Save As. In the Save As window, navigate to the Lesson04 folder and open it. Type **path1.ai** in the File name text field. In the Save as Type drop-down menu, choose Adobe Illustrator (.AI). In the Illustrator Options window, leave the default settings and choose OK.

4 Use Ctrl+0 (zero) (Windows) or Command+0 (Mac OS) to fit the entire page into the window and then close all the palettes, except for the tools, by clicking their Close boxes or by holding down Shift and pressing Tab once. You won't need to use them for this lesson.

5   Select the Pen tool (✒). Notice that when the Pen has not yet placed its first point, an "x" appears to the right of the pen icon. This indicates that you are starting a new path. Click and release once in the bottom work area. Then, move the mouse away from the original anchor point, the "x" no longer appears.

Note: If instead of the pen icon, you see a crosshair, the Caps Lock key is active. Caps Lock On turns tool icons into crosshairs for increased precision.

6   Move the mouse to the right of the original point, and click once to create the next anchor point in the path.

Note: The first segment you draw will not be visible until you click a second anchor point. Also, if direction handles appear, you have accidentally dragged with the Pen tool; choose Edit > Undo, and click again. (Direction handles are used to reshapes curved paths, but do not print.)

The first point connects to the new anchor point. Click back under the initial anchor point to create a zigzag pattern. Your zigzag is complete when it has a total of six anchor points.

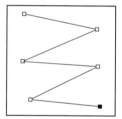

*Click and release from point
to point to create the zigzag.*

Choose the Selection tool (▶). One of the many benefits of using the Pen tool is that you can create custom paths and continue to edit the anchor points that make up the path. Next, see how the Selection tools relate to the Pen tool.

7   Using the Selection tool, click on the zigzag path and note how all the anchor points become solid, signifying that all anchor points are selected. Click and drag the path to a new location anywhere on the artboard, and notice that all the anchor points travel together, maintaining the zigzag path.

8   Deselect the zigzag path any of these four ways:

• Use the Selection tool and click on an empty section of the artboard.

• Use Select > Deselect from the menu.

• While on the Pen tool, hold down the Ctrl (Windows) or Command (Mac OS) key and click to deselect; this temporarily gives you the Selection tool. When the Control or Command key is released, you return to the Pen tool.

• Click once on the Pen tool. Even though it looks like the path is still active, it will not connect to the next anchor point created.

9   Choose the Direct Selection tool (↖) and click on any one point in the zigzag. Clicking and dragging a marquee selection around an anchor point with the Direct Selection tool can make selecting individual anchor points easier. The selected anchor point turns solid, the unselected anchor points are hollow.

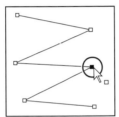

*Only the active point
appears solid.*

10   With the anchor point selected, click and drag to reposition the anchor point. The anchor point is moving but the others are stationary. Use this technique to edit a path.

11   At times you will need to recreate just one line segment in a path. Choose Select > Deselect, then with the Direct Selection tool, click on any line segment that is between two anchor points and choose Edit > Cut.

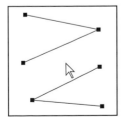

Select a segment of a path.

12 Return to the Pen tool and position the cursor over one of the anchor points that was connected to the line segment. Note that the pen icon has a forward slash (/) to the right of it, signifying a continuation of an existing path. Click and release the mouse.

13 Position the cursor over the other point that was connected to the original line segment. An icon of a circle with a line through it (⟟) appears. This signifies that you are connecting to another path. Click the point to reconnect the paths.

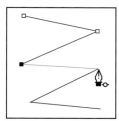

Reconnect the paths.

14 Choose File > Save and then File > Close this file.

Creating straight lines

In Lesson 3, "Transforming Objects," you discovered that using the Shift key in combination with shape tools constrains the shape of objects you create using Illustrator. This is also true with the Pen tool, except that the procedure constrains the paths you create in multiples of 45°.

In this part of the lesson, you will learn how to draw straight lines.

1 Open the file named L4strt_02.ai from the Lesson04 folder, located inside the Lessons folder within the AICIB folder on your hard drive. The top portion of the artboard shows the path that you will create. Use the bottom half of the page for this exercise.

2 Choose File > Save As. In the Save As window, navigate to the Lesson04 folder and open it. Type **path2.ai** in the File name text field. In the Save as Type drop-down menu, choose Adobe Illustrator (.AI). In the Illustrator Options window, leave the default settings and choose OK.

3 Select the Pen tool (✒) and click once in the work area of the page.

4   Hold down the Shift key and click about an inch to the right of the original anchor point. Note that if you are not in the exact straight line position, that you are snapped to that point.

5   While holding down the Shift key, click with the mouse and try to replicate the path in the exercise file.

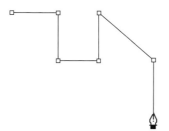

Hold down the Shift key while clicking to constrain the path.

6   Choose File > Save and close the file.

Creating curved paths

In this part of the lesson, you'll learn how to draw smooth, curved lines with the Pen tool. In vector-drawing programs such as Adobe Illustrator CS2, you draw a curve, called a Bézier curve, with control points. By setting anchor points and dragging direction handles (controls), you can define the shape of the curve. Although drawing curves this way takes some getting used to, it gives you the greatest control and flexibility in creating paths.

1   Before we get started with a lesson file, choose File > New to create a new letter-sized document in Adobe Illustrator, leaving settings at the page defaults. Consider this page a "scratch" page to practice the Bézier curve.

2   Using the Control palette, click on the Fill box and choose the None swatch (⊠) Then click on the Stroke box and choose the Black swatch.

3   Click on the Stroke Weight drop-down menu in the Control palette and change the stroke weight to 1 pt.

4   Click and release the mouse anywhere on the page to create the initial anchor point. Then click in another location on the page (don't release the mouse), and drag, creating a curved path.

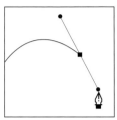

Click and drag to create a curved path.

Continue clicking and dragging at various locations on the page. The goal for this exercise is not to create anything specific, but to get you accustomed to the feel of the Bézier curve.

Notice that as you click and drag, direction handles that end in round direction points appear. The angle and length of the direction handles determine the shape and size of the curved segments. Direction lines do not print and are not visible when the anchor is inactive.

5   Choose Select > Deselect.

6   Choose the Direct Selection tool (⬚) and select a curved segment to display the direction handles again. Moving the direction points reshapes the curves.

Note: *Anchor points are square, and when selected, appear filled; unselected, they appear unfilled, like hollow squares. Direction points are round. These lines and points do not print with the artwork.*

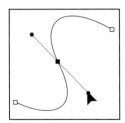

Select anchor points to access the direction handles.

7   Choose File > Close and do not save this file.

Components of a path

A smooth anchor point always has two direction handles that move together as a single, straight unit. When you drag the direction anchor point of either direction line on a smooth anchor point, both direction handles move simultaneously, maintaining a continuous curve at that anchor point.

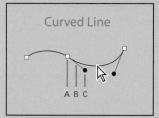

Curved Line

A B C

In comparison, a corner point can have two, one, or no direction handles, depending on whether it joins two, one, or no curved segments, respectively. Corner point direction handles maintain the corner by using different angles. When you drag a direction point on a corner point's direction line, the other direction line, if present, does not move.

*A. Anchor point. **B**. Direction line.*
***C**. Direction point (or handle).*

Building a curve

In this part of the lesson, you will learn how to control the direction handles in order to control curves.

1   Open the file named L4strt_03.ai from the Lesson04 folder. On this page you can see the paths that you will create. A template layer has been created in this file so that you can practice using the Pen tool (✒) by tracing. (See Lesson 7, "Working with Layers," for information about creating layers.) The work area below the path is for additional practice on your own.

2   Choose File > Save As. In the Save As window, navigate to the Lesson04 folder and open it. Type **path3.ai** in the File name text field. In the Save as Type drop-down menu, choose Adobe Illustrator (.AI). In the Illustrator Options window, leave the default settings and choose OK.

3   Press Z to switch to the Zoom tool (🔍) and drag a marquee around the first curve.

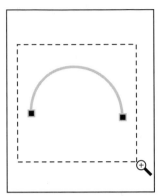

Zoom in to a specified area by dragging
a marquee when on the Zoom tool.

4   Select the Pen tool and click and hold at the base of the left side of the arch and drag up to create a direction line going the same direction as the arch. It helps to remember to always follow the direction of the curve. Release the mouse when the direction line is slightly above the arch.

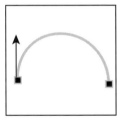

When a curve goes up, the
direction line should also go up.

Note: *The artboard may scroll as you drag the anchor point. If you lose visibility of the curve, choose View > Zoom out until you see the curve and anchor point. Pressing the spacebar will temporarily give you the Hand tool and allow you to reposition the artwork.*

5   Click on the lower right base of the arch path and drag down. Release the mouse when the top direction line is slightly above the arch.

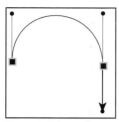

*To control the path, pay attention
to where the direction handles fall.*

6   If the path you created is not aligned exactly with the template, return to the Direct Selection tool (⬚) and select the anchor points one at a time. Then, adjust the direction handles until your path follows the template more accurately.

Note: *Pulling the direction handle longer makes a higher slope, while pulling it shorter makes the slope flatter.*

7   Use the Selection tool (▶) and click on the artboard anywhere there are no other objects, or choose Select > Deselect. If necessary, zoom out to see the next path on this page.

If you click with the Pen tool while the original path is still active, the path will connect to the next point. Deselecting the first path allows you to create a new path.

8   Save the file by choosing File > Save.

Note: *You can also hold down the Ctrl (Windows) or Command (Mac OS) key to temporarily switch you to the Selection or Direct Selection tool, whichever was last used. Hold down Ctrl/Command and click on the artboard where there are no objects to deselect.*

9 Select the Pen tool and click and drag at the left base of path "B," again in the direction of the arch. Click and drag down on the next square point, adjusting the arch with the direction handle before you release the mouse. Don't worry if it is not exact; you can correct this with the Direct Selection tool when the path is complete.

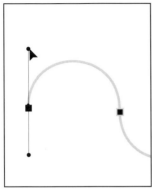

Click and drag up to create the upward arch.

Continue along the path, alternating between clicking and dragging up and down. Put anchor points only where you see the square boxes. If you make a mistake as you draw, you can undo your work by choosing Edit > Undo. Adobe Illustrator CS2, by default, lets you undo a series of actions—limited only by your computer's memory—by repeatedly choosing Edit > Undo or Ctrl+Z (Windows) or Command+Z (Mac OS).

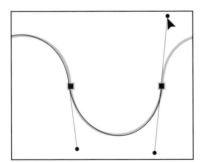

Alternate between dragging up and down with the Pen tool.

10 When the path is complete, choose the Direct Selection tool and select an anchor point. When the anchor is selected, the direction handles reappear, and you can readjust the slope of the path.

11 Practice repeating these paths in the work area.

12 Choose File > Save and close the file.

Curves and corner anchor points

When creating curves, the directional handles help to determine the slope of the path. Returning to a corner point requires a little extra effort. In this next portion of the lesson, we will practice converting curve points to corners.

1 Open the file named L4strt_04.ai from the Lesson04 folder. On this page you can see the path that you will create. Use the top section as a template for the exercise. Create your paths directly on top of those that you see on the page. The work area below is for additional practice on your own.

2 Choose File > Save As. In the Save As window, navigate to the Lesson04 folder and open it. Type **path4.ai** in the File name text field. In the Save as Type drop-down menu, choose Adobe Illustrator (.AI). In the Illustrator Options window, leave the default settings and choose OK.

3 Use the Zoom tool (🔍) and drag a marquee around the top path.

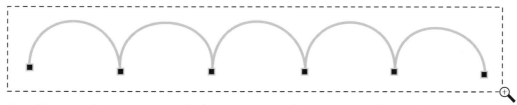

You will get a much more accurate path when you are zoomed in to an increased magnification.

4 Choose the Pen tool (✒), click on the first anchor point and drag up, then click on the second anchor point and drag down, just as you have been doing for previous exercises. Holding the Shift key when dragging constrains the angle of the handle to a straight line.

5 Hold down Alt (Windows) or Option (Mac OS) and position the mouse over either the last anchor point created or its direction handle. Look for the caret (^) symbol and click and drag up when it is visible.

An alert window will appear if you don't click exactly on the anchor point. If that appears, click OK and try again.

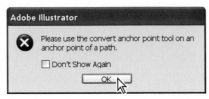

This alert will appear if you do not click on the anchor point.

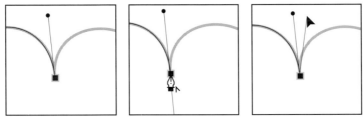

When the caret is visible, click and drag.

You can practice adjusting the direction handles with the Direct Selection tool (↑) when the path is completed.

6   Release the Alt/Option key and click on the next square point on the template path and drag down.

7   Hold down the Alt/Option key again and grab the last anchor point or direction line and pull it up for the next curve. Remember, you must see the caret or you will create an additional loop.

8   Continue this pattern of clicking and dragging, and using the Alt/Option key, to create corner points, until the path is completed. Use the Direct Selection tool to fine-tune the path, and then deselect the path.

9   Choose File > Save.

10   Choose View > Fit in Window. You can also use Ctrl+0 (zero) (Windows) or Command+0 (Mac OS). Use the Zoom tool (🔍) to drag a marquee around the second path and enlarge its view.

11 With the Pen tool, click on the first anchor point and drag up, then click and drag down on the second anchor point. This motion of creating an arch should be familiar to you by now. You will now go from the curve to a straight line. Simply pressing the Shift key and clicking will not produce a straight line, since this last point is a curved anchor point.

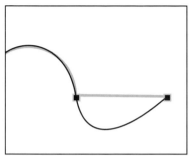

The path when a curved point is not turned into a corner point.

12 To create the next path as a straight line, click on the last point created to delete one handle from the path. Then hold down the Shift key and click to the next point.

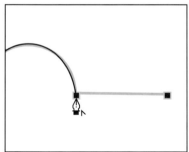

Click on the last anchor point created to force a straight path from it.

13 For the next arch, click and drag down (since the arch is going down) on the point you just created. This creates a directional handle.

14 Click on the next point and drag up to complete the downward arch.

15 Click and release on the last anchor point of the arch.

16 Shift+click to the next point.

17 Click and drag up, and then click and drag down on the last point, to create the final arch.

18 Practice repeating these paths in the lower portion. Use the Direct Selection tool to adjust your path if necessary.

19 Choose File > Save and then File > Close the file.

Creating the pear illustration

In this next part of the lesson, you'll create an illustration of a pear pierced by an arrow. This procedure will incorporate what you have learned in the previous exercises, and will also teach you some additional Pen tool techniques.

1 Choose File > Open, and open the L4end.ai file in the Lesson04 folder, located inside the Lessons folder within the AICIB folder on your hard drive.

2 Choose View > Zoom Out to make the finished artwork smaller and leave it on your screen as you work. (Use the Hand tool (✋) to move the artwork to where you want it in the window.) If you don't want to leave the image open, choose File > Close. Now you'll open the start file to begin the lesson.

3 Choose File > Open, and open the L4begin.ai file in the Lesson04 folder.

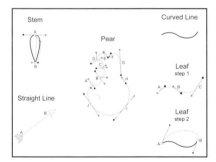

4 Choose File > Save As, name the file **Pear.ai**, and select the Lesson04 folder in the Save In menu. Leave the type of format set to Adobe Illustrator Document, and click Save. In the Illustrator Options palette, leave the options set at the defaults and click OK.

Creating the arrow

You'll begin by drawing the straight line for the arrow. The template layer allows you to follow along directly over the artwork.

1 Choose View > Straight Line to zoom into the left corner of the template.

Separate views that show different areas of the template at a higher magnification were created for this document and added to the View menu.

To create a custom view, choose View > New View. For information, see "To use multiple windows and views" in Illustrator Help.

2 Choose View > Hide Bounding Box to hide the bounding boxes of selected objects. Select the Pen tool (✒) in the toolbox, and move the cursor to the dashed line of the arrow in the artwork. Notice that the Pen tool cursor has a small "x" next to it. If you recall, this indicates that clicking will begin a new path.

3 Click point A at the left end of the line to create the starting anchor point—a small solid square.

Click point B at the right end of the line to create the ending anchor point.

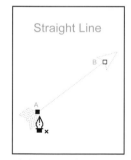
Click once to begin a straight line.

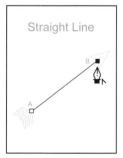
Click again to end it.

When you click a second time, a caret (^) appears next to the Pen tool. The caret indicates that you can split the anchor point to create a direction line for a curve by dragging the Pen tool from this anchor point. The caret disappears when you move the Pen tool away from the anchor point.

4   Remember that you must end the path before you can draw other lines that aren't connected to this path. Choose Select > Deselect, or use any of the other methods discussed in the previous exercises.

Now you'll make the straight line thicker by changing its stroke weight.

5   With the Selection tool (⬆) from the toolbox, click the straight line to select it.

6   Choose Window > Stroke to display the Stroke palette.

7   In the Stroke palette, type **3 pt** in the Weight text field, and press Enter or Return to apply the change.

Splitting a path

To continue creating the arrow for this illustration, you'll split the path of the straight line using the Scissors tool, and adjust the segments.

1   With the straight line still selected, select the Scissors tool (✄) in the toolbox and click in the middle of the line to make a cut.

Cuts made with the Scissors tool must be on a line or a curve rather than on an endpoint.

Where you click with the Scissors tool, you will see a newly selected anchor point. The Scissors tool actually creates two anchor points each time you click, but because they are on top of each other, you can see only one.

2   Select the Direct Selection tool (⬆) in the toolbox and position it over the cut. The small hollow square on the cursor indicates that it's over the anchor point. Select the new anchor point, and drag it up to widen the gap between the two split segments.

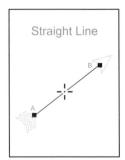
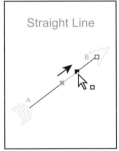

Click with the Scissors tool to cut the line.

Drag to separate the new line segments.

Adding arrowheads

Adobe Illustrator lets you add pre-made arrowheads and tails to open paths by applying an Effect. The Add Arrowhead feature is available under the Filter menu as well as in the Effect menu. The benefit to using an Effect is that the arrow dynamically changes with the stroke to which it is applied. A filter, on the other hand, has no relationship to the stroke.

When a path with the Add Arrowhead Effect is changed, the arrowhead follows the path, whereas the Filter arrowhead remains in its created position. Read more about Effects and how to use them in Lesson 11 "Applying Appearance Attributes, Graphic Styles, and Effects."

 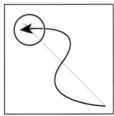

The Add Arrowhead Filter. *The Add Arrowhead Effect.*

Now you'll add an arrowhead to the ending point of one line segment and a tail to the starting point of the other line segment.

1   With the top line segment selected, choose Effect > Stylize > Add Arrowheads.

Note: Choose the top, or first, Effect > Stylize command. The second Effect > Stylize command applies painted or impressionistic effects to RGB images.

2   In the Add Arrowheads dialog box, leave the Start section set to None. For the End section, click an arrow button to select the number 2 style of arrowhead (a thumbnail preview appears in the dialog box), and click OK.

Illustrator adds the arrowhead to the end of the line (the last anchor point created on the uncut line).

3   Using the Selection tool (▶), select the bottom line segment, and choose Effect > Stylize > Add Arrowheads to open the dialog box again. Select the number 18 style of arrowhead from the Start section, select None for the End section, and click OK to add a tail to the starting point of the line.

You can reapply the same arrowhead style to other selected objects by choosing Effect > Stylize > Add Arrowheads.

4   Choose Select > Deselect to deselect the artwork, and then choose File > Save.

Drawing curves

In this part of the lesson, you will review drawing curves by drawing the pear, its stem, and a leaf. You'll examine a single curve and then draw a series of curves together, using the template guidelines to help you.

Selecting a curve

1   Choose View > Curved Line to display a view of a curved line on the template.

2   Using the Direct Selection tool (▸), click one of the segments of the curved line to view its anchor points and its direction handles, which extend from the points. The Direct Selection tool lets you select and edit individual segments in the curved line.

With a curve selected, you can also select the paint attributes of the curve. When you do this, the next line you draw will have those same attributes. For more on paint attributes, see Lesson 5, "Color and Painting."

Drawing the leaf

Now you'll draw the first curve of the leaf.

1   Choose View > Leaf or scroll down to see the guides for Leaf step 1.

Instead of dragging the Pen tool (✎) to draw a curve, you will drag it to set the starting point and the direction of the line's curve. When you release the mouse button, the starting point is created and two direction handles are formed. Then you drag the Pen tool to the end of the first curve to set the starting point and direction of the next curve on the line.

2   Select the Pen tool and position it over point A on the template. Press the mouse button and drag from point A to the red dot. Then release the mouse button.

Next you'll set the second anchor point and its direction handles.

3   Press the mouse button and drag from point B to the next red dot. Release the mouse button. Illustrator connects the two anchor points with a curve that follows the direction handles you have created. Notice that if you vary the angle of dragging, you change the amount of curve.

4   To complete the curved line, drag the Pen tool from point C on the template to the last red dot and release the mouse button.

5   Control+click (Windows) or Command+click (Mac OS) away from the line to indicate the end of the path. (You must do this to indicate when you have finished drawing a path. You can also do this by clicking the Pen tool in the toolbox, or by choosing Select > Deselect.)

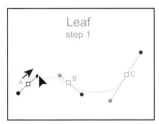

Drag to start the line and set direction of first curve.

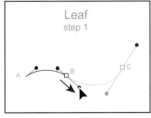

Drag to end first curve and set direction of second curve.

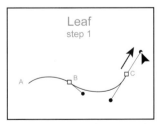

Drag to end second curve and adjust its direction.

Drawing different kinds of curves

Now you'll finish drawing the leaf by adding to an existing curved segment. Even after ending a path, you can return to the curve and add to it. The Alt (Windows) or Option (Mac OS) key lets you control the type of curve you draw.

Before starting this lesson, choose the arrow to the right of the status bar in the lower left corner of the Illustrator workspace and select Show > Current Tool.

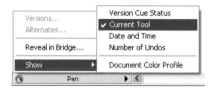

1　Scroll down to the instructions on the template for Leaf step 2.

You'll add a corner point to the path. A corner point lets you change the direction of the curve. A smooth point lets you draw a continuous curve.

2　Position the Pen tool (✎) over the end of the line at point A. The slash next to the Pen tool indicates that you'll continue the path of the existing line, rather than start a new line.

3　Hold down Alt (Windows) or Option (Mac OS) and notice that the status bar in the lower left corner of the window displays "Pen: Make Corner." Now Alt/Option+drag the Pen tool from anchor point A to the red dot. Then release the mouse button.

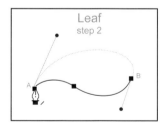
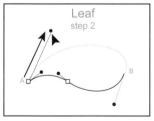

A slash indicates the Pen tool is aligned with anchor.

Alt/Option+dragging creates corner point.

So far, all the curves you have drawn have been open paths. Now you'll draw a closed path, in which the final anchor point is drawn on the first anchor point of the path. (Examples of closed paths include ovals and rectangles.) You'll close the path using a smooth point.

4   Position the cursor over anchor point B on the template. A small, open circle appears next to the Pen tool, indicating that clicking will close the path. Press the mouse button and drag from this point to the second red dot.

Notice the direction handles where you close the path. The direction handles on both sides of a smooth point are aligned along the same angle.

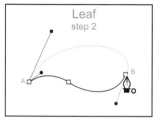

A small circle indicates that clicking with the Pen tool closes the path.

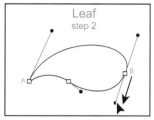

Drag to red dot to lengthen curved line.

5   Control+click (Windows) or Command+click (Mac OS) away from the line, and choose File > Save.

Changing a smooth curve to a corner and vice versa

Now you'll create the leaf stem by adjusting a curved path. You'll be converting a smooth point on the curve to a corner point and a corner point to a smooth point.

1   Choose View > Stem to display a magnified view of the stem.

2   Select the Direct Selection tool (↖) in the toolbox, position the cursor over point A at the top of the curve to display a hollow square on the cursor, and then click the anchor point to select it and display its red direction handles for the smooth point.

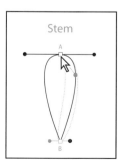

3   Select the Convert Anchor Point tool (⌐) from the same group as the Pen tool (✍) in the toolbox, or use the shortcut for Convert Anchor Point tool by pressing the Alt (Windows) or Option (Mac OS) key while the Pen tool is selected.

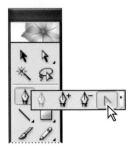

4   Using the Convert Anchor Point tool, select the left direction point (on top of the red dot) on the direction line, drag it to the gold dot on the template, and then release the mouse button.

Dragging with the Convert Anchor Point tool converts the smooth anchor point to a corner point and adjusts the angle of the left direction line.

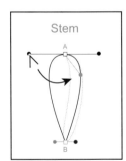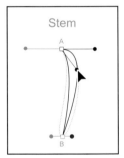

Use Convert Anchor Point tool to convert curves to corners.

5   Using the Convert Anchor Point tool, select the bottom anchor point and drag from point B to the red dot to convert the corner point to a smooth point, rounding out the curve, and then release the mouse button.

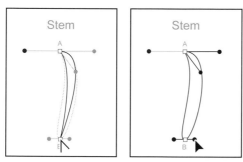

Use Convert Anchor Point tool to convert corners to curves.

Two direction handles emerge from the anchor point, indicating that it is now a smooth point.

When using the Convert Anchor Point tool, keep these guidelines in mind:

• Drag from the curve's anchor point for a smooth point and continuous curve.

• Click the curve's anchor point, or drag a handle (direction point) of the curve for a corner point on a discontinuous curve.

6   Choose File > Save.

Drawing the pear shape

Now you'll draw a single, continuous object that consists of smooth points and corner points. Each time you want to change the direction of a curve at a specific point, you'll hold down Alt (Windows) or Option (Mac OS) to create a corner point.

1   Choose View > Pear to display a magnified view of the pear.

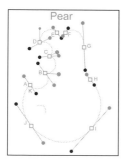

First you'll draw the bite marks on the pear by creating corner points and changing the direction of the curve segments.

2   Select the Pen tool (✎) from the same group as the Convert Anchor Point tool (⊾). Drag the Pen tool from point A on the template to the red dot to set the starting anchor point and direction of the first curve. Release the mouse button.

3   Drag the Pen tool from point B to the red dot—but don't release the mouse button—and, while holding down Alt (Windows) or Option (Mac OS), drag the direction handle from the red dot to the gold dot. Release the mouse button.

4   Continue drawing to points C and D by first dragging from the anchor point to the red dot and then Alt/Option+dragging the direction handle from the red dot to the gold dot.

At the corner points B, C, and D, you first drag to continue the current segment, and then Alt/Option+drag to set the direction of the next curved segment.

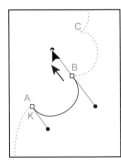
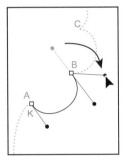

Drag to adjust curve.   *Alt/Option+drag direction point to set corner point.*

Next, you'll complete your drawing of the pear by creating smooth points.

5   Drag each of the points from E through J to their red dots, and then click anchor point K to close the pear shape. Notice that when you hold the cursor over anchor point K, a small open circle appears next to the pen, indicating that the path will close when you click.

6   Hold down Control (Windows) or Command (Mac OS) and click away from the path to deselect it, and then choose File > Save.

Editing curves

To adjust the curves you've drawn, you can drag either the curve's anchor points or its direction handles. You can also edit a curve by moving the line.

1   Select the Direct Selection tool (⭢) and click the outline of the pear.

Clicking with the Direct Selection tool displays the curve's direction handles and lets you adjust the shape of individual curved segments. Clicking with the Selection tool (⭠) selects the entire path.

2   Click the anchor point G at the top right of the pear to select it, and adjust the segment by dragging the top direction handle as shown in the illustration.

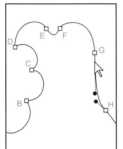

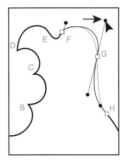

Use Direct Selection tool   Select anchor point.   Adjust anchor point.
to select individual
segments.

3   Make sure the fill is set to none. If not, click the Fill box in the Control palette. When the Swatches palette appears click the None box.

4   Now select the Pen tool (✎) and drag to draw the small curve on the pear where the arrow pierces it. (Use the dashed line on the template as a guide.)

Note: If you can't see the dashed, curved line on the template, make sure that the Fill in the toolbox is set to None and that the Stroke is set to black.

5   Choose File > Save.

Finishing the pear illustration

To complete the illustration, you'll make some minor modifications and assemble and paint all the objects. Then you will position parts of the arrow to create the illusion of the pear being pierced.

Assembling the parts

1   Double-click the Zoom tool (🔍) to zoom to 100%.

2   Choose Window > Layers to display the Layers palette.

3   In the Layers palette, click the template icon (🖺), next to the Template layer name, to hide the template.

4   Choose View > Show Bounding Box so that you can see the bounding boxes of selected objects as you transform them.

5   Choose the Selection tool (▶) in the toolbox, and Shift+click to select the two single curved lines that you no longer need for the leaf. Press Backspace (Windows) or Delete (Mac OS) to delete them.

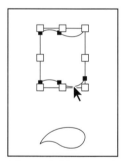

Select and delete extra lines.

Now you'll make the stem and leaf smaller, and rotate them slightly using the Transform commands.

6   Select the stem and choose Object > Transform > Scale. Select Uniform and enter **50%** in the Scale text field. Select the Scale Strokes & Effects Option, and click OK.

The Scale Strokes & Effects Option scales stroke weights and effects automatically. You can also set this Option as a preference, choose Edit > General > Preferences (Windows) or choose Illustrator > Preferences > General (Mac OS).

7   Choose Object > Transform > Rotate. Enter **45** in the Angle text field, and click OK.

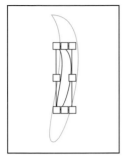 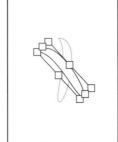

Scale stem 50%.   *Rotate stem 45°.*

Now you'll repeat the scaling and rotation on the leaf.

8   Select the leaf and choose Object > Transform > Scale. Leave the settings as they are, and click OK to scale the leaf by 50%. Then choose Object > Transform > Rotate, enter **15** in the Angle text field, and click OK.

You can also scale and rotate objects by using the Scale and Rotate tools, respectively, or by using the Free Transform tool to do either. For information, see Lesson 3, "Transforming Objects."

9   Select the Selection tool, and move the stem and the leaf to the top of the pear.

10   Move the parts of the arrow over the pear to make it look as if the arrow is entering the front of the pear and exiting the back.

Objects are arranged in the order in which they are created, with the most recent in front.

11   Select the bottom part of the arrow, and Shift+click to select the curve where the arrow pierces the pear. Then choose Object > Arrange > Bring to Front to arrange them in front of the pear.

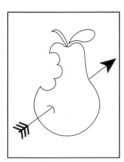

Painting the artwork

Now paint the objects as you like. In our color illustration, we have removed the stroke on the leaf, the stem, and the pear, and we've painted the fills with custom-made gradients called Pear leaf, Pear stem, and Pear body, which are provided in the Swatches palette. We painted the arrow with a dark blue color, and then we added some detail lines to the leaf, the stem, and the round part of the pear using the Paintbrush tool (✐) and the Pen tool (✎). We also stroked the curve where the arrow pierces the pear.

1　Select an object, and then select Fill on the Control palette to view the Swatches palette. Use the named swatches: Pear leaf, Pear stem, and Pear body for the appropriate parts and Dark Blue for the arrow.

To learn how to create your own gradients, see Lesson 8, "Blending Shapes and Colors." To learn more about painting options in Illustrator, see Lesson 5, "Color and Painting."

2　Choose File > Save to save your work, then File > Close.

You've completed the lesson on drawing straight lines and curves. For additional practice with the Pen tool, try tracing over images with it. As you practice more with the Pen tool, you'll become more adept at drawing the kinds of curves and shapes you want.

Exploring on your own

Experiment by placing your own images and recreating them using a template. Find an image, logo, or other simple artwork that you would like to create save it as any number of image file formats that Illustrator CS2 can accept, including: .pdf, .psd, .tiff, .eps, .jpg and more.

1　Create a new Illustrator document, choose the size and color mode based upon your needs, or simply leave the defaults settings unchanged.

2　Choose File > Place. When you browse to locate the artwork you wish to recreate, select it and check the Template checkbox. Choose OK. The image is placed on a locked template with a clean layer at the top of the stacking order.

3　Select your Pen tool (✎) and start using the techniques you learned throughout this lesson to help recreate your graphic.

Review

▶ **Review questions**

1   Describe how to draw straight vertical, horizontal, or diagonal lines using the Pen tool.

2   How do you draw a curved line using the Pen tool?

3   How do you draw a corner point on a curved line?

4   How do you change a smooth point on a curve to a corner point?

5   Which tool would you use to edit a segment on a curved line?

▶ **Review answers**

1   To draw a straight line, you click twice with the Pen tool—the first click sets the starting anchor point, and the second click sets the ending anchor point of the line. To constrain the straight line vertically, horizontally, or along a 45° diagonal, hold down the Shift key as you click with the Pen tool.

2   To draw a curved line using the Pen tool, hold down the mouse button and drag to create the starting anchor point and set the direction of the curve, and then click to end the curve.

3   To draw a corner point on a curved line, hold down Alt (Windows) or Option (Mac OS) and drag the direction handle on the endpoint of the curve to change the direction of the path, and then continue dragging to draw the next curved segment on the path.

4   Use the Direct Selection tool to select the anchor point, and then use the Convert Anchor Point tool to drag a direction handle to change the direction.

5   To edit a segment on a curved line, select the Direct Selection tool and drag the segment to move it, or drag a direction handle on an anchor point to adjust the length and shape of the segment.

Spice up your illustration with colors by taking advantage of new controls available in Illustrator CS2. Discover how to use Live Trace and Live Paint, as well as how to traditionally paint fills and strokes in this information packed lesson.

5 | Color and Painting

In this lesson, you'll learn how to do the following:

- Use the new Live Trace and Live Paint features.

- Paint with, create, and edit colors using the new control palette and shortcuts.

- Name and save colors, and build a color palette.

- Copy paint and appearance attributes from one object to another.

- Paint with gradients, patterns, and brushes.

Getting started

In this lesson, you will jump right in, creating Vector Man, the scalable superhero that was created traditionally with pencil and scanned into Photoshop as a raster (bitmap) image. Vector Man, obviously, wants to be converted into vector paths. In this lesson, you will discover how to automatically trace scanned images, create vector paths, and then paint intuitively using the new Live Paint feature.

1   To ensure that the tools and palettes function exactly as described in this lesson, delete or deactivate (by renaming) the Adobe Illustrator CS2 preferences file. See "Restoring default preferences" on page 3.

2   Start Adobe Illustrator CS2.

3   Choose File > Open, and open the L5_End.ai file in the Lesson05 folder, located inside the Lessons folder within the AICIB folder on your hard drive.

4   If you like, choose View > Zoom Out to make the finished artwork smaller and leave it on your screen as you work. (Use the Hand tool (✋) to move the artwork where you want it in the window.) You may want the complete illustration open for color reference as you work. If you don't want to leave the image open, choose File > Close. Now open the start file to begin the lesson.

5   Choose File > Open, and open the L5_ Start.ai file in the Lesson05 folder.

6   Choose File > Save As, name the file **vectorman.ai**, and select the Lesson05 folder in the Save As window. Leave the type of format set to Adobe Illustrator Document, and click Save. In the Illustrator Options dialog box, accept the default settings by clicking OK.

Using Live Trace

Live Trace automatically turns placed images into beautifully detailed vector graphics that are easy to edit, resize, and manipulate. Live Trace reduces the amount of time it takes to recreate a scanned drawing on-screen from days to minutes, without loss of quality.

1   With vectorman.ai open, take the Selection tool (k) and select the vectorman sketch.

Note that the Control palette, options change when the scanned image is activated.

2   Click on the Live Trace button on the Control palette. The image has been converted to a vector image.

Choose the Live Trace button to recreate the artwork as vector.

Understand that the reason it is called Live Trace is that you can change the settings, or even the original placed image, and see immediate updates in Illustrator.

3   In this example, you selected the default trace setting, which worked fine for this image, but click on the Tracing options dialog button (▣) on the Control Panel, and check Preview to experiment with other presets and options.

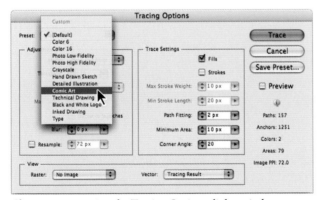

Change options using the Tracing Options dialog window.

As you see, the Live Trace feature can interpret black and white sketches as well as full-color images.

4   After experimenting with other settings, choose Cancel.

5   Choose File > Save.

Tracing options

Preset specifies a tracing preset.

Mode specifies a color mode for the tracing result.

Threshold specifies a value for generating a black and white tracing result from the original image. All pixels lighter than the Threshold value are converted to white, all pixels darker than the Threshold value are converted to black. (This option is available only when Mode is set to Black and White.)

Palette specifies a palette for generating a color or grayscale tracing from the original image. (This option is available only when Mode is set to Color or Grayscale.) To let Illustrator determine the colors in the tracing, select Automatic.

Max Colors specifies a maximum number of colors to use in a color or grayscale tracing result. (This option is available only when Mode is set to Color or Grayscale and when Palette is set to Automatic.)

Output To Swatches creates a new swatch in the Swatches palette for each color in the tracing result.

Blur blurs the original image before generating the tracing result. Select this option to reduce small artifacts and to smooth jagged edges in the tracing result.

Resample resamples the original image to the specified resolution before generating the tracing result. This option is useful for speeding up the tracing process for large images but can yield degraded results. **Note:** The resample resolution is not saved when you create a preset.

Fills creates filled regions in the tracing result.

Strokes creates stroked paths in the tracing result.

Max Stroke Weight specifies the maximum width of features in the original image that can be stroked. Features larger than the maximum width become outlined areas in the tracing result.

Min Stroke Length specifies the minimum length of features in the original image that can be stroked. Features smaller than the minimum length are omitted from the tracing result.

Path Fitting controls the distance between the traced shape and the original pixel shape. Lower values create a tighter path fitting; higher values create a looser path fitting.

Minimum Area specifies the smallest feature in the original image that will be traced. For example, a value of 4 specifies that features smaller than 2 pixels wide by 2 pixels high will be omitted from the tracing result.

Corner Angle specifies the sharpness of a turn in the original image that is considered a corner anchor point in the tracing result.

Raster specifies how to display the bitmap component of the tracing object.

Vector specifies how to display the tracing result.

Select Preview in the Tracing Options dialog box to preview the result of the current settings. To set the default tracing options, deselect all objects before you open the Tracing Options dialog box. When you're finished setting options, click Set Default.

—From Illustrator Help

Applying Live Paint

Live Paint lets you paint vector graphics intuitively by automatically detecting and correcting gaps that previously would have affected how fills and strokes were applied. Instead of having to plan every detail of an illustration, you can work more as you would coloring by hand on paper.

1   With the vectorman.ai file still open, use the Selection tool (↖) to select the traced image and choose the Live Paint button in the Control palette. This creates a Live Paint group which can now be easily painted.

There are some gap issues to work with before painting. Gaps are the little spaces that leave openings in shapes that allow for paint to leak from one shape to another. Before starting the paint work on Vectorman, choose Object > Live Paint > Gap Options. The Gap Options window appears.

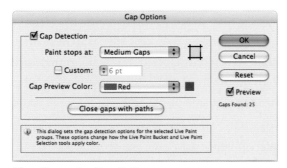 

Close Gaps using Gap Options.

2   Check the Gap Detection checkbox, the gaps are highlighted in red.

3   Change the Paint stops at: drop-down menu to Medium Gaps. This will stop paint from leaking through some of the large spaces as you apply paint. Click OK.

4   Choose File > Save. Leave this file open.

5   Select the Live Paint Bucket tool (🪣) from the toolbox. Before painting, choose Fill in the Control panel and select Canary Yellow in the Swatches palette. In the CS2 version, the Fill and Swatch control palette items link to the Swatches palette.

6 Move the mouse over the cape strap. As you move over Live Paint objects in the traced image, they highlight. Click when part of the cape strap becomes highlighted.

Coloring a shape using the Live Paint Bucket tool.

7 Repeat this step, filling in the side edge of the cape strap with the Canary Yellow.

8 Keeping the Live Paint Bucket tool active, select Va Va Va Voom Red from the Swatches palette. You can use Window > Swatches, to access the Swatches palette, or click once on Fill in the Control palette. With Red selected, move the mouse over the left side of the Adobe logo "A" emblem on the front of Vectorman and click when it becomes highlighted. Repeat this for the right side of the emblem. The A becomes Red.

9 Referencing the L5_End.ai illustration, complete the painting of this illustration. You can use the colors in the example, or create your own interpretation.

It is helpful to zoom in to see details. Don't worry if you fill a region with the wrong color, just choose the right color and fill again.

10 When completed, choose File > Save, and close the file.

Editing Live Paint regions

Once you've made a Live Paint group, each path remains fully editable. When you move or adjust a path's shape, the colors that had been previously applied don't just stay where they were, like they do in natural media paintings or image editing programs. Instead, Illustrator automatically reapplies them to the new regions that are formed by the edited paths.

To experience this feature further, create a blank new file on which you will create a simple illustration.

1   Using File > New, create a new letter-sized document. Leave at the default settings, and choose OK.

2   On the blank document, use the Ellipse Shape tool (○) to create a circle anywhere on the artboard. The size of the circle shape is not important.

3   Using the Selection tool (▶), hold down the Alt (Windows) or Option (Mac OS) key to clone the circle shape, drag it so the duplicated circle is overlapping the initial circle shape.

4   Choose Select > All. Choose None from Fill in the Control palette, and then choose None from Stroke on the Control palette.

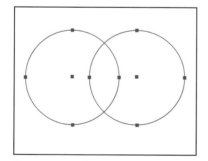

Create two overlapping circle shapes. Paint both the Fill and Stroke None.

5   Select the Live Paint Bucket tool (◐), and cross over the center overlapping area; when it becomes highlighted, click once to activate the center shape as a Live Paint group

6   Select a color from the Swatches palette and click on the center Live Paint object to color it.

7   Select a color. Then using the Live Paint Bucket tool, click the left Live Paint object and click inside of it. Repeat this with a different color for the right Live Paint object.

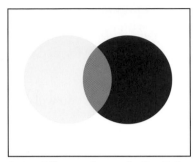

Assign different colors to the Live Paint objects.

8   Select > Deselect. Choose the Direct Selection tool (▸). Select and reposition one of the circles, keeping some of the overlap. Notice that the intersecting area is dynamic. It changes the fill based upon the relationship of the two circles.

Note: *The Selection tool selects an entire Live Paint group; the Direct Select tool selects the individual paths inside a Live Paint group. For instance, clicking once with the Selection tool selects the entire Live Paint group, and clicking once with the Direct Selection tool or the Group Selection tool selects individual paths that make up the Live Paint group.*

You can use the different selection tools depending on what you want to select and affect in a Live Paint group. For instance, use the Live Paint Selection tool (▸) to apply different gradients across different faces in a Live Paint group, and use the Selection tool to apply the same gradient across the entire Live Paint group.

Note that if you delete a path that divides a circle in half, the circle is filled with one of the fills previously in the circle. You can help guide what fill is used as a result. For instance, before deleting a path that divides a circle, first move it so that the fill you want to keep is larger than the fill you want to remove.

You have completed the Live Paint and Live Trace portion of this lesson. Read on to use more traditional painting methods in Illustrator CS2.

9   Choose File > Close. Choose to not save the file.

Color Mode

First, and most importantly, before starting a new illustration, you must determine if the image should use CMYK colors or RGB.

CMYK—Cyan, Magenta, Yellow, Black colors are part of the four-color process. These four colors are combined and overlapped in a screen pattern to create what appears to be a multitude of other colors.

RGB—Red, Green, Blue is the natural method of viewing color using light. Select this mode if using images for screen presentations or the Internet.

The mode is selected when you choose File > New and pick the appropriate Color Mode radio box.

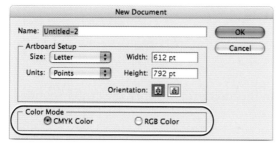

Select the Color mode when creating a new Illustrator document.

When a Color Mode is selected, Illustrator opens the applicable palettes built with colors in either the CMYK or RGB mode. A document's color mode can be changed after the file is created by using File > Document Color Mode > CMYK Color or RGB Color.

Understanding the color controls

In this lesson, you will discover the traditional method of coloring objects in Adobe Illustrator CS2. This includes painting objects with colors, gradients, or patterns, and is done using a combination of palettes and tools—including the Control palette, Color palette, the Swatches palette, the Gradient palette, the Stroke palette, and the paint buttons in the toolbox—that let you select and change an object's paint and line attributes. You'll begin by investigating finished artwork that has been applied with color.

Even though you can access many of the palettes using the New Control palette in Illustrator CS2, go to the Window menu and open these palettes if they are not already visible: Appearance, Color, Gradient, and Swatches.

1 Choose File > Open and open the illustration in the Lesson05 folder named vectorcity_done.ai.

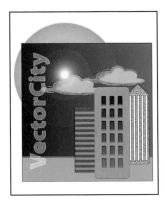

2 Choose the Selection tool (➤) in the toolbox, then click the center rounded rectangular building.

In the toolbox, notice that the Fill box appears in the foreground, indicating that it is selected. (This is the default.) The box has a fill of a gray color. Behind the Fill box, the Stroke box has no outline, represented by a red slash. When the Stroke box or Fill box is in the background, its color is not the current selection.

The Fill and Stroke attributes of the selected object also appear in Window > Appearance palette. Appearance attributes can be edited, deleted, saved as Graphic Styles, and applied to other objects, layers, and groups. You'll use this palette later in this lesson.

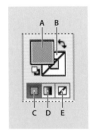

A. Fill. *B.* Stroke. *Appearance palette*
C. Color. *reflects selected object's*
D. Gradient. *paint attributes.*
E. None.

3 On the Color palette, hold down the mouse button on the triangle in the upper right corner of the palette, and choose Show Options from the palette menu. The Color palette displays the current color for the fill and stroke, and its CMYK sliders show the colors' percentages of cyan, magenta, yellow, and black. At the bottom of the Color palette is the color bar. If you choose CMYK, you will notice that the Gray color is a 30% tint of Black.

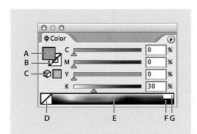

A. Fill box. B. Stroke box. C. Out of Web Color Warning.
D. None button. E. Color bar.
F. Black color box. G. White color box.

The color bar lets you quickly and visually select a fill or stroke color from a spectrum of colors. You can also choose white or black by clicking the appropriate color box at the right end of the color bar.

Shift+click on the Color bar at the bottom of the Color palette to rotate through the different color modes.

4 Using the Selection tool, click on various shapes in the vectorcity_done.ai file to see how their paint attributes are reflected in the various palettes.

5 You will complete this illustration later in the lesson. You can choose to leave it open at this time, or choose File > Close.

Color fundamentals

Before opening the project file for this lesson, you will open a basic document to gain a better understanding of how color is applied in Illustrator.

1 Choose File > Open and select the file named color.ai in the Lesson05 folder inside the AICIB folder.

2   Choose File > Save As, name the file **color_practice.ai**, and select the Lesson05 folder in the Save In menu. Leave the type of format set to Adobe Illustrator Document, and click Save. In the Illustrator Options dialog box, accept the default settings by clicking OK.

3   Using the Selection tool (↖), select some of the objects and note that they have a white fill and a black stroke.

4   Choose any one of the stars, and click once on Fill box in the Control palette. Choose the Pure Yellow Swatch from the Swatches palette that appears.

5   With the same star selected, choose the color box to the right of Stroke on the Control palette and select the Pumpkin swatch.

6   Using the Stroke Weight drop-down menu, choose 4 pt.

7   Select the word Stroke on the Control palette to link to the Stroke palette. Note that in Illustrator CS2, you can choose to have the stroke of an object centered on the path or on the inside or outside. For this exercise, put the stroke on the outside of the path.

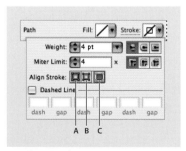

A. Align Stroke to Center.
B. Align Stroke to Inside.
C. Align Stroke to Outside.

8   If the Stroke palette is not visible, choose the traditional method to show the palette by selecting Window >Stroke. Choose Show Options from the palette menu.

9   Check the Dashed Line checkbox, the path defaults to 12 pt dashes.

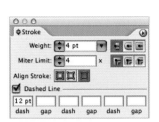

Show options in the Stroke palette.

Change the stroke to a dashed line.

10   Choose File > Save.

Copying attributes

1   Using the Selection tool (⬉), select one of the stars that has not yet been colored, then Shift+click to add all other unpainted stars to the selection.

2   Using the Eyedropper tool (⬈), click on the star you painted. All stars that are unpainted pick up the attributes from the painted star.

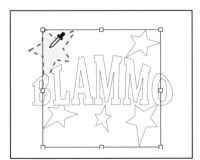

Sample fill and stroke attributes using the Eyedropper tool.

All selected stars pick up the painted star's attributes.

Adding a spot color

Perhaps the Blammo Company always uses red for their company logo. When this color of red is defined, it could be warm red, dark red, or light red. This is why most printers and designers rely on a color matching system, like the Pantone® system, a color system that helps color consistency.

In this section, you will see how to load a color library, such as the Pantone color system, and how to add a Pantone (PMS) color to your Swatches palette.

1   Choose Select > Deselect to make sure no objects are selected.

2   Choose Fill from the Control palette to open the Swatches palette, or you can choose Window > Swatches.

3   From the Swatches Palette menu, choose Open Swatch Library, and then scroll down until you can find Pantone Solid Coated and click to select it. The Pantone solid coated library appears in its own palette.

4   Using the Pantone solid coated palette menu, choose Show Find Field. Type the value **187** into the Find field. Pantone 187 is highlighted. Double-click on the highlighted swatch to add it to your Swatches palette.

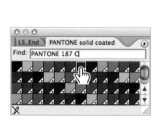
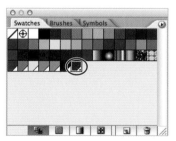

Why does my Pantone Swatch look different from the other swatches?

When you add the Pantone solid coated swatch, you should notice a black spot and triangle in the lower right corner of the swatch.

As a default, the Pantone solid coated swatch is defined as a Spot color; hence, the black dot. A spot color is not created from a combination of Cyan, Magenta, Yellow, and Black (CMYK) inks but is its own solid ink color. A press operator uses a pre-mixed PMS (Pantone Matching System) color in the press, offering consistency and better color accuracy.

The triangle indicates that this color is Global. If this color is edited, all color references used in the illustration are updated. Any color can be Global, not only Pantone colors.

Using the Appearance palette for fills and strokes

Up to this point you have mostly used the Control palette to paint Fills and Strokes, but you can also use the Appearance palette to paint and apply other attributes specific to the Fill or Stroke.

1   Using the Selection tool (▸), select the Blammo text.

2   If the Appearance palette is not open, choose Window > Appearance. Notice that the selected text is listed as a group in the Appearance palette. Double-click on Contents to show the Fill and Stroke attributes for the text.

3   Click on Fill in the Appearance palette, and then select the Pantone 187 swatch in your Swatches palette. The text fill is now red.

4   Select the word Stroke in the Appearance palette, and choose the same Pantone 187 swatch from the Swatches palette.

5   With Stroke still selected in the Appearance palette, choose the Stroke Weight drop-down menu, from the Control palette, and select 5 pt.

6   Select Opacity from the Control palette; enter **50** into the Opacity text field. Notice that because only the Stroke was selected in the Appearance palette, the Fill is still at 100% Opacity.

7   Choose File > Save and close the file.

Paint the city!

In this next part of the lesson, you will open the uncolored vectorcity image and apply the paint attributes yourself. This will include custom-created colors, spot colors, patterns, and gradients.

1   Choose File > Open and open the file in the Lesson05 folder named vectorcity.ai.

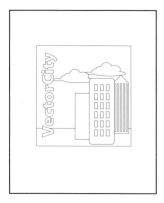

2   Choose File > Save As. Name the file **vectorcity2.ai** and select the Lesson05 folder in the Save As window. Leave the type of format set to Adobe Illustrator Document, and click Save. In the Illustrator Options dialog box, accept the default settings by clicking OK.

3   Choose the center rounded rectangle building, click once on the Fill box in the Control palette, and select the swatch Smoke. The building is now colored with a gray fill.

4   Click once on the color box to the right of Stroke in the Control palette and select the None swatch (red slash). The building now has a gray fill and no stroke.

Building your own custom color

This illustration is in the CMYK color mode, which means that you can create your own color from any combination of Cyan, Magenta, Yellow, and Black.

1   Choose Select > Deselect.

2   If the Color palette is not visible, choose Window > Color. From the palette menu, choose CMYK.

3 Enter this combination in the CMYK text fields: C = **50**, M = **0**, Y = **100**, K = **0**.

4 Choose Create New Swatch from the Swatches palette menu.

5 Name the color **lawn green,** and click OK.

You can also Alt+click (Windows) or Option+click (Mac OS) on the New Swatch button in the Swatches palette to open up the New Swatch dialog window.

Note: *The Swatches palette stores the colors, gradients, and patterns that have been preloaded into Adobe Illustrator CS2, as well as those you create and save for reuse. New colors added to the Swatches palette are saved with the current file. Opening a new artwork file displays the default set of swatches that comes with the Adobe Illustrator CS2 program. If you want to load a Swatches palette from one saved document into another, choose Open Swatch Library from the Swatches palette menu and select Other palette, then locate the document with the Swatches palette you wish to import.*

6 Click on the rectangle representing grass in the vector city image and click on the Fill box in the Control palette. When the Swatches palette appears, choose your new swatch.

7 Click on Stroke in the Control palette and choose the None swatch, or choose Window > Swatches, make sure stroke is forward and select the None swatch.

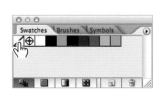

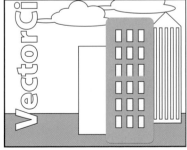

Painting with patterns and gradients

In addition to process and spot colors, the Swatches palette can also contain pattern and gradient swatches. Adobe Illustrator CS2 provides sample swatches of each type in the default palette and lets you create your own patterns and gradients. Click on the buttons at the bottom of the palette to see All or specific types of swatches.

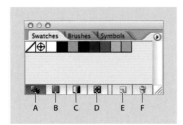

A. Show All Swatches. B. Show Color Swatches.
C. Show Gradient Swatches. D. Show Pattern Swatches.
E. New Swatch. F. Delete Swatch.

1   Make sure nothing is selected by choosing Select > Deselect.

2   Choose Window > Gradient if your Gradient palette is not visible. Choose Show Options from the palette menu. Click once on the Gradient ramp at the bottom of the palette to make the color stops visible.

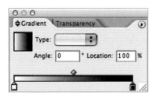

The Gradient Ramp with a
color stop at either end.

You can create your own gradient by activating the color stops on the Gradient slider, or by dragging existing swatches directly on top of the existing Gradient color stops.

3   Click and hold down on the color Twilight Blue, don't release. Then drag the swatch to the color stop on the right side of the Gradient ramp. If you select the color and release without dragging it to the Gradient ramp, you will fill the shape with a solid color. If this occurred, choose Edit > Undo Color, and try again.

4   Select the Purple swatch and drag it to the color stop on the left side of the Gradient ramp.

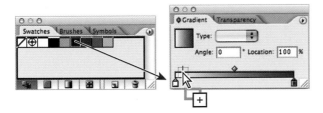

Note: *If you miss the existing indicator, you will add an extra color stop. Delete any extra colors in a Gradient slider by clicking and dragging them off the slider.*

5   Choose New Swatch from the Swatches palette menu, and name this **gradient sky**.

6   Select the large rectangle representing the sky behind the buildings. Click on the Fill box in the Control palette and choose your new sky gradient. The sky gradient has been applied.

7   Select one of the windows in the center building. Since these windows are part of a group, all become selected.

8   Click on the Fill box in the Control palette, and apply the sky gradient to the windows.

9   Choose the Gradient tool (◼) from the toolbox, and click and drag from the top to the bottom of the group of windows.

Notice that the Gradient is now smoothly transitioned through all windows, as though they are one object.

10   Choose File > Save.

Using patterns

You can use preset patterns that load with Adobe Illustrator CS2, or create your own. In this section, you will do both.

1 Choose Other Library from the Open Swatch Library menu from the Swatches palette menu. If you are not immediately directed to the Presets folder, browse to the Adobe Illustrator CS2 application folder. This is at Local Disk/Programs/Adobe/Adobe Illustrator CS2/Presets (Windows) or Macintosh HD/Applications/Adobe Illustrator CS2/ Presets (Mac OS).

2 Open Patterns > Basic Graphics > Basic Graphics_Textures.

A separate palette appears with supplied patterns. These patterns aren't clear but contain a texture pattern.

3 Using the Selection tool (✸), select the outside of the building furthest to the right. If the Appearance palette is not visible, choose Window > Appearance. Since the pattern has a clear background, you will give this object two separate fills.

4 Select the word Fill in the Appearance palette. From the Appearance palette menu, choose Duplicate Item. Two Fills appear in the Appearance palette.

5 With the top Fill selected in the Appearance palette, choose the pattern named Bird Feet from the Basic Graphics_Textures palette.

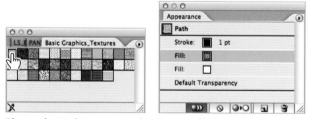

Choose the Bird Feet texture for the top Fill of the object.

6   Make the Pattern larger, without affecting the shape, by double-clicking on the Scale tool (▣). Uncheck Objects, and Patterns becomes checked. Type **200** in the Uniform Scale text field, press OK. Only the pattern is enlarged.

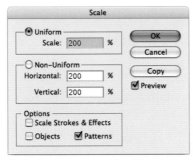

Scale the pattern, not the object, using the Scale tool options.

7   Select the bottom Fill in the Appearance palette, and select the Swatch named Sunshine. The object now has a solid yellow/orange fill, as well as a pattern fill.

8   Choose File > Save.

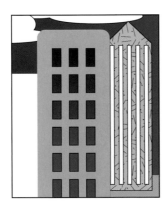

Creating your own pattern

In this section of the lesson, you will create your own striped pattern and add it to the Swatches palette. You will then discover how to edit an existing pattern and update it in the Swatches palette. If your Swatches palette is not visible, choose Window > Swatches.

1   Choose Select > Deselect to make sure no objects are selected.

For this section, you will assign colors using the toolbox.

2   Click on the Fill swatch at the bottom of the toolbox to make sure it is forward. It does not matter if it has the last-used colors selected.

*Make sure Fill
is forward before
applying color.*

3   With the Fill forward, choose the Twilight Blue swatch from the Swatches palette.

4   Press "X" to swap the Fill and Stroke in the toolbox. When Stroke is forward, choose None by choosing the None button (☑) at the bottom of the toolbox.

5   Choose the Rectangle Shape tool (■) from the toolbox and click once on the Artboard (do not click and drag!). In the Rectangle options dialog box, enter **125 pt** for the width and **8 pt** for the Height, press OK.

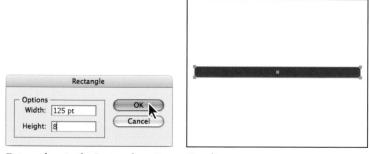

Enter values in the Rectangle options.   Result.

A blue-colored rectangle appears. Using the Selection tool (➤), position it off the artwork if it is touching any of your existing illustration.

6   With the new Rectangle still selected, double-click on the Selection tool to reveal the Move dialog window. In the Position section, enter **0** in the Horizontal text field, and **-8 pt** in the Vertical text field. It is important that you verify that Objects is checked and that you press Copy, not OK. A rectangle directly beneath your existing rectangle appears.

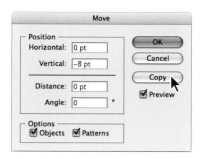

7   Press "X" to bring the Fill forward on the toolbox, and choose the White swatch for the bottom rectangle.

8   Using the Selection tool (▶), select one of your new rectangles and Shift+click to add the other to the selection.

9   Click and drag the selected rectangles into the Swatches palette. You have created a new pattern.

10 Double-click on the pattern swatch you added to assign the name **stripe**.

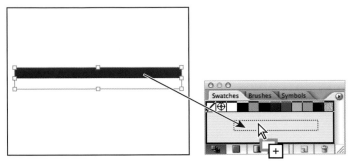

Drag rectangles into the Swatches palette.

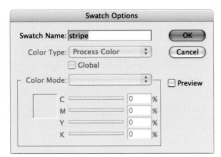

Double-click on the new pattern swatch to name it.

Applying the pattern

1 Select the left rectangular building in the illustration.

You can assign the pattern using a number of different methods. It is preferable to use the Control palette in most cases, as it allows you to put away the Swatches palette, and link to it only when necessary.

2   Choose Fill in the Control palette, and choose the new pattern swatch (stripe) you created.

The pattern is applied to the fill of the building.

💡 *As you add more custom swatches, it may be beneficial to view the Swatches palette by the Swatch names. You can change the view by choosing List View from the Swatches palette menu.*

3   Select the two rectangles used to create the pattern, and press Delete, as you will no longer need the originals.

4   Using the Selection tool (✦), select the rectangular building, and choose 6 pt from Stroke Weight in the Control palette, and Black from the Color box to the right of Stroke on the Control palette.

5   If your Appearance palette is not open, choose Window > Appearance; click on Stroke in the Appearance palette.

6   Choose Opacity from the Control palette, and enter **50** into the Opacity text field. The stroke becomes 50% transparent.

7   Choose Stroke on the Control palette and change the stroke to apply to the inside of the path.

8 Choose File > Save.

Editing the pattern

Perhaps you have used a pattern several times in an illustration and want to update its contents. Not a problem, just follow these steps:

1 Using the Selection tool (▶), click and drag the pattern swatch (stripe) you created from the Swatches palette to an empty location on the artboard. The pattern returns to your artboard.

2 Choose Select > Deselect, and choose the Direct Selection tool (▷). Select only the bottom white rectangle.

3 Choose Fill in the Control palette, and select Twilight Blue for the bottom rectangle. They both look the same, but you will create a tint of the Twilight Blue using the Color palette.

4 Choose Window > Colors if the Colors palette is not visible, and make sure Fill is forward in the Color palette. With the bottom Rectangle still selected, hold down the Shift key, and drag either the Cyan or Magenta slider to create a "tint" of this color. Notice that when you hold down the Shift key, the sliders move relative to each other. Use this method to create a lighter blue color; an exact tint is not necessary.

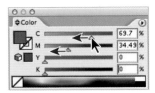

5   Using the Selection tool, select both the rectangles and hold down the Alt (Windows) or Option (Mac OS) key while dragging them back on top of the existing pattern Swatch. The pattern is updated.

6   Select the two rectangles that you edited to create the updated pattern and delete them.

7   Choose File > Save.

Using Brushes

Brushes are fun to use to add texture to objects. Follow these steps to add a brush effect to the clouds. Learn more about Brushes in Lesson 10, "Working with Brushes and Scribbles."

1   Select the left cloud, and choose the Chalk Scribble brush from the Brushes drop-down menu on the Control palette.

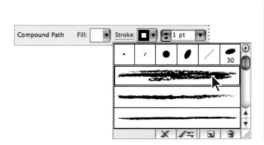

2 Choose Stroke from the Control palette, and assign the color Smoke. The Brush stroke is now gray.

3 Choose Opacity from the Control palette, and type **75** into the Opacity text field.

4 Choose File > Save.

Saving a Graphic Style

Anytime you invest time-consuming decisions in painting objects that you think you might want to use again, you should save them as Graphic Styles. For example, you may want to apply the same color attributes to the cloud next to it. Choose Window > Graphic Styles before starting this part of the lesson. You can learn more about Graphic Styles in Lesson 11, "Applying Appearance Attributes, Graphic Styles, and Effects."

1 Select the cloud that you applied the brush stroke to.

2 From the Graphic Styles palette menu, choose New Graphic Style.

3 In the Graphic Styles Options window, enter the name **Cloud**, press OK.

The Cloud Graphic Style is added to the end of the Graphic Style palette.

4 Select the other cloud, and choose the Cloud Graphic Style on the Graphic Styles palette. The same attributes are now applied to the second cloud.

Congratulations! You have completed the lesson portion of this exercise. Read "Exploring on your own" to gain some additional practice in applying painting and coloring attributes.

Exploring on your own

When you select groups or compounds, you may not see the individual attributes of the Fill and Stroke in the Appearance palette. Follow these steps to discover how to separately apply Fill and Stroke attributes to groups.

Using the Selection tool (▸), select the VectorCity text, and notice that it appears as a Group in the Appearance palette. Double-click on Contents to reveal the text objects Fill and Stroke attributes.

Using the techniques you learned in this lesson, apply a 2-point white stroke to this text, and change the opacity of the fill only to 50% white.

Experimenting with Lens Flare

If you want to add some spunk to your illustration, experiment with the Lens Flare tool (hidden tool in the shape tools.)

You can double-click on the Lens Flare tool to change options prior to creating the Flare. Then click and drag to create the Lens Flare object on your illustration.

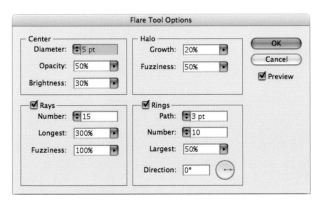
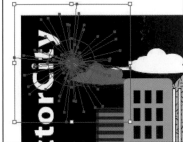

Review

▶ **Review questions**

1   Describe at least three ways to fill an object with color.

2   How can you save a color?

3   How do you name a color?

4   How do you assign an object a transparent color?

5   How do you add pattern swatches to the Swatches palette?

▶ **Review answers**

1   To fill an object with color, select the object and the Fill box in the toolbox. Then do one of the following:

• Click on the Fill box in the Control palette.

• Drag the color sliders, or type in values in the text boxes in the Color palette.

• Click a color swatch in the Swatches palette.

• Select the Eyedropper tool, and click a color in the artwork.

• Choose Window > Swatch Libraries to open another color library, and click a color swatch in the Color Library palette.

2   You can save a color for painting other objects in your artwork by adding it to the Swatches palette. Select the color, and do one of the following:

• Drag it from the Fill box, and drop it over the Swatches palette.

• Click the New Swatch button at the bottom of the Swatches palette.

• Choose New Swatch from the Swatches palette menu.

You can also add colors from other color libraries by selecting them in the Color Library palette and choosing Add to Swatches from the palette menu.

3   To name a color, double-click the color swatch in the Swatches palette, or select it and choose Swatch Options from the palette menu. Type the name for the color in the Swatch Options dialog box.

4   To paint a shape with a transparent color, select the shape and fill it with any color. Then adjust the opacity percentage in the Transparency palette or Control palette to less than 100%.

5   Create a pattern (patterns cannot contain patterns themselves), and drag it into the Swatches palette.

Text as a design element plays a major role in your illustrations. Like other objects, type can be painted, scaled, rotated, and so on. In this lesson discover how to create basic text and interesting text effects in Illustrator CS2. Also learn how to use the new Control palette for easy access to text attributes.

6 Working with type

In this lesson on type, you'll learn how to do the following:

- Import text.

- Create columns of type.

- Change text attributes.

- Use and Save Styles.

- Sample type.

- Wrap type around a graphic.

- Reshape text with an envelope.

- Create text on paths and shapes.

- Create type outlines.

Getting started

You'll be working in one art file during this lesson, but before you begin, restore the default preferences for Adobe Illustrator CS2. Then open the finished art file for this lesson to see the illustration.

1   To ensure that the tools and palettes function exactly as described in this lesson, delete or deactivate (by renaming) the Adobe Illustrator CS2 preferences file. See "Restoring default preferences" on page 3.

2   Launch Adobe Illustrator CS2.

3   Choose File > Open. Locate the file named L6_finish.ai in the Lesson06 folder inside the AICIB that you copied onto your hard drive. This art is a poster for Sammy's ShoeWorld, and you will create the text in this lesson. Leave it open for reference, or choose File > Close.

The finished Type Poster.

4   Choose File > Open. From the Open window, navigate to the Lesson06 folder inside the AICIB folder. Open the file named L6_begin.ai.

This file has some non-text components ready; you will build all text elements necessary to complete the poster.

5   Choose File > Save As. In the Save As window, navigate to the Lesson06 folder and open it. Type **shoe_poster.ai** in the File name text field. In the Save as Type drop-down menu, choose Adobe Illustrator (.AI). In the Illustrator Options window, leave at the default and choose OK.

Importing a text file

You can import text into your artwork from a file that was created in another application. Illustrator supports the following formats for importing text:

- Microsoft Word 97, 98, 2000, and 2002.

- RTF (Rich Text Format).

- Plain text (ASCII) with ANSI, Unicode, Shift JIS, GB2312, Chinese Big 5, and Cyrillic encoding.

You can also copy and paste text, but one of the advantages of importing text from a file, rather than copying and pasting it, is that imported text retains its character and paragraph formatting. For example, text from an RTF file retains its font and style specifications in Illustrator.

1   Before importing text, create a text area by selecting the Type tool (T) and clicking and dragging from the upper left corner of the provided guide box to the lower right corner.

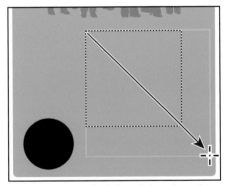

Using the Type tool, click and drag from the upper left to the lower right.

2   Choose File > Place. Navigate to the Lesson06 folder inside the AICIB folder, select the file named L6_copy.txt, and choose Place.

3   The Text Import Options window offers you additional options that you can set prior to importing text. For this example, leave the default settings and choose OK. The text is now placed in the text area. Don't be concerned about formatting the text, you will discover how to apply attributes later in this lesson.

4   Choose File > Save, leave this file open.

Creating columns of text

Create columns and rows of text easily in Illustrator by using the Area Type options.

1   If the text area is no longer selected, use the Selection tool (➤) to select it now.

2   Choose Type > Area Type Options. When the Area Type Options window appears, you see many choices that include settings for not only rows, but columns.

3   For this example, check Preview and change the Number text field under the heading of Columns to **2**, and click OK.

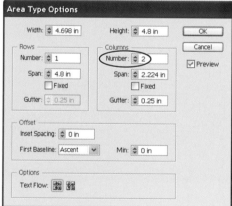

Creating columns of text.   *Result.*

4   Choose File > Save. Leave this document open.

What are the other Area Type options?

You can use the Area Type options to create rows and columns of text. Read about additional options below:

• *Number specifies the number of rows and columns you want the object to contain.*

• *Span specifies the height of individual rows and the width of individual columns.*

• *Fixed determines what happens to the span of rows and columns if you resize the type area. When this option is selected, resizing the area can change the number of rows and columns, but not their width. Leave this option deselected if you want row and column widths to change when you resize the type area.*

Create a statement with your shoes Nothing makes you look more put together than a new clean pair of polished shoes. Sammy's ShoeWorld can help you make the statement you want by providing to you an enor- mous selection of boots, high heels, sneakers, walk- ing and running shoes in wall-high displays that span over a mile. There is no style, no size that we can't provide for you. (Special order the size and size you want at no extra charge.)

Original columns.

Create a statement with your shoes Nothing makes you look more put together than a new clean pair of polished shoes. Sammy's ShoeWorld can help you make the statement you want by providing to you an enor- mous selection of boots, high heels, sneakers, walk- ing and running shoes in wall-high displays that span over a mile. There is no style, no size that we can't provide for you. (Special order the size and size you want at no extra charge.) Come and see for yourself, we are not pulling your leg. we just want to fit your leg with an incredible shoe deal! Throw away your old tired shoes With this sale, there is no reason to run around in

Columns resized with Fixed selected.

Create a statement with your shoes Nothing makes you look more put together than a new clean pair of polished shoes. Sammy's ShoeWorld can help you make the statement you want by providing to you an enormous selection of boots, high heels, sneakers, walking and running shoes in wall- high displays that span over a mile. There is no style, no size that we can't provide for you. (Special order the size and size you want at no extra charge.) Come and see for yourself, we are not pulling your leg, we just want to fit your leg with an incredible shoe deal! Throw away your old tired shoes With this sale, there is no reason to run around in unfashionable and tired shoes. Check out the two for one sale going on from July 17th

Columns resized with Fixed deselected.

• *Gutter specifies the distance between rows or columns.*

• *Inset controls the margin between the text and the bounding path. This margin is referred to as the inset spacing.*

• *First Baseline controls the alignment of the first line of text with the top of the object.*

• *Text Flow determines how text flows between rows and columns.*

–From Illustrator Help

Understanding text flow

For this next section, you will keep the shoe_poster.ai file open, but create a new blank document in addition to it. The purpose is to find out more details about flowing text in Adobe Illustrator CS2.

1   Choose File > New. In the Document Setup, choose Inches for Units, and keep other defaults the same. Click OK.

2   Create a fixed type area by selecting your Rectangle tool (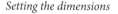) and clicking once on the page...do not click and drag! The Rectangle dialog window appears.

3   Type **2 inches** into both the Width and Height text fields. Click OK.

A square appears. It may have a fill or stroke color. Both fill and stroke will change to None when the shape is converted into a type area.

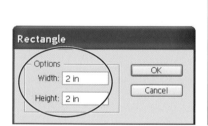

Setting the dimensions   *Result.*

Note: *If you inadvertently dragged the cursor, you have a small rectangle. Delete this using Edit > Undo, or Ctrl+Z (Windows)/Command+Z (Mac OS). You can also delete by pressing the Delete or Backspace key.*

4 Select the Type tool (T) and cross it over the edge of the square. The text insertion point swells, or becomes curved, indicating that when you click, the text cursor will appear inside this shape.

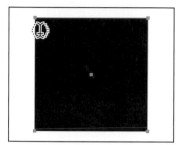

The text insertion point when crossed over an edge of a shape.

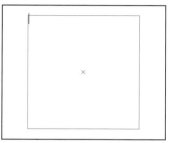

Result. The text cursor is inside the shape, strokes and fills are changed to none.

Note: *Even though there is a hidden Area Type tool in the toolbox, it is not necessary to switch to this tool.*

5 With the cursor still active in the square, choose File > Place and navigate to the Lesson06 folder inside the AICIB folder on your hard drive. Select the file order_copy.doc, and then choose Place. You have selected a native Microsoft Word document to place so you will have additional options to choose from.

6 In the Microsoft Word Options dialog window, leave at the default settings and click OK.

The text appears in the square. Text remembers the last used settings, so your type may appear slightly different from that in our example; this is not a problem.

Order your shoes today!
At Sammy's ShoeWorld you can place an order with total confidence.
Free shipping and free returns are standard policy. You won't pay sales tax*, and our price guarantee means you'll never find a better deal. Also, your transactions

Working with overflow text and text reflow

Each area type object contains an in port and an out port, which enable you to link to other objects and create a linked copy of the type object. An empty port indicates that all the text is visible and that the object isn't linked or overflowing. A red plus sign (⊞) in an out port indicates that the object contains additional text. This remaining unseen text is called overflow text.

Order your shoes today!
At Sammy's ShoeWorld you
can place an order with total
confidence.
Free shipping and free
returns are standard policy.
You won't pay sales tax*, and
our price guarantee means
you'll never find a better
deal. Also, your transactions ⊞

Note that since the text area created is too small, there is a plus sign in the out port.

There are two main methods for remedying overflow text.

• Thread the text to another text area.

• Re-size the text area.

Threading text

Thread, or connect, one text area to another to create a dynamic connection between the areas by following these steps:

1   Use the Selection tool (▸) to select the type area.

2   With the Selection tool, click on the out port of the selected type area. The cursor changes to the loaded text icon (▨).

3   Click and drag on an empty part of the artboard.

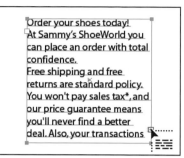

*Click on the out port of the overflowed text area. Click and drag to create
a threaded text area.*

*Click off the existing type area to create an object of the same size and shape as the
original text area.*

Note: *Another method for threading text between objects is to select an area type object,
select the object (or objects) you want to link to, and then choose Type > Threaded Text >
Create.*

Threading text between objects

You can break threads and have the text flow into either the first or the next object, or you can remove
all threads and have the text stay in place.

• To break the thread between two objects, double-click the port on either end of the thread. The text
flows into the first object.

• To release an object from a text thread, choose Type > Threaded Text > Release Selection. The text
flows into the next object.

• To remove all threads, choose Type > Threaded Text > Remove Threading. The text stays in place.

—From Illustrator Help

Resizing the text area

For this next lesson, you will see how to re-size the text area to make room for additional text.

1   If you have created additional text areas using the threading method, switch to the Selection tool (↖) and click to select and delete all but the original text area. Make sure the overflow text icon is still visible.

2   Using the Selection tool, drag a handle on the bounding box. Drag the handle on the middle of the right side, the text area increases or decreases in size only horizontally. Click and drag to make the text area larger.

Resizing the text using a middle handle.

3   Grab the lower right corner handle to see how dragging a corner handle will increase the size of the area both horizontally and vertically.

Resizing the text area using a corner handle.

♀ Create unique text area shapes by deselecting the text area and choosing the Direct Selection tool. Click and drag the edge or corner of the type to adjust the shape of the path. This method is easier to use when View > Hide Bounding Box is selected.

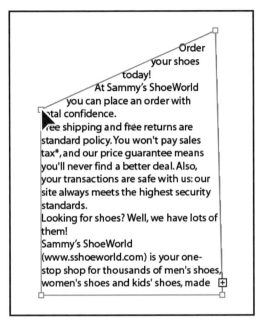

Adjusting the type path using the Direct Selection tool is easiest when you're in Outline view.

4   You have completed the text flow section of this lesson. Choose File > Close. In the Adobe Illustrator alert window, choose No to close without saving this file. This returns you to your original project shoe_poster.ai.

Changing text attributes

In this section, you'll discover how to change text attributes, such as size, font, and style. Fortunately with this version, most attributes can be changed quickly and easily using the new Control palette across the top of the Illustrator work area.

1   With the project shoe_poster.ai open, select the Type tool (T) and insert the cursor anywhere in the text area created earlier.

2   Choose Select > All, or Ctrl+A (Windows) or Command+A (Mac OS). All text becomes selected.

In this next section, you will discover two different methods for font selection, both using the new Control panel.

3 Change the font of selected text by using the Font drop-down menu in the Control palette. Click on the arrow to the right of the menu and scroll until you find the font Times, or Times New Roman.

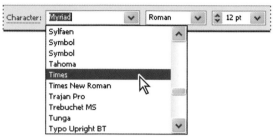

Choose fonts using the Control palette.

4 With the text still selected, choose from the menu items Type > Font to see the font display to the right of the font name. This may take a little more time because of the display, but scroll to change the selected font to Arial Regular.

5 This next method is the most dynamic method for selecting a font. Make sure the text is still selected and then follow these instructions:

• Click and drag over the Font Name in the Font text field on the Control palette.

Select the font name in the Control palette.

• Now, press the up or down arrow keys on your keyboard. This navigates up and down through your font list, in alphabetical order. Using this method, change to the font named Myriad Pro, an OpenType font.

💡 *If you know the font that you wish to select, you can also type the first few letters in the Font drop-down menu in the Control palette.*

6   Font styles are specific to each font family. Though you may have the Tekton font family on your system, you may not have bold and italic styles of that family. Find the available styles by clicking on the arrow in the Font Style drop-down menu.

What is OpenType?

If you frequently send files back and forth between platforms, you should be designing your text files using the OpenType format.

OpenType is a cross-platform font file format developed jointly by Adobe and Microsoft. Adobe has converted the entire Adobe Type Library into this format and now offers thousands of OpenType fonts.

The two main benefits of the OpenType format are its cross-platform compatibility (the same font file works on Macintosh and Windows computers), and its ability to support widely expanded character sets and layout features, which provide richer linguistic support and advanced typographic control.

OpenType fonts can include an expanded character set and layout features, providing broader linguistic support and more precise typographic control. Feature-rich Adobe OpenType fonts can be distinguished by the word "Pro," which is part of the font name and appears in application font menus. OpenType fonts can be installed and used alongside PostScript Type 1 and TrueType fonts.

—From Adobe.com/type/opentype

Changing font size

1   If the text is not still active, use the Type tool (T) to insert the cursor in the text area and choose Select > All.

2 Using the Font Size drop-down menu on the Control palette, choose from a preset size, or click and drag over the present size and enter a value in points. If the font size is not 12, choose **12** now.

Changing the font size in the Control palette.

💡 *Change selected text font size dynamically by using the keyboard shortcut Ctrl+Shift+> (Windows), Command+Shift+> (Mac OS) to make the font size larger, or Ctrl+Shift+< (Windows), Command+Shift+< (Mac OS) to make the font size smaller by increments of 2.*

Changing font color

In this next section, you'll change the font color; you can change both the fill and/or the stroke of selected text. In this example we simply change the fill.

1 Click and drag to select the first line of copy in your text area, or click three times.

💡 *Click twice to select a word, three times to select an entire paragraph. The end of a paragraph is defined as where a return has been entered.*

2 Click on the Fill box in the Control palette. When the Swatches palette appears choose White. The text fill changes to white.

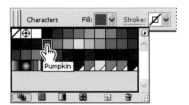

3 While you still have the first line of text selected, change the font size by selecting **14** from the Font size drop-down menu on the Control palette.

4 Change the font style for the selected text by selecting the Font Style drop-down menu on the Control palette and choosing Bold.

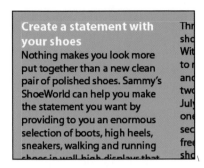

Changing additional text attributes

By clicking on the Character palette link on the Control palette you can change many other attributes that are worth investigating but not covered in this particular exercise.

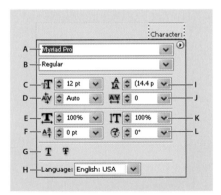

A. Set the font family. B. Set the font style.
C. Font size. D. Kerning. E. Horizontal Scale
F. Baseline Shift. G. Underline and Strikethrough
H. Language. I. Leading. J. Tracking.
K. Vertical Scale. L. Rotation.

Changing paragraph attributes

Just like with character attributes, you can set paragraph attributes (such as alignment or indenting) before you enter new type, or reset them to change the appearance of existing, selected type. If you select several type paths and type containers, you can set attributes for them all at the same time.

Now you'll add more space before all the paragraphs in the column text.

1   Using the Type tool (T), insert the cursor anywhere in the text area and choose Select > All.

2   Select the word Paragraph on the Control palette. This links you to the Paragraph palette.

3   Type **6** in the Space Before Paragraph text field (in the bottom left corner) and press Enter. Spacing before paragraphs, rather than pressing the Return key, is recommended when creating large text areas.

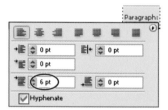

Enter a space before the paragraphs.

Saving and using styles

In Illustrator, you can save and use styles. This keeps text consistent and is helpful when text attributes need to be updated. Once a style is created, a change needs to be made only to the saved style. Then, all text with that style applied is updated.

There are two types of styles in Adobe Illustrator CS2:

•   Character—This retains the text attributes and applies them to selected text only.

•   Paragraph—This retains text and paragraph attributes and applies them to an entire paragraph.

Creating and using a Paragraph style

1   Using the Text tool (T), insert the cursor someplace in the first line of text. No text needs to be selected to create a Paragraph Style, but you do have to have the text insertion point in the line of text containing the attributes you wish to store.

2   Choose Window > Type > Paragraph Styles, and choose New Paragraph Style from the palette menu.

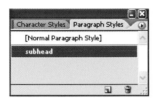

Use the palette menu to create Paragraph Styles.

3   In the New Paragraph Style window, type **subhead** for the Style Name, click OK. The text attributes used in the paragraph have been saved in a Paragraph style named subhead.

4   Apply the new paragraph style by selecting the text: "Throw away your old tired shoes." Then, select the named subhead style from the Paragraph Styles palette. The text attributes are applied to the selected text.

5   Select the text: "We are all over the place!" and apply the subhead style by holding down the Alt (Windows) or Option (Mac OS) key while you select the subhead style name in the Paragraph Styles palette.

Note: If you see a plus (+) to the right of your style name, another attribute, not part of the named style, is used on the selected text. Holding down on the Alt (Windows) or Option (Mac OS) key when you select the style name overwrites any existing attributes.

Creating and using Character Styles

Whereas Paragraph styles apply attributes to an entire paragraph, Character styles can be applied to selected text only.

1   Using the Type tool (T), select "Sammy's ShoeWorld" in the first column of the paragraph text.

2   Using the Font Style drop-down menu in the Control palette, change the font style to Bold.

3   Click on the Fill box on the Control palette and select the Red swatch from the Swatches palette.

The selected text is now bold and red.

Now save these attributes as a Character Style, and apply it to other instances in the text.

4   Choose Window > Type > Character Styles.

5   Alt+click (Windows) or Option+click (Mac OS) on the Create New Style button at the bottom of the Character Styles palette. Alt/Option+clicking on the New Style button allows you to name the style as it is added to the palette. You can also double-click at any time on a style to name and edit it.

6   Name the style **Bold** and click OK. The style records the attributes applied to your selected text.

Now you will apply that Character Style to other instances.

7   With the Sammy's ShoeWorld still selected, Alt+click (Windows) or Option+click (Mac OS) on the named style Bold in the Character Styles palette to assign the style to that text. Remember, the Alt/Option+click is used to clear any attributes from the text that are not part of the Character Style.

8   Select the text "sshoeworld.com" and assign it the Bold style as well.

9   Choose Select > Deselect.

Perhaps you decide that the color just isn't working and you want to change it. Using styles, you have to change the color only once, and all instances are updated.

10 From the Character Styles palette, choose the palette menu, then Character Style Options. Select a type attribute option from the window on the left, and then assign specific attributes by selecting characteristics on the right.

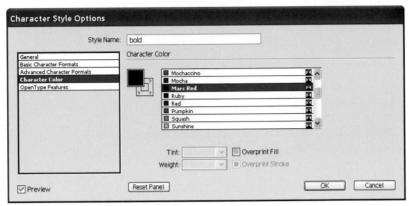

Update Styles using the Character Style Options Dialog box.

11 For this exercise, click on Character Color. In the window that appears on the right, choose the swatch named Mars Red.

12 Click OK. The text that was assigned the Character style is all updated to the new color.

13 Choose File > Save. Leave the file open.

Sampling text

Perhaps you just want to quickly sample text to retrieve its attributes without creating a style. Use the Eyedropper tool to pick-up type attributes and apply them to selected text.

1 Using the Type tool (T) select the text: "Special order the style and size you want at no extra charge." in the first paragraph.

2 Using the Control palette, change the font Fill color to White and the Font Style to Italic.

3 Now select the text: "Check out the two for one sale going on from July 17th to August 1st."

4   Choose the Eyedropper tool (✒) and click on any of the text in the line of text, Special order the size…the attributes are immediately applied to your selected text.

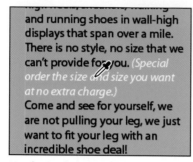

Use the Eyedropper tool to sample and apply text attributes.

5   Choose File > Save. Leave the file open.

Wrapping text around a graphic

Create interesting and creative results by wrapping text around a graphic.

1   With the file shoe_poster.ai still open, choose File > Open. In the Open dialog window, choose shoe.ai.

2   Using the Selection tool (➤), select the shoe on the page and choose Edit > Copy, then File > Close.

3   Return to the shoe_poster.ai file, and choose Edit > Paste. The shoe graphic is placed on the page.

4   Position the Shoe graphic so it is in the middle of the two columns.

5   With the shoe graphic still selected, click on the Fill box in the Control palette. When the Swatches palette appears choose the White swatch.

6 Using the Opacity text field in the Control palette, change the opacity to **30%**.

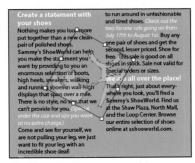

*The Shoe Graphic positioned between
the columns.*

7 With the shoe graphic still selected, choose Object > Text Wrap > Make. The text wraps around the graphic.

Note: *Objects that are to be used to create a text wrap must be above the text area.*

8 If you still have text flowing in areas that you would rather close off, choose Object > Text Wrap > Text Wrap Options. In the Text Wrap Options window, change the Offset to **16**. Click OK.

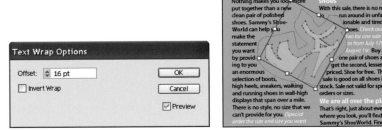

You can increase or decrease the Offset in the Text Wrap Options window.

9 Using the Selection tool, reposition the shoe graphic so as to create a better text flow. For this example, it is OK if some of your text overflows out of the text area.

10 Choose File > Save. Keep the file open.

Reshaping text with a warp

This is fun and exciting. Use an Effect on your text to give it a more interesting shape. Using Effects allow you to change the text in this way, yet change and edit the text at any time.

1   Choose Select > Deselect and choose the Type tool (T). Before typing, change the Font Family in the Control palette to Myriad Pro (if it is not already selected), the Font Style to Black and the font size to **85**.

2   Select the silhouette of the people and choose Object > Lock > Selection. Reselect the Type tool and then click once on the poster art slightly above the silhouette of the people. Exact placement is not important. A text cursor appears.

3   Type the words **KICK IT UP!** Then switch to the Selection tool and reposition the text so it is centered over the silhouette art.

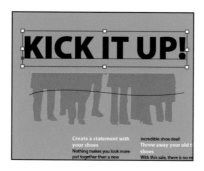

4   With the text still selected, choose Effect > Warp > Arc Upper. The Warp Options window appears. Check the Preview checkbox. The Text stays flat on the bottom and arcs only in the upper part.

Using the Settings and Style drop-down menu, you can experiment with many different combinations. Click OK when you have finished with this window. Use the Selection tool to reposition your text if necessary.

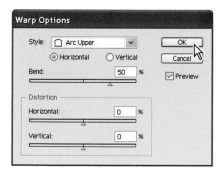

The Arc Upper Effect options window.   *Result.*

5   Using the Type tool, click and drag to select the words "KICK IT UP!".

6   In the Control palette, click on the Fill box and select White from the Swatches palette.

7   Click on the Stroke Color box and choose Pumpkin.

8   Choose the arrow to the right of the Stroke Weight on the control panel and select or type in **2**.

Notice that additional attributes are applied easily to the warped text.

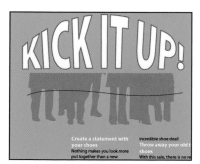

Easily apply new text attributes to text warped with an Effect.

Next you will add an additional Drop Shadow Effect.

9   Switch to the Selection tool and select "KICK IT UP!"

10   Choose Effects > Stylize > Drop Shadow. In the Drop Shadow Options window, leave at the defaults and choose OK. Read more about applying and editing effects in Lesson 11, "Applying Appearance Attributes, Graphic Styles, and Effects."

11   Choose Select > Deselect and File > Save. Leave the file open.

Creating text on paths and shapes

Using the Type tools in Illustrator CS2, you can type on paths and on shapes.

1   With the Selection tool (▶), select the wavy path crossing the silhouette artwork.

> 💡 *To quickly switch to the Selection tool and back to the Type tool, hold down Ctrl (Windows) or Command (Mac OS).*

2   With the Type tool (T), cross the cursor over the left side of the path to see an insertion point with an intersecting wavy path (⌖). Click when this cursor appears. The stroke attributes of the stroke change to None and a cursor appears. Don't type yet.

3   In the Font Size text field, in the Control palette, type **36** then press the Enter key.

4 Type **Don't just stand there...** The text follows the path.

Type on a path.

5 With the Type tool, click and drag over the text you just entered. Click the Fill box in the Control palette to link to the Swatches palette. Then select the White swatch.

Now you will put text on a closed path.

6 Using the Selection tool, select the small black circle in the lower left corner of the poster.

7 Switch to the Type tool, and holding down the Alt (Windows) or Opt (Mac OS) key, cross over the left side of the circle. The type on a path icon (ℐ) appears. Click, but don't type.

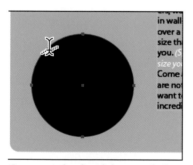
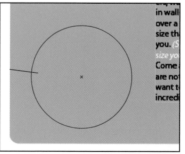

Cross over the closed shape with the Type tool and the Alt/Opt key.

After clicking, the text cursor appears.

The fill and stroke attributes of the circle are changed to None, and you have a cursor on the path.

Note: If you do not want to use the keyboard shortcut (Alt/Opt), you can choose to use the Type on a Path tool hidden in the Text tool.

8 Using Font Size drop-down menu in the Control palette, change the text size to **24**.

9 Choose the Align center button to the right of Paragraph on the Control palette.

10 Type **SAMMY'S SHOEWORLD**. The text flows on the circular path.

11 To adjust the placement on the path, switch to the Selection tool. The type object is selected. A bracket appears at the beginning of the type, at the end of the path, and at the midpoint between the start and end brackets.

12 Position the cursor over the type's center bracket until a small icon (⊾) appears next to the cursor, and drag the center bracket along the path. Hold down Ctrl (Windows) or Command (Mac OS) to prevent the type from flipping to the other side of the path. Position the text so it is centered across the top of the circle.

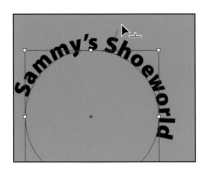

💡 *To flip the direction of text along a path, drag the bracket across the path. Alternatively, choose Type > Type On A Path > Type On A Path Options, select Flip, and click OK.*

Creating text outlines

When creating artwork for multiple purposes, it is a wise idea to create outlines of text so the recipient doesn't need your fonts to create, open, and use the file correctly. Note that you will want to keep an original of your artwork, as you cannot change outline text back to editable text.

1 Choose the Type tool (T). Click out on the Scratch area (away from the poster art) off to the left.

2 Type **WALK! RUN! DANCE!**

3 Double-click on the Rotate tool (⟳). The Rotate options window appears, type 90. The text is rotated 90 degrees counterclockwise.

Rotate text 90 degrees   *Result.*

4 With the Selection tool (▸), position the text so it is in the lower left corner of the poster art.

5 Using the Selection tool, click and drag the upper right handle of the text's bounding box, while holding down the Shift key, to proportionally enlarge the text to the size of the height of the poster.

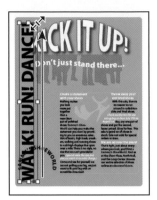

*Enlarge a text area using
the bounding box.*

6 With the text area still selected, click on the Fill box in the Control palette and choose White from the Swatches palette.

7 Click once on the word Opacity in the Control palette to link to the Opacity palette. Use the Blend Mode drop-down menu to select Soft Light. Change the Opacity to **75%** in the Opacity text field.

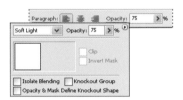

8 With the text area still selected, choose Type > Create Outlines. The text is no longer linked to a particular font, but has become artwork, much like any other vector art in your illustration.

One of the benefits of creating outlines from text is that it allows you to fill the text with a gradient. If a gradient fill is what you wish to achieve, but you still want to maintain text editing control, select the text with the Selection tool and choose Effect > Path > Outline Object.

9 Choose File > Save.

Congratulations! You have completed the lesson.

Exploring on your own

Experiment with Illustrator CS2 text features by integrating paths with illustrations. Use the clip art provided in the Lesson06 folder and try some of these type techniques:

• pizza.ai—Using the Pen tool create paths representing steam rising from the slice. Create text on a the wavy paths and apply varying levels of opacity.

• airplane.ai—Complete a banner following the airplane with text of your own.

Take the project further by using your graphic in a one-page sales flyer and has the following text elements on the page:

• Using the placeholder.txt found in the Lesson06 folder, create a three-column text area.

• Use the graphic of the pizza or plane for a text wrap.

• Create a masthead across the top of your page that has text on a curve.

• Create a Paragraph Style.

Review

▶ ## Review questions

1 Name two methods for creating text area in Adobe Illustrator CS2.

2 What are two benefits of using an OpenType font?

3 What is the difference between a Character and Paragraph Style?

4 What are the advantages and disadvantages of converting text to outlines?

Review answers

1 There are several methods for creating text areas; you can choose from any of these three:

• Using the Type tool, click on the artboard. A cursor appears; start typing. After typing, note that a text area has been created to accommodate the text.

• Using the Type tool, click and drag to create a text area. A cursor appears in the text area; start typing.

• Using the Type tool, click on a path or closed shape to convert it to text on a path or a text area. Alt/Opt+Click when crossing over the stroke of a closed path creates text around the shape.

2 The two main benefits of the OpenType format are its cross-platform compatibility (the same font file works on Macintosh and Windows computers), and its ability to support widely expanded character sets and layout features, which provide richer linguistic support and advanced typographic control.

3 A Character Style can be applied to selected text only. A Paragraph style is applied to an entire paragraph. Paragraph styles are best when indents, margins, and line spacing attributes need to be saved.

4   A benefit of converting type to outlines is that doing so eliminates the need to send the font along with the file when sharing with others. You can also fill the type with a gradient and create interesting effects on individual letters.

However, when you create outlines from text, you must consider:

• Text is no longer editable. The content and font cannot be changed on outlined text. It is best to save a layer with the original text, or use the Outline Object Effect.

• You can not convert bitmap fonts or outline-protected fonts to outlines.

• It is not suggested that you outline text that is less than 10 points in size. When you convert type to outlines, the type loses its hints—instructions built into outline fonts to adjust their shape so that your system displays or prints them optimally at a wide range of sizes. Therefore, if you plan to scale the type, do so by adjusting its point size before converting it to outlines.

• You must convert all the type in a selection to outlines; you cannot convert a single letter within a string of type. To convert a single letter into an outline, create a separate type area containing only that letter.

Layers let you organize your work into distinct levels that can be edited and viewed as individual units. Every Adobe Illustrator CS2 document contains at least one layer. Creating multiple layers in your artwork lets you easily control how artwork is printed, displayed, and edited.

7 | Working with Layers

In this lesson, you'll learn how to do the following:

- Work with the Layers palette.
- Create, rearrange, and lock layers, nested layers, and groups.
- Move objects between layers.
- Paste layers of objects from one file to another.
- Merge layers into a single layer.
- Apply a drop shadow to a layer.
- Make a layer clipping mask.
- Apply an appearance attribute to objects and layers.

Getting started

In this lesson, you'll finish the artwork of a wall clock as you explore the various ways to use the Layers palette. Before you begin, you must restore the default preferences for Adobe Illustrator and then you will open the finished art file for this lesson to see what you'll create.

1 To ensure that the tools and palettes function exactly as described in this lesson, delete or deactivate (by renaming) the Adobe Illustrator CS2 preferences file. See "Restoring default preferences" on page 3.

2 Start Adobe Illustrator CS2.

3 Choose File > Open, and open the L07end.ai file in the Lesson07 folder, located inside the Lessons folder within the AICIB folder on your hard drive.

Separate layers are used for the objects that make up the clock's frame, striped clock face, hands, and numbers—as indicated by their layer names in the Layers palette.

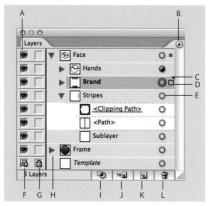

A. *Eye icon (Hide/Show).*
B. *Layers palette menu.*
C. *Current layer indicator.*
D. *Selection indicator.*
E. *Target and appearance indicator.*
F. *Template Layer icon.*
G. *Edit column (Lock/Unlock).*
H. *Expand/Collapse triangle.*
I. *Make/Release Clipping Mask.*
J. *Create New Sublayer button.*
K. *Create New Layer button.*
L. *Delete button.*

4   If you like, you may leave the file open as a visual reference. Do this by reducing the size of your window then select View > Fit in Window. If you don't want to leave the image open, choose, File > Close.

To begin working, you'll open an existing art file.

5   Choose File > Open, and open the L07start.ai file in the Lesson07 folder, located inside the Lessons folder within the AICIB folder on your hard drive.

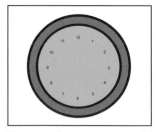

*The artwork contains some of the
basic objects for the clock illustration.*

6   Choose File > Save As, name the file **Clock.ai**, and select the Lesson07 folder. Leave the type of file format set to Adobe Illustrator Document, and click Save. In the Illustrator Options dialog box, leave at the defaults and click OK.

Using layers

Using the Layers palette, you can create multiple levels of artwork that reside on separate, overlapping layers, sublayers, and groups in the same file. Layers act like individual, clear sheets containing one or more objects. Where no filled (or nontransparent) objects overlap, you can see through any layer to the layer below.

You can create and edit objects on any layer without affecting the artwork on any other layer. You can also display, print, lock, and reorder layers as distinct units.

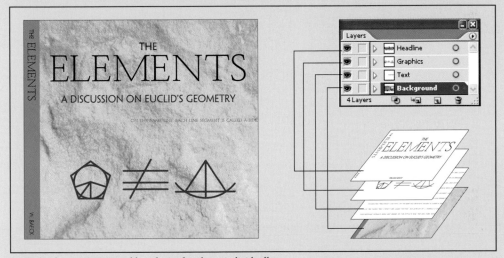

Example of composite art and how layers break out individually.

Creating layers

Every document in Illustrator contains one layer by default. You can rename the layer and add more layers at any time as you create the artwork. Placing objects on separate layers lets you easily select and edit them by their organization. For example, by placing type on a separate layer, you can change the type all at once without affecting the rest of the artwork.

You'll change the layer name to "Clock," and then you'll create another layer.

1 If the Layers palette isn't visible on-screen, choose Window > Layers to display it. Layer 1 (the default name for the first layer) is highlighted, indicating that it is active. The layer also has a triangle (▾), indicating that objects on the layer can be edited when you use the tools.

2 In the Layers palette, double-click the layer name to open the Layer Options dialog box. Type **Clock** in the Name text field, and then click OK.

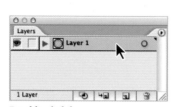
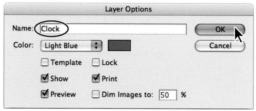

Double-click layer name.   *Change layer name to Clock.*

Now you'll create a sublayer for the clock numbers.

3 Click once on the named layer, Clock, in the Layers palette and then Alt+click (Windows) or Option+click (Mac OS) the Create New Sublayer button (⬓) at the bottom of the Layers palette to create a new sublayer and display the Layer Options dialog box. Creating a new sublayer also opens the layer to show existing sublayers.

(If you want to create a new sublayer without setting any options or naming the layer, you can click the Create New Sublayer button. New sublayers created without Alt+clicking are numbered in sequence, for example, Layer 2.)

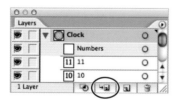

Create sublayer named Numbers.

4 In the Layer Options dialog box, type **Numbers** in the Name text field, and click OK. The new sublayer appears directly beneath its main layer name (Clock) and is selected.

Moving objects and layers

By rearranging the layers in the Layers palette, you can reorder layered objects in your artwork. You can also move selected objects from one layer or sublayer to another.

First you'll move the clock numbers onto their own sublayer.

1   In the Layers palette, grab the thumbnail for the 11 object and drag it onto the thumbnail for the Numbers layer. Release the mouse button when you see the large black triangles at either end of the Numbers layer in the palette. (The large triangles indicate that you are adding something to that layer.)

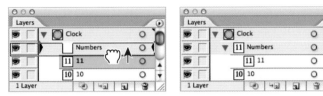

Grab thumbnail and move it onto sublayer thumbnail.

💡 *To select multiple layers or sublayers quickly, select a layer and then Shift+click on additional layers.*

2   Repeat step 1 for each of the twelve numbers in the Layers palette.

3   Choose Select > Deselect. Then choose File > Save.

Now you'll move the face of the clock to a new layer, to use later when you add the stripes, hands, and brand name of the clock, and you'll rename the Clock layer to reflect the new organization of the artwork.

4   In the artwork, click behind the numbers to select the clock face. In the Layers palette, the object named <Path> becomes active (as indicated by the small square selection indicator (■) in the far right column.)

5   Alt+click (Windows) or Option+click (Mac OS) the Create New Layer button at the bottom of the Layers palette, or choose New Layer from the Layers palette menu.

6   In the Layer Options dialog box, enter **Face** in the Name text field, choose a different layer color from the drop-down menu (such as Orange), and click OK.

The new Face layer is added above the Clock layer and becomes active.

7 In the Layers palette, select the small square selection indicator on the <Path> layer, and drag it directly up to the right of the target indicator (○) on the new Face layer.

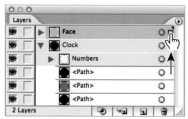

Drag selection indicator up to move object to another layer.

This action moves the selected object to the new layer. The color of the selection lines in the artwork changes to the color of the new Face layer (such as Orange).

Now that the Face layer is on top of the Clock layer and the Numbers sublayer, the clock numbers are covered up. You'll move the Numbers sublayer onto a different layer and rename the Clock layer to reflect the new organization of the artwork.

8 In the Layers palette, drag the Numbers sublayer thumbnail onto the Face layer thumbnail. Release the mouse button when you see the indicator bar with large black triangles at either end of the Face layer in the palette.

Now you can see the numbers again.

9 Double-click the Clock layer to display the Layer Options dialog box, and change the layer name to **Frame**. Then click OK.

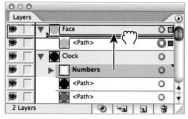 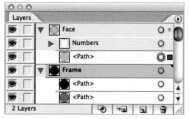

Drag sublayer thumbnail to move it to another layer.   *Change layer name.*

10 Choose Select > Deselect to deselect all active objects, and then choose File > Save.

Locking layers

As you edit objects on a layer, use the Layers palette to lock other layers and prevent selecting or changing the rest of the artwork.

Now you'll lock all the layers except the Numbers sublayer so that you can easily edit the clock numbers without affecting objects on other layers. Locked layers cannot be selected or edited in any way.

1 To simplify your work, click the triangle to the left of the Frame layer to collapse the layer view.

2 Click the edit column to the right of the eye icon on the Frame layer to lock the layer.

The padlock icon (🔒) indicates that a layer and all its objects are locked.

3 Click the edit column to the right of the eye icon on the <Path> sublayer below the Numbers layer.

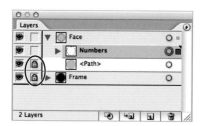

Click the edit column to lock a layer.

You can unlock individual layers by clicking the padlock icon to make it disappear from the edit column. Clicking again in the edit column relocks the layer. Holding down Alt (Windows) or Option (Mac OS) as you click in the edit column alternately locks and unlocks all other layers.

Now you'll change the type size and font of the numbers.

4 In the Layers palette to the right of the Numbers layer, click the selection column to select all objects on that layer.

A quick way to select all the type or objects on a layer is to click the selection column—the blank area to the right of the target indicators—in the Layers palette.

The Numbers layer now has a large red square, indicating that everything on the layer is selected.

5   Click Character in the Control palette to display the Character palette.

6   In the Character palette, select another font or size for the group of numbers. (We used Myriad Pro Bold, size 28 points.)

Note: *Myriad Pro is an OpenType font included with Illustrator CS2. Click on Browse Cool Extras on the Welcome Screen for more information about fonts.*

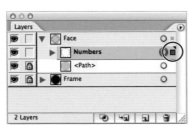
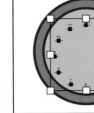
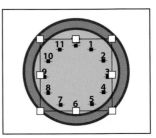

Click the selection column.   *All type is selected.*   *Change font and size globally.*

7   If you wish, use the Color palette or Swatches palette to change the color of the selected numbers.

8   In the Layers palette, click the padlock icons next to the <Path> and the Frame layers to unlock them.

Viewing layers

The Layers palette lets you hide layers, sublayers, or individual objects from view. When a layer is hidden, objects on the layer are also locked and cannot be selected or printed. You can also use the Layers palette to display layers or objects in either Preview or Outline to view independently from other layers in the artwork.

Now you'll edit the frame on the clock, using a painting technique to create a three-dimensional effect on the frame.

1 In the Layers palette, click the Frame layer to select it, and then Alt+click (Windows) or Option+click (Mac OS) the eye icon (👁) next to the Frame layer name to hide the other layers.

💡 *Alt/Option+clicking the layer eye icon alternately hides and shows a layer. Hiding layers also locks them and prevents them from being changed.*

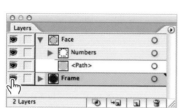

Alt/Option+click eye icon.

Only objects on Frame layer appear.

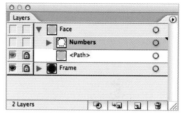

Only Frame layer is showing and unlocked.

2 Using the Selection tool (⬉), click the inside circle of the frame to select it. Then holding down the Shift key, click the next largest circle to add it to the selection.

3 With the two inner circles selected, click the Fill box in the Control palette, and then click the Clock.frame swatch in the Swatches palette to paint the circles with a custom gradient.

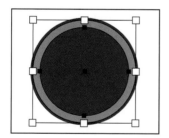

Select two inner circles.

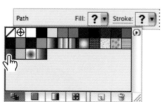

Paint with gradient fill.

4 Shift+click the second largest circle to deselect it and keep the inside circle selected.

5   Select the Gradient tool (▨) in the toolbox. Drag the tool in a vertical line from the top of the circle straight down to the bottom to change the direction of the gradient.

The Gradient tool works only on selected objects that are filled with gradients. To learn more about using the Gradient tool, see Lesson 8, "Blending Shapes and Colors."

 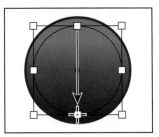

Select the   *Drag over selected object.*
Gradient
tool.

6   Choose Select > Deselect to deselect the artwork, and then choose File > Save.

7   In the Layers palette, choose Show All Layers from the palette menu.

As you edit objects in layered artwork, you can display individual layers in Outline view, keeping the other layers in Preview view.

8   Ctrl+click (Windows) or Command+click (Mac OS) the eye icon next to the Face layer to switch to Outline view for that layer.

This action lets you see the gradient-filled circle behind the clock face. Displaying a layer in Outline view is also useful for viewing the anchor points or center points on objects without selecting them.

White fill in eye icon indicates   *Preview view of other layers shows*
Outline view.   *through Face layer in Outline view.*

9 Ctrl/Command+click the eye icon next to the Face layer to return to Preview view for that layer.

Pasting layers

To complete the clock, you'll copy and paste the finishing parts of artwork from another file. You can paste layered files into another file and keep all the layers intact.

1 Choose File > Open, and open the Details.ai file, located in the Lesson07 folder, inside the Lessons folder within the AICIB folder on your hard drive.

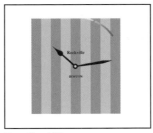
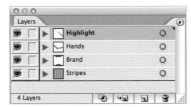

Clock.ai file.   *Details.ai file.*   *Layers palette for Details.ai file.*

2 If you want to see how the objects are organized on the layers, Alt/Option+click the eye icons in the Layers palette to alternately display each layer and hide the others. You can also click the triangles (▶) to the left of the layer names to expand and collapse the layers for further inspection. When you've finished, make sure that all the layers are showing and that they are fully collapsed.

If a layer is hidden, its objects are locked and cannot be selected or copied.

3 Choose Select > All and then Edit > Copy to select and copy the clock details to the Clipboard.

4 Choose File > Close. If an Adobe Illustrator alert window appears, click No (Windows) or Don't Save (Mac OS) to close the Details.ai file without saving any changes.

5   In the Clock.ai file, choose Paste Remembers Layers from the Layers palette menu to select the option. (A check mark next to the option indicates that it's selected.)

Selecting the Paste Remembers Layers option indicates that when multiple layers from another file are pasted into the artwork, they're added as individual layers in the Layers palette. If the option is not selected, all objects are pasted into the active layer.

6   Choose Edit > Paste In Front to paste the details into the clock.

The Paste In Front command pastes the objects from the Clipboard to a position relative to the original position in the Details.ai file. The Paste Remembers Layers option causes the Details.ai layers to be pasted as four separate layers at the top of the Layers palette (Highlight, Hands, Brand, Stripes).

7   Drag the Layers palette by its lower right corner to resize it and display all the layers in the palette. As you can see, some of the layers need to be repositioned.

8   Close any open layers and move the Frame layer above the Highlight layer and then the Face layer above Frame.

Release the mouse button when the indicator bar with large black triangles extends the full column width above the Highlight and Frame layer. (You want to create a separate layer, not a sublayer.)

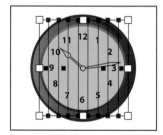
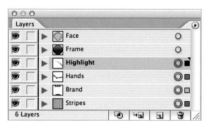

Paste artwork from   *Layers are added from Details.ai file.*
Details.ai file.

Now you'll move the brand and hands into the Face layer and the highlight in front of the Frame layer.

9   Choose the Selection tool (➤), and click away from the artwork to deselect it.

10 In the Layers palette, select the Highlight layer, and drag it up between the Face and Frame layers.

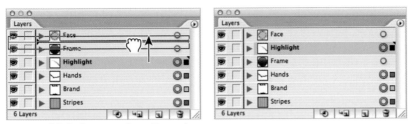

Move Highlight layer up above Frame layer.

11 Click on the arrow to the left of the Face layer to show the sublayers.

12 Click the Hands layer and Shift+click the Brand layers in the Layers palette.

13 Drag the selected layers up between the Numbers and <Path> sublayers; when the insertion bar appears between those sublayers, release the mouse button to make the Hands and Brand layers sublayers of the Face layer.

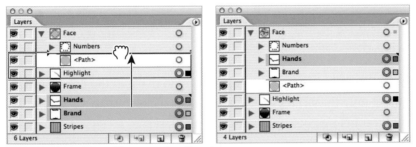

Drag Hands and Brand layers up into Face layer.

14 Choose File > Save to save the changes.

Creating clipping masks

The Layers palette lets you create clipping masks to control how artwork on a layer (or in a group) is hidden or revealed. A *clipping mask* is an object or group of objects whose shape masks artwork below it so that only artwork within the shape is visible.

Now you'll create a clipping mask with the circle shape in the Face layer. You'll group it with the Stripes sublayer so that only the stripes show through the circle shape.

1 In the Layers palette, drag the Stripes layer up until the insertion bar's double lines are highlighted above the <Path> layer within the Face layer. Release the mouse button when the indicator bar appears.

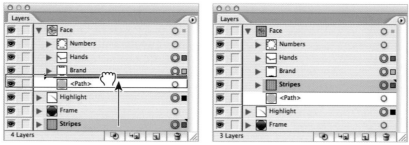

Drag Stripes layer up above <Path> sublayer within the Face layer.

A masking object must reside above the objects it will mask in the Layers palette. Since you want to mask only the stripes, you'll move the circular <Path> object to the top of the Stripes sublayer before you create the clipping mask.

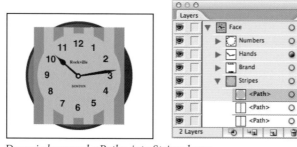

Drag circle named <Path> into Stripes layer.

2 Drag the <Path> sublayer with the circle color fill onto the Stripes thumbnail to add it to that layer as the top sublayer.

3 In the Layers palette, click the triangle (▸) to the left of the Stripes layer to expand the layer view.

4 Make sure that the <Path> with the circle color fill is the topmost sublayer in the Stripes layer, moving it if necessary. (Clipping masks are always the first object in a layer or group.)

5 Select the Stripes layer to highlight it. Then click the selection area to the right of the Stripes layer to select all the stripes and the colored circle path.

6 Click the Make/Release Clipping Mask button at the bottom of the Layers palette. Notice that all the layer's dividing lines are now dotted and the first path's name has changed to <Clipping Path>. The clipping path name is also underlined to indicate that it is the masking shape.

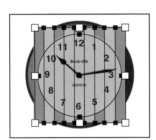 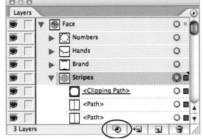 

Select Stripes layer.   *Click Make/Release Clipping Mask button.*   *Result.*

7 Click the triangle next to the Stripes layer name to collapse the layers in the Layers palette.

8 Choose Select > Deselect. Then choose File > Save.

Merging layers

To streamline your artwork, you can merge layers. Merging layers combines the contents of all selected layers onto one layer.

1   In the Layers palette, click the Numbers layer to highlight it, and then Shift+click to highlight the Hands layer.

Notice the current layer indicator (▾) shows the last highlighted layer as the active layer. The last layer you select will determine the name and color for the merged layer.

2   Choose Merge Selected from the Layers palette menu to merge the objects from the Numbers layer into the Hands layer.

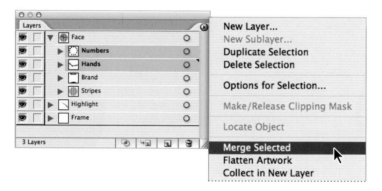

The objects on the merged layers retain their original stacking order, and are added above the objects in the destination layer.

3   Now click the Highlight layer to highlight it, and then Shift+click to highlight the Frame layer.

4   Choose Merge Selected from the Layers palette menu to merge the objects from the Highlight layer into the Frame layer.

5   Choose File > Save.

Applying appearance attributes to layers

You can apply appearance attributes such as styles, effects, and transparency to layers, groups, and objects with the Layers palette. When an appearance attribute is applied to a layer, any object on that layer will take on that attribute. If an appearance attribute is applied only to a specific object on a layer, it affects only that object, not the entire layer.

You will apply an effect to an object on one layer. Then you'll copy that effect to a layer to change all objects on that layer.

1   In the Layers palette, collapse the Face layer and expand the Frame layer to reveal all its objects.

2   Select the bottom path in the Frame layer.

3   To the right of the bottom path's layer name, click the target indicator (◎) to target the bottommost object. Clicking the target indicator indicates that you want to apply an effect, style, or transparency change.

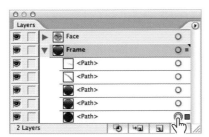

*Click the target indicator to target
the bottom path.*

4   Choose Effect > Stylize > Drop Shadow. Leave the settings at their default values and click OK. A drop shadow appears on the outer edge of the clock.

Note: Select the first Stylize option from the Effect submenu. Effect > Stylize > Drop Shadow command.

5   Notice that the target indicator is now shaded, indicating that the object has appearance attributes applied to it.

6   Click the Appearance tab to bring the palette to the front of its group. (If the Appearance palette isn't visible on-screen, choose Window > Appearance.) Notice that Drop Shadow has been added to the list of appearance attributes for the selected shape.

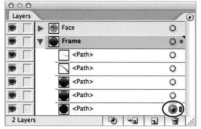

Apply drop shadow effect to clock edge.   *Shaded target indicator indicates appearance attributes.*   *Appearance palette lists selection's attributes.*

You will now use the Layers palette to copy an appearance attribute onto a layer and then edit it.

7   Expand the Face layer to reveal its contents. Drag the bottom right corner of the Layers palette to display the entire list.

8   Hold down Alt (Windows) or Option (Mac OS) and drag the shaded target indicator of the <Path> sublayer to the target indicator of the Hands layer, without releasing the mouse button. The hand cursor with a plus sign indicates that the appearance is being copied.

9   When the target indicator of the Hands layer turns light gray, release the mouse button. The drop shadow is now applied to the entire Hands layer, as indicated by the shaded target indicator.

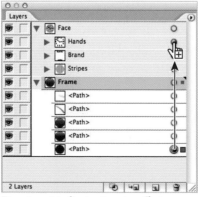

Drag target indicator to copy effect.   *Result.*

Now you'll edit the drop shadow attribute for the type and clock hands, to tone down the effect.

10 In the Layers palette, click the target indicator for the Hands layer. This automatically selects the objects on the Hands layer and deselects the object on the Frame layer.

11 In the Appearance palette, double-click the Drop Shadow attribute. In the Drop Shadow dialog box, enter **3 pt** for the X and Y offsets and the Blur amount. Click OK.

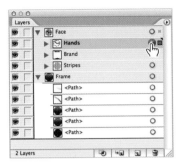

Target Hands layer.   *Edit Drop Shadow effect.*   *Result.*

For more information on appearance attributes, see Lesson 11, "Applying Appearance Attributes, Graphic Styles, and Effects."

12 Choose Select > Deselect.

13 Choose File > Save. Choose File > Close to close the file.

You have completed building a layered file.

In some cases after the artwork is complete, you may want to place all the layers of art onto a single layer and delete the empty layers. This is called flattening artwork. Delivering finished artwork in a single layer file can prevent accidents, such as hiding layers and not printing parts of the artwork, from happening.

To flatten specific layers without deleting hidden layers, select the layers you want to flatten, and then choose Merge Layers from the Layers palette menu.

To consolidate layers and groups

Merging and flattening layers are similar in that they both let you consolidate objects, groups, and sublayers into a single layer or group. With merging, you can select which items you want to consolidate; with flattening, all visible items in the artwork are consolidated in a single layer. With either option, the stacking order of the artwork remains the same, but other layer-level attributes, such as clipping masks, aren't preserved.

• *To merge items into a single layer or group, hold down Ctrl (Windows) or Command (Mac OS) and click the names of the layers or groups that you want to merge. Alternatively, hold down Shift to select all listings in between the layer or group names you click. Then select Merge Selected from the Layers palette menu. Note that items will be merged into the layer or group that you selected last.*
Layers can only merge with other layers that are on the same hierarchical level in the Layers palette. Likewise, sublayers can only merge with other sublayers that are within the same layer and at the same hierarchical level. Objects can't be merged with other objects.

• *To flatten layers, click the name of the layer into which you want to consolidate the artwork. Then select Flatten Artwork from the Layers palette menu.*

—From Illustrator Help

For information on opening layered Photoshop files in Illustrator and working with layered Illustrator files in Photoshop, see Lesson 13, "Combining Illustrator CS2 Graphics with the Creative Suite."

? For a complete list of shortcuts that you can use with the Layers palette, see "Keyboard Shortcuts" in Illustrator Help.

Exploring on your own

When you print a layered file, only the visible layers print in the same order in which they appear in the Layers palette—with the exception of template layers, which do not print even if they're visible. Template layers are locked, dimmed, and previewed. Objects on template layers neither print nor export.

Now that you've learned how to work with layers, try creating layered artwork by tracing an image on a template layer. We've provided a bitmap photo image of a goldfish that you can use to practice with, or use your own artwork or photo images.

1 Choose File > New to create a new file for your artwork.

2 Choose File > Place. In the dialog box, select the Goldfish.eps file, located in the Lesson07 folder, inside the Lessons folder within the AICIB folder on your hard drive; or locate your file containing the artwork or image you want to use as a template and click Place to add the placed file to Layer 1.

3 Create the template layer by choosing Template from the Layers palette menu or choosing Options for Layer 1 and selecting Template in the Layer Options dialog box.

4 Click the New Layer button to create a new layer on which to draw.

5 With Layer 2 active, use any drawing tool to trace over the template, creating new artwork.

6 Create additional layers to separate and edit various components of the new artwork.

7 If you wish, delete the template when you've finished, to reduce the size of the file.

💡 *You can create custom views of your artwork with some layers hidden and other layers showing, and display each view in a separate window. To create a custom view, choose View > New View. To display each view in a separate window, choose Window > New Window.*

🔲 For information on custom views, see "To use multiple windows and views" in Illustrator Help.

Review

▶ ## Review questions

1   Name two benefits of using layers when creating artwork.

2   How do you hide layers? Display individual layers?

3   Describe how to reorder layers in a file.

4   How can you lock layers?

5   What is the purpose of changing the selection color on a layer?

6   What happens if you paste a layered file into another file? Why is the Paste Remembers Layers option useful?

7   How do you move objects from one layer to another?

8   How do you create a layer clipping mask?

9   How do you apply an effect to a layer? How can you edit that effect?

Review answers

1   Benefits of using layers when creating artwork include: You can protect artwork that you don't want to change, you can hide artwork that you aren't working with so that it's not distracting, and you can control what prints.

2   To hide a layer, you click the eye icon to the left of the layer name; you click in the blank, leftmost column to redisplay a layer.

3   You reorder layers by selecting a layer name in the Layers palette and dragging the layer to its new location. The order of layers in the Layers palette controls the document's layer order—topmost in the palette is frontmost in the artwork.

4   You can lock layers several different ways:

• You can click in the column to the left of the layer name; a padlock icon appears, indicating that the layer is locked.

• You can choose Lock Others from the Layers palette menu to lock all layers but the active layer.

• You can hide a layer to protect it.

5   The selection color controls how selected anchor points and direction lines are displayed on a layer, and helps you identify the different layers in your document.

6   The Paste commands paste layered files or objects copied from different layers onto the active layer by default. The Paste Remembers Layers option keeps the original layers intact when the objects are pasted.

7   Select the objects you want to move and drag the Square Selection Indicator icon (to the right of the target indicator) to another layer in the Layers palette.

8   Create a clipping mask on a layer by selecting the layer and clicking the Make/Release Clipping Mask button. The topmost object in the layer will become the clipping mask.

9   Click the target indicator for the layer to which you want to apply an effect. Then choose an effect from the Effect menu. To edit the effect, make sure that the layer is selected; then double-click the name of the effect in the Appearance palette. The effect's dialog box will open, and then you can change the values.

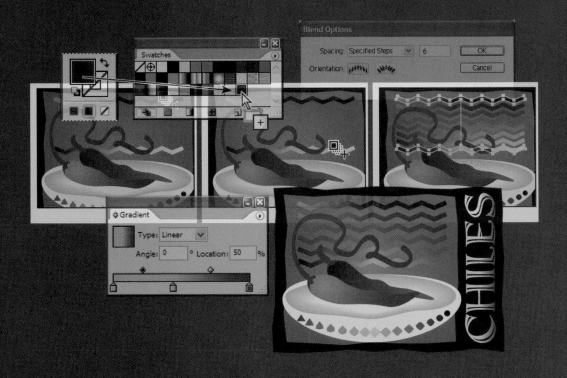

Gradient fills are graduated blends
of two or more colors. You use the
Gradient palette to create or modify a
gradient fill. The Blend tool blends the
shapes and colors of objects together
into a new blended object or a series
of intermediate shapes.

8 Blending Shapes and Colors

In this lesson, you'll learn how to do the following:

• Create and save gradients.

• Add colors to a gradient.

• Adjust the direction of a gradient blend.

• Create smooth-color blends between objects.

• Blend the shapes of objects in intermediate steps.

• Modify a blend, including adjusting its path and changing the shape or color of the original objects.

Getting started

You'll explore various ways to create your own color gradients, and blend colors and shapes together using the Gradient palette and the Blend tool.

Before you begin, you'll restore the default preferences for Adobe Illustrator. Then you'll open the finished art file for this lesson to see what you'll create.

1   To ensure that the tools and palettes function exactly as described in this lesson, delete or deactivate (by renaming) the Adobe Illustrator CS2 preferences file. See "Restoring default preferences" on page 3.

2   Start Adobe Illustrator CS2.

3   Choose File > Open, and open the L08end.ai file in the Lesson08 folder, located within the AICIB folder on your hard drive.

4   The chile peppers, CHILES type, and wavy lines are all filled with gradients. The objects that make up the inside of the bowl, the objects on the outside of the bowl, and the top and bottom wavy lines on the blanket have all been blended to create new objects.

5   If you like, choose View > Zoom Out to make the finished artwork smaller, adjust the window size, and leave it on your screen as you work. (Use the Hand tool (✋) to move the artwork where you want it in the window.) If you don't want to leave the image open, choose File > Close.

To begin working, you'll open an existing art file.

6   Choose File > Open, and open the L08start.ai file in the Lesson08 folder, located within the AICIB folder on your hard drive.

7   Choose File > Save As, name the file **Chiles.ai**, and select the Lesson08 folder in the Save In menu. Leave the type of file format set to Adobe Illustrator Document, and click Save. In the Illustrator Options dialog box, leave at the default settings and click OK.

8   Click the close box in the Layers palette or choose Window > Layers to close the Layers palette group. You won't need these palettes for this lesson.

Creating a gradient fill

Gradients can be used very much like colors to fill objects that you create. A gradient fill is a graduated blend between two or more colors. You can easily create your own gradients, or you can use the gradients provided with Adobe Illustrator and edit them for the desired effect.

To begin the lesson, you'll create a gradient fill for one of the chile peppers.

1   Using the Selection tool (▸), click to select the chile pepper in the back.

The pepper is painted with a solid color fill and no stroke, as indicated in the Fill and Stroke boxes in the toolbox. The Gradient button below the Fill and Stroke boxes indicates the current gradient fill (which is by default a black-and-white gradient until you select a gradient-filled object or a gradient swatch in the Swatches palette).

2   Click the Gradient button (▨) in the toolbox.

The default, black-and-white gradient appears in the Fill box in the toolbox and is applied to the selected chile pepper.

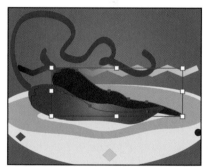  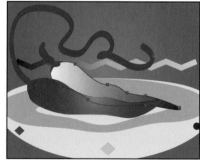

Click Gradient button to paint selected object with default or current gradient fill.

Choose Window > Gradient if your Gradient palette is not visible. You use the Gradient palette to create your own gradients and to modify the colors of existing gradients.

3   In the Gradient palette, position the cursor on the triangle in the upper right corner of the palette, press the mouse button, and choose Show Options from the palette's menu. (Use the same technique for choosing options from other palette menus.)

4　Now click the Gradient tab on the palette and drag it to move the palette to another area on your screen. This action separates, or undocks, the Gradient palette from any other palettes.

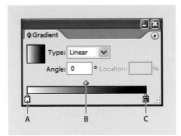

A. *Starting gradient stop.*
B. *Midpoint between blended colors.*
C. *Ending gradient stop.*

In the Gradient palette, the left gradient square, or stop, under the gradient bar marks the gradient's starting color; the right gradient stop marks the ending color. A gradient stop is the point at which a gradient changes from one color to the next. A diamond above the bar marks the midpoint where two colors blend equally.

5　Click the left gradient stop to select the starting color of the gradient. The tip of the gradient stop appears darker to indicate that it's selected.

In the Color palette, choose to Show Options from the palette menu. A gradient stop appears beneath the Fill box, indicating which color in the gradient is currently selected. Now you'll paint the selected color in the gradient with a new color.

6　In the Color palette, position the cursor on the triangle in the upper right corner of the palette, press the mouse button, and choose CMYK to switch from the Grayscale palette to the CMYK palette.

7   With the gradient stop selected, position the eyedropper cursor (✐) in the color bar at the bottom of the Color palette, and drag or click to select a new color. Notice the change to the gradient fill in the selected chile pepper.

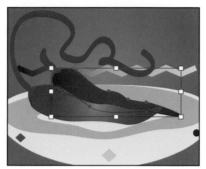

Gradient stop color selected.   *Result.*

You can also drag the Color palette sliders or enter values in the percent text fields to select a color. The selected gradient stop changes to reflect your choice.

8   With the left gradient stop still selected, enter these CMYK values in the Color palette: C=**20**, M=**100**, Y=**80**, and K=**0**. (To move between text fields, press Tab.) Press Enter (Windows) or Return (Mac OS) to apply the last value typed.

9   In the Gradient palette, select the ending gradient stop on the right.

10   In the Color palette, choose CMYK from the palette menu to switch to the CMYK palette from the Grayscale palette.

11   Change the ending color by entering these values in the Color palette: C=**100**, M=**30**, Y=**100**, and K=**0**. (Press Tab to select each text field.) Press Enter or Return to apply the last value typed.

Now you'll save the new gradient in the Swatches palette.

12 Click the Swatches tab to bring the palette to the front of its group. (If the Swatches palette isn't visible on-screen, choose Window > Swatches to display it.)

13 To save the gradient, drag it from the Fill box in the toolbox or the Gradient palette and drop it on the Swatches palette; or select it in the Fill box in the toolbox or in the Gradient palette, and click the New Swatch button at the bottom of the Swatches palette.

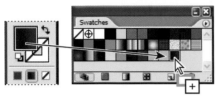

Drag gradient swatch from Fill box to Swatches palette.

14 In the Swatches palette, double-click the new gradient swatch to open the Swatch Options dialog box. Type **Pepper2** in the Swatch Name text field, and click OK.

15 To display only gradient swatches in the Swatches palette, click the Show Gradient Swatches button at the bottom of the Swatches palette.

Display only gradient swatches.

16 Try out some of the different gradients in the selected chile pepper.

Notice that some of the gradients have several colors. You'll learn how to make a gradient with multiple colors later in this lesson.

17 Deselect the artwork by choosing Select > Deselect, and then choose File > Save.

Adjusting the direction of the gradient blend

Once you have painted an object with a gradient fill, you can adjust the direction that the gradient colors blend in the object. Now you'll adjust the gradient fill in the other chile pepper.

1   Use the Selection tool (↖) to select the chile pepper in front. Notice that it's painted with a radial-type gradient (as indicated in the Gradient palette).

You can create linear or radial gradients. Both types of gradient have a starting and an ending color of the fill. With a radial gradient, the starting color of the gradient defines the center point of the fill, which radiates outward to the ending color.

2   Select the Gradient tool (▭) in the toolbox.

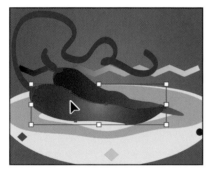
Select gradient-filled object.

The Gradient tool.

The Gradient tool works only on selected objects that are filled with a gradient.

3   Click or drag the Gradient tool across the selected chile pepper to change the position and direction of the gradient's starting and ending colors.

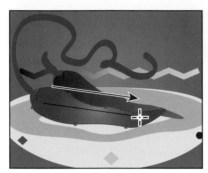

Drag Gradient tool at an angle.   *Result.*

For example, drag within the pepper to create a short gradient with distinct color blends; drag a longer distance outside the pepper to create a longer gradient with more subtle color blends. You can also drag from the ending color to the starting color and vice versa to transpose the colors and reverse the direction of the blend.

4   Deselect the artwork by choosing Select > Deselect, and then choose File > Save.

Adding colors to a gradient

Every gradient in Adobe Illustrator has at least two gradient stops. By editing the color mix of each stop and by adding gradient stops in the Gradient palette, you can create your own custom gradients.

Now you'll paint some type that has been converted to path outlines with a linear gradient fill, and edit the colors in it.

1   Select the Magic Wand tool (✎), and click to select the letters in the type CHILES. The CHILES type has already been converted to path outlines so you can fill it with a gradient. (To convert type to path outlines, select it and choose Type > Create Outlines. See Lesson 6, "Working with type," for more information.)

2   Choose Object > Group to group the letters.

Select letter outlines and group type.

By grouping the letters, you'll fill each individual letter with the same gradient at once. Grouping them also makes it easier to edit the gradient fill globally.

3   In the toolbox, click the Gradient button (below the Fill and Stroke boxes) to paint the type outlines with the current gradient fill—in this case, with the radial gradient that was last selected in the chile pepper.

Paint selected type with last-selected gradient fill.

To edit the colors in a gradient, you click their gradient stops below the gradient bar.

4   In the Gradient palette, for Type choose Linear to change the fill to a linear gradient, and then click the left gradient stop to select it so that you can adjust the starting color of the gradient.

The Color palette displays the color of the currently selected gradient stop in the Fill box.

Now you'll change the display of the Swatches palette so that you can choose any color from it.

5   At the bottom of the Swatches palette, click the Show All Swatches button to display all the color, gradient, and pattern swatches in the Swatches palette.

Display all swatches.

6   With the left gradient stop selected in the Gradient palette, hold down Alt (Windows) or Option (Mac OS) and click a color swatch in the Swatches palette to assign the color to the gradient. (We selected the Lime color swatch.)

Holding down Alt/Option as you click a color swatch applies the color to the selected gradient stop in the gradient rather than to the selected objects in the artwork.

Colors in gradients can be assigned as CMYK process colors, RGB process colors, Web Safe RGB colors, or spot colors. When a gradient is printed or separated, mixed-mode gradient colors are all converted to CMYK process color.

Now you'll add intermediate colors to the gradient to create a fill with multiple blends between colors.

7   In the Gradient palette, click anywhere below the gradient bar to add a stop between the other gradient stops.

You add a color to a gradient by adding a gradient stop. When you add a new gradient stop, a diamond appears above the gradient bar to mark the color's new midpoint.

8   With the new gradient stop selected, hold down Alt (Windows) or Option (Mac OS) and click a color swatch in the Swatches palette to assign it to the gradient. (We selected the Yellow color swatch.)

Observe how the new color looks in the CHILES type.

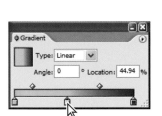 

Select gradient stop and change   Result.
middle color of gradient.

9   To adjust the midpoint between two colors, drag the diamond above the gradient bar to the right or left.

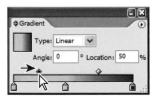

Drag diamond to adjust color midpoint.

Note: *You can delete a color in a gradient by dragging its gradient stop downward and out of the Gradient palette.*

Another way to apply a color to the gradient is to sample the color from the artwork using the Eyedropper tool.

10 Select the right gradient stop in the Gradient palette. Select the Eyedropper tool ( ) in the toolbox. Then hold down Shift and click a color in the artwork. (We sampled the light red color in the front chile pepper.)

Holding down Shift as you click with the Eyedropper tool applies the color sample to the selected gradient stop in the gradient rather than replacing the entire gradient with the color in the selected CHILES type.

Shift+click to apply sample to selected stop in gradient.

Now you'll save the new gradient.

11 In the Swatches palette, choose New Swatch from the palette menu, type a name for the gradient in the Swatch Name text field (we named it "Chiles type"), and click OK to save the new gradient.

12 Deselect the artwork by choosing Select > Deselect, and then choose File > Save.

Creating smooth-color blends

You can choose several options for blending the shapes and colors of objects to create a new object. When you choose the smooth-color blend option, Illustrator combines the shapes and colors of the objects into many intermediate steps, creating a smooth graduated blend between the original objects.

Now you'll combine the two inner shapes of the bowl into a smooth-color blend.

1 Select the Selection tool ( ), click the smallest shape inside the bowl to select it, and then Shift+click to select the second shape inside the bowl.

Both objects are filled with a solid color and have no stroke. Objects that have strokes blend differently than those that have no stroke.

2 Choose Object > Blend > Blend Options.

3 In the Blend Options dialog box, for Spacing choose Smooth Color (selected by default), and click OK.

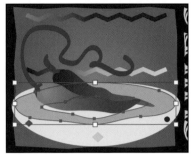

Select two inner shapes. *Set blend options.*

This action sets up the blend options, which remain set until you change them. Now you'll apply the blend.

4 Choose Object > Blend > Make.

Result.

When you make a smooth-color blend between objects, Illustrator automatically calculates the number of intermediate steps necessary to create a smooth transition between the objects.

Note: *To release a blend and revert to the original objects, select the blend and choose Object > Blend > Release.*

Blending intermediate steps

Now you'll create a series of blended shapes among three different-colored shapes on the outside of the bowl by specifying the number of steps in the blend and using the Blend tool to create the blend.

1   Click away from the artwork to deselect it, and then double-click the Blend tool (⬚) to open the Blend Options dialog box.

2   For Spacing, choose Specified Steps, type **6** for the number of steps, and click OK.

3   Using the Blend tool, click the red diamond with the tool's upper hollow square, and then click the green diamond to make a blend between them.

A new object is created that blends the shapes of the diamonds and their colors together in six steps.

4   Now click the blue circle to complete the blended path.

Click objects with Blend tool to   *Result.*
create a blend.

Note: *To end the current path and continue blending other objects on a separate path, click the Blend tool in the toolbox first, and then click the other objects.*

Modifying the blend

Now you'll modify the shape of the path or spine of the blend using the Convert Anchor Point tool.

1 Select the Convert Anchor Point tool (⌐) from the same group as the Pen tool (✒) in the toolbox.

2 Select the endpoint of the spine at the center of the blue circle (don't release the mouse button). Drag slowly down until you see two direction lines, and continue dragging down and a little to the left until the path runs parallel to the bottom edge of the bowl. Release the mouse button.

3 Repeat step 2 with the endpoint of the spine at the center of the red diamond, but drag up instead of down.

Now you'll adjust the spacing between the center shapes on the blend.

4 Using the Convert Anchor Point tool, select the middle anchor point of the spine (at the center of the green diamond)—don't release the mouse button—and drag to the left to lengthen the direction line and stretch out the spacing between the blend steps.

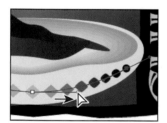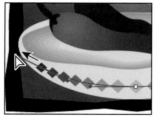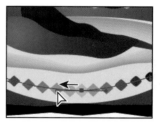

Select end and middle anchor points and drag direction handles to reshape blend path.

💡 *A quick way to reshape the blend's path is to wrap it around another path or object. Select the blend, select the other object or path, and then choose Object > Blend > Replace Spine.*

You can modify the blend instantly by changing the shape or color of the original objects.

Now you'll delete an anchor point on an object and reshape the object to modify the blend.

5   Zoom in closer on the red diamond by using the Zoom tool (🔍) or the Navigator palette.

6   Hold down Ctrl (Windows) or Command (Mac OS), and click the red diamond to select it.

7   Select the Delete Anchor Point tool (✒) from the same group as the Convert Direction Point tool in the toolbox and click a corner point on the red diamond to delete it.

Notice how changing the shape of the diamond affects the shape of the intermediate steps in the blend.

8   Select the Direct Selection tool (▷) in the toolbox and drag another anchor point on the diamond out to extend the shape of the corner.

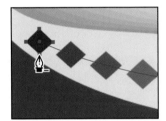  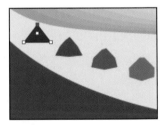

Delete anchor point on original object. *Drag anchor point to reshape object.* *Result.*

💡 *You can switch the starting and ending objects in the blend without affecting the shape of the spine by selecting the blend, and choosing Object > Blend > Reverse Spine.*

9   Choose Select > Deselect, then File > Save.

Combining blends with gradients

You can blend objects that are filled with gradients to create different effects of color blending. The two zigzag lines in the artwork are filled with gradients. (See "Exploring on your own" at the end of this lesson to learn how to create them.)

Now you'll blend the gradient-filled lines to create a multicolored blend in the artwork.

1 Double-click the Hand tool (✋) in the toolbox to fit the artwork in the window.

2 Select the Blend tool (🖫) in the toolbox and click the top zigzag line to select the first object for the blend. Then click the corresponding point on the bottom zigzag line to create the blend. (If you don't click the corresponding point, you'll get a distorted result.)

The current blend settings for six specified steps are applied to the blend. You can change these settings for an existing blend.

Click top line to select first object for blend.

Click corresponding point on bottom line.

Result.

3 Click the Selection tool (▶) to select the bounding box of the new blend, and choose Object > Blend > Blend Options.

4 In the Blend Options dialog box, select Preview, type a number in the text field (we specified 4 steps), and press Tab to see the effect in the artwork. Click OK.

Change number of steps in the blend.

Result.

5   Click away from the artwork to deselect it.

Now you'll adjust the blend by changing a gradient color in one of the original objects.

6   Select the Direct Selection tool (🔍), and select one of the original zigzag lines. (We selected the bottom zigzag line.)

Select original object.

7   In the Gradient palette, click a gradient stop to select a color in the gradient fill. (We selected the right gradient stop to select the ending color of the gradient.)

8   Hold down Alt (Windows) or Option (Mac OS), and click a color in the Swatches palette to apply it to the selected gradient stop. (We selected the Teal color swatch.) Holding down Alt/Option as you click applies the color swatch to the selected gradient stop rather than to the selected zigzag line.

💡 *You can paint the individual steps in the blend with separate gradients or colors by expanding the blend. Select the blend and choose Object > Blend > Expand.*

9   To view your final artwork, press Tab to hide the toolbox and all the open palettes. Pressing Tab toggles between hiding and showing the toolbox and palettes. Pressing Shift+Tab toggles between hiding and showing just the palettes (and not the toolbox).

10   Deselect the artwork.

11   Choose File > Save. Choose File > Close to close the file.

To learn how to use the color modes or transparency to blend colors together, see Lesson 11, "Applying Appearance Attributes, Graphic Styles, and Effects."

Exploring on your own

The two wavy lines in the artwork were created by applying the Zig Zag distort filter to two straight lines, and then they were converted to path outlines so that they could be filled with gradients.

To create a gradient-filled zigzag line like those in the artwork, do the following:

1   Choose File > New to create a new document and draw a straight line using the Pen tool.

2   Select the line, remove the fill, paint the stroke with a color, and increase the stroke weight to **10 pt**.

3   With the line selected, choose Filter > Distort > Zig Zag. (Choose the top filter command in the menu.)

4   In the Zig Zag dialog box, enter **0.15 inch** in the Size text field and **11** in the Ridges per segment text field. Click OK.

5   Choose Object > Path > Outline Stroke.

Notice that the stroke color has switched with the fill of None, so now you can fill the object with a gradient.

Review

▶ **Review questions**

1 What is a gradient fill?

2 Name two ways to fill a selected object with a gradient.

3 What is the difference between a gradient fill and a blend?

4 How do you adjust the blend between colors in a gradient?

5 How do you add colors to a gradient?

6 How do you adjust the direction of a gradient?

7 Describe two ways to blend the shapes and colors of objects.

8 What is the difference between selecting a smooth-color blend and specifying the number of steps in a blend?

9 How do you adjust the shapes or colors in the blend? How do you adjust the path of the blend?

▶ **Review answers**

1 A gradient fill is a graduated blend between two or more colors, or tints of the same color.

2 Select an object and do one of the following:

• Click the Gradient button in the toolbox to fill an object with the default white-to-black gradient or with the last selected gradient.

• Click a gradient swatch in the Swatches palette.

• Make a new gradient by clicking a gradient swatch in the Swatches palette and mixing your own in the Gradient palette.

• Use the Eyedropper tool to sample a gradient from an object in your artwork, and then apply it to the selected object.

3 The difference between a gradient fill and a blend is the way that colors combine together—colors blend together within a gradient fill and between objects in a blend.

4   You drag the gradient's stops, or diamonds in the Gradient palette.

5   In the Gradient palette, click beneath the gradient bar to add a gradient stop to the gradient. Then use the Color palette to mix a new color, or in the Swatches palette Alt+click (Windows) or Option+click (Mac OS) a color swatch.

6   You click and drag with the Gradient tool to adjust the direction of a gradient. Dragging a long distance changes colors gradually; dragging a short distance makes the color change more abrupt.

7   You can blend the shapes and colors of objects by doing one of the following:

• Clicking each object with the Blend tool to create a blend of intermediate steps between the objects according to preset blend options.

• Selecting the objects and choosing Object > Blend > Blend Options to set up the number of intermediate steps, and then choosing Object > Blend > Make to create the blend.

Objects that have painted strokes blend differently than those with no strokes.

8   When you select the Smooth Color blend option, Illustrator automatically calculates the number of intermediate steps necessary to create a seamlessly smooth blend between the selected objects. Specifying the number of steps lets you determine how many intermediate steps are visible in the blend. You can also specify the distance between intermediate steps in the blend.

9   You use the Direct Selection tool to select and adjust the shape of an original object, thus changing the shape of the blend. You can change the colors of the original objects to adjust the intermediate colors in the blend. You use the Convert anchor point tool to change the shape of the path, or spine, of the blend by dragging anchor points or direction handles on the spine.

The Symbols palette lets you apply multiple objects by painting them onto the page. Symbols used in combination with the symbolism tools offer options that make creating repetitive shapes, such as grass, or stars in the sky, easy and fun. You can also use the Symbol palette as a database to store artwork and map symbols to 3D objects.

9 Working with Symbols

In this lesson, you'll learn how to do the following:

- Create a symbol.

- Apply symbol instances.

- Use the symbolism tools.

- Modify and redefine a symbol.

- Store and retrieve artwork in the Symbols palette.

- Use a symbol for 3D mapping.

Getting started

In this lesson, you'll finish artwork for a poster. Before you begin, restore the default preferences for Adobe Illustrator; then open a file containing the final version of the finished artwork to see what you are going to create.

1   To ensure that the tools and palettes function exactly as described in this lesson, delete or deactivate (by renaming) the Adobe Illustrator CS2 preferences file. See "Restoring default preferences" on page 3.

2   Start Adobe Illustrator CS2.

3   Choose File > Open and open the file named 09_symbol_end.ai in the Lesson09 folder within the AICIB folder on your hard drive.

If you like, choose View > Zoom Out to reduce the view of the finished artwork, adjust the window size, and leave it on your screen as you work. (Use the Hand tool (✋) to move the artwork where you want it in the window.) If you don't want to leave the image open, choose File > Close.

4   To begin working, you'll open an existing art file set up for the artwork. Choose File > Open to open the 09_symbol_start.ai file in the Lesson09 folder, located inside the Lessons folder within the AICIB folder on your hard drive.

5   Choose File > Save As, name the file **ballgame.ai** and save in the Lesson09 folder. Leave the type of file format set to Adobe Illustrator Document (.AI), and click Save. In the Illustrator Options dialog box, leave the defaults settings and click OK.

Creating a symbol

A symbol is an art object that you store in the Symbols palette, and can be reused over and over again. For example, if you create a symbol from an object in the shape of a blade of grass, you can then add instances of that grass multiple times to your artwork by spraying it on using the Symbol Sprayer tool. The grass instance is linked to the symbol in the palette and can be altered using symbolism tools or edited and replaced; all instances of the symbol linked to that original symbol are also updated. You can turn that grass from brown to green instantly! Symbols save time and greatly reduce file size.

Illustrator objects that can be used are these; paths, compound paths, text, raster images, mesh objects, and groups of objects. Symbols can even include active objects, such as brush strokes, blends, effects, or other symbol instances in a symbol.

Note: *You cannot use non–embedded placed art as a symbol, nor can you use some groups, such as groups of graphs.*

You will first start by adding a crowd to this image.

1	Using the Control palette, select Stroke and in the linked Swatches palette, select None (☑). Then select Fill in the Control palette, and choose the Custard swatch.

2	Select the Ellipse tool (○) and click and drag to create the shape of a head.

Create the shape of a head with the Ellipse tool.

3	If the Symbols palette is not visible, choose Window > Symbols. Select the ellipse that you created and Alt+click (Windows) or Option+click (Mac OS) on the New Symbol button (☒) at the bottom of the Symbols palette. Name the symbol **face**. Click OK.

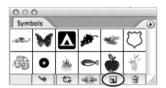
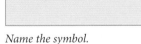

Click the New Symbol button.	*Name the symbol.*

Note: *Alt/Option+clicking on the New Symbol button gives you the opportunity to name the symbol as it is being added to the palette.*

4　Using the Selection tool (↖), select and delete the original ellipse used to create the symbol.

Applying a symbol instance

Now you will use the Symbol Sprayer tool to apply the face to your illustration.

1　Select the Symbol Sprayer tool (🖊) from the toolbox.

2　Click on the symbol that you created in the Symbols palette.

3　Click and drag using the Symbol sprayer, much like an airbrush or can of spray paint, to create a crowd with your symbol.

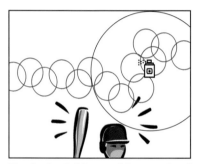

Use the Symbol Sprayer like an airbrush.

Symbol instances

Keep the following in mind when creating a symbol instance with the Symbol Sprayer:

• All the symbols that appear from each spray become one instance set that you manipulate and edit as a whole.

• You can enlarge or reduce the spraying radius by using the bracket keys ,"[" for a smaller spraying radius, "]" for a larger spraying radius.

• Holding down the Alt (Windows) or Option (Mac OS) key while using the Symbol Sprayer deletes instances.

4　While the symbol instance is still selected, choose Object > Arrange > Send to back. The crowd is placed behind the baseball player.

About the symbolism tools

There are seven symbolism tools hidden inside the Symbol Sprayer tool. Symbolism tools are used for changing the density, color, location, size, rotation, transparency, or style of symbol sets.

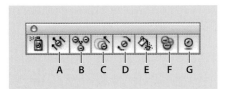

*A. Symbol Shifter tool. **B.** Symbol Scruncher tool.
C. Symbol Sizer tool. **D.** Symbol Spinner tool.
E. Symbol Stainer tool. **F.** Symbol Screener tool.
G. Symbol Styler tool.*

What do the Symbolism tools do?

Symbol Shifter tool—Moves symbol instances around. It can also change the relative paint order of symbol instances in a set.

Symbol Scruncher tool—Pulls symbol instances together or apart.

Symbol Sizer tool—Increases or decreases the size of symbol instances in an existing symbol set.

Symbol Spinner tool—Orients the symbol instances in a set. Symbol instances located near the cursor orient in the direction you move the cursor. As you drag the mouse, an arrow appears above the cursor to show the current orientation of symbol instances.

Symbol Stainer tool—Colorizes symbol instances. Colorizing a symbol instance changes the hue toward the tint color, while preserving the original luminosity, so black or white objects don't change at all.

Symbol Screener tool—Increases or decreases the transparency of the symbol instances in a set.

Symbol Styler tool—Applies the selected style to the symbol instance.

You can switch to the Symbol Styler tool when using any other symbolism tool, by clicking a style in the Styles palette.

Using the symbolism tools

In this next lesson, you will use the Symbol Sizer and Stainer tools to alter the look of individual symbol instances.

1   Select the Sizer tool (⌀), and click and drag over your symbol instances to scale up some of the faces. Hold down Alt (Windows) or Option (Mac OS) while you are using the Symbol Sizer tool to reduce the size of the selected instances.

Note: *The Symbol Sizer works better when you click and release over symbol instances, rather than holding down. If the symbols resize too quickly for you, choose Edit > Undo and try again.*

Now you will apply colorization to the symbols.

2   Select the color Malt from the Swatches palette. Select the Symbol Stainer tool (⌀) and click and drag over the faces to add tints of the malt color.

The longer you hold down on the mouse, the more colorization occurs. Hold down the Alt key (Windows) or Option key (Mac OS) while holding down the mouse to decrease the colorization amount.

Change the size and color using the symbolism tools.

3   Choose File > Save.

Editing symbols

In the next steps, you will add an additional symbol, then edit and update it.

1   Choose Select > Deselect.

2   Using the Selection tool (↖), click on the Fill box in the Control palette and select None (⊘) from the Swatches palette. Click on the Stroke box in the Control palette and select Green from the Swatches palette for the stroke.

3   Click on the Stroke weight field in the Control palette, and select **1 pt** from the drop-down menu.

4   Using the Line Segment tool (╲), create several blades of grass. Use at least 10 line segments to make a tuft of grass.

Create blades of grass to be used as a symbol.

5   Switch to the Selection tool and marquee select the blades of grass. (You could also select one blade and Shift+click to add the others.)

6   With the blades of grass selected, hold down Alt (Windows) or Option (Mac OS), and click on the New Symbol button on the Symbols palette. Name the new symbol **grass**. Click OK.

Create a new symbol from the grass.

7 Use the Selection tool to delete the original blades of grass used to create the symbol.

8 Choose the Symbol Sprayer tool (🖋), and click on the grass symbol you just added to the Symbols palette. Return to the artboard and click and drag to apply the grass symbol over the dirt.

9 Select the Symbol Scruncher tool (🖋), and click and drag over the grass instances, scrunching them together. Use Alt (Windows) or Option (Mac OS) to unscrunch some of the instances of grass.

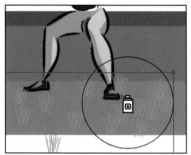
Spray on the grass using the
Symbol Sprayer.

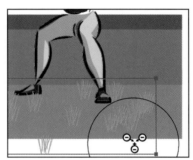
Scrunch the grass using the
Symbol Scruncher.

10 Choose File > Save.

Updating a symbol

Perhaps 1 pt blades of grass are too small. In this next section, you will edit the blades of grass once, and all instances will be updated.

1 To reactivate a symbol as an art object, click on the Place Symbol Instance button at the bottom of the Symbols palette. This will place the symbol one time in the middle of your page.

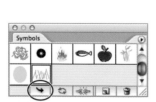

Click the Place Symbol Instance button to edit the symbol.

2   Using the Selection tool (➤), move the blades of grass that you just placed to a location that will let you view it away from other artwork.

3   Choose Object > Expand to put the artwork back into an editable mode. Leave the options of the Expand window at the defaults, and click OK.

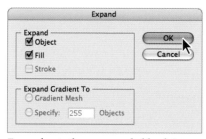

Expand puts the grass symbol back into an editable mode.

4   While the grass is selected, choose 2 pt from the Stroke weight drop-down menu in the Control palette.

5   Choose File > Save.

Now you will update all instances of the grass symbol with the new art.

6   Hold down Alt (Windows) or Option (Mac OS), and drag the edited blades of grass on top of the original grass symbol in the Symbols palette. Release when you see a black border appear around the grass symbol.

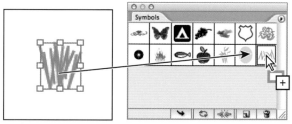

Replace the original symbol with the new one by Alt/Option dragging it on top of the original symbol.

The symbol instances are now using the thicker blades of grass.

7   Edit > Clear the grass image used to create the symbol.

8   Choose File > Save this artwork.

Storing and retrieving artwork in the Symbols palette

Save frequently used logos or other artwork as a symbol to readily access them when needed.

In this next lesson, you will take the illustration you created and save it as a symbol. You will then close the file, import it into a new document, and make changes to it.

1   If the Layers palette is not visible, choose Window > Layers. In the Layers palette, click on the padlock icon on the left of the background layer to unlock it.

2   Choose Select > All to activate all the components of your illustration.

3   Alt+click (Windows) or Option+click (Mac OS) on the New Symbol button at the bottom of the Symbols palette. Name the symbol **baseball**. Click OK.

4   Click and drag the baseball symbol back onto the page. This symbol can be placed back onto the page as many times as you need and can be a big help when using artwork repeatedly.

You will only be referencing the Symbols palette from this file later, so do not worry about how many symbol instances are on the page.

5   Choose File > Save and close the file.

6   Create a new document using File > New. Leave the settings at the defaults and click OK.

7   Choose File > Save and name the file **ballgame2.ai** and save in the Lesson09 folder. Leave the type of file format set to Adobe Illustrator Document (.AI), and click Save. In the Illustrator Options dialog box, leave the default settings and click OK.

8 From the Symbols palette menu, choose Open Symbol Library > Other Library, locate the file named ballgame.ai in the Lesson09 folder of the AICIB folder. A palette will appear with the name of the original file. In it are any symbols created when the file was last saved.

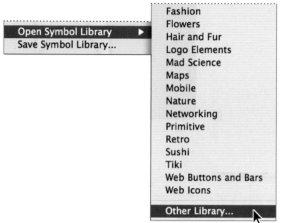

Take advantage of precreated symbols like borders and 3D effects in the palette menu of the Symbols palette.

9 Locate the symbol you named baseball and use the Place Symbol Instance button at the bottom of the Symbols palette, or drag it out from the Symbols palette onto your page.

The artwork comes in the same size as the original, but is considered an object, or symbol instance, until you expand it.

10 Choose Object > Expand. Leave the expand options at the default and click OK,

11 The artwork is now editable but is also grouped. Use the Direct Selection tool (⬎) to select the shirt, and then click on various colors in the Swatches palette until you find one you like.

💡 *Need an extra source of clip art? Any of the symbols from the palette menu can be dragged out of the Symbols palette onto the page and expanded to have colors and sizes changed.*

12 Choose File > Save. Leave the file open.

Mapping a symbol to 3D artwork

Symbols can be mapped to 3D artwork to create labels and textures. In this next lesson, you will create a cereal box with your baseball player on the front panel, and a text symbol on the top and side.

1 Choose Select > All.

2 Double-click on the Scale tool (⬚), and enter the value of **50%** in the Uniform text field. Click OK.

3 Choose Window > Type > Character, or Ctrl+T (Windows)/Command+T (Mac OS) to open the Character palette. Choose any font (we selected Chaparral Pro Bold), and change the size to **45 pt**. Select the Type tool (T) and click above the artwork to create a text insertion point. Type the word **Superstar**.

Add text to the graphic.

4 Choose the Selection tool (➤) and then Select > All. Alt+click (Windows) or Option+click (Mac OS) on the New Symbol button on the Symbol palette. Name the symbol **superstar**. Click OK. The symbol has been added to the Symbols palette.

5 Choose Select > Deselect.

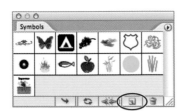

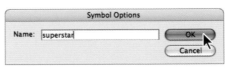

Alt/Option+click on the New Symbol button.   *Name the symbol.*

Creating a symbol for the side panel

Now you will create the word Cereal that will be mapped to the box's side panel.

1 Choose the Type tool (T) and select any font (we chose Chaparral Pro Semibold). Leave the font size at 45 pt. Find a blank area on the artboard and click to create a text insertion point. Type the word **Cereal**.

2 Choose the Selection tool and select the text. Alt+Click (Windows) or Option+Click (Mac OS) on the New Symbol button on the Symbols palette to add this text as a symbol. Name the symbol **Cereal**. Click OK.

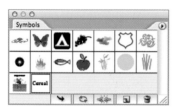

Add the text, Cereal, to the Symbols palette.

3 Choose Select > All, and use the Delete key to eliminate any artwork on the artboard.

4 Click on the Default color swatches button (▣) at the bottom of the toolbox, or press the letter **D** to return to the default fill of white and stroke of black.

5 Choose the Rectangle tool (▣), and click once on the artboard, the Rectangle options window appears. Enter the values **225 pt** in the Width text field and **300 pt** for in the Height text field. Click OK.

6 With the Rectangle still selected, choose Effect > 3D > Extrude and Bevel. Check the Preview checkbox.

Using the Extrude Effect, you will make the rectangle appear to be three-dimensional. Read more details about the 3D Effect in Lesson 12, "Using the 3D Effect," or in Illustrator Help.

7   Choose Off-Axis Front for the position, and type **75** for Extrude Depth. Leave this window open.

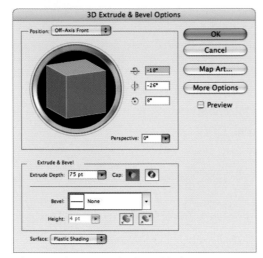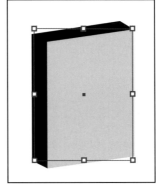

The Extrude and Bevel Effect adds dimension to our rectangle.

8   Click on More Options to change the light source. Change the surface to Diffuse Shading and the Shading Color to None.

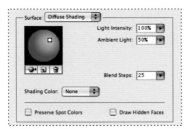

Additional light options are available by pressing More Options.

9   Change the direction of the light source by clicking on the light indicator on the image of the sphere, and dragging it to the lower left.

Click and drag the light to change its location.

Now you will map the symbols to our newly created cereal box.

10   Click on the Map Art button in the upper right. Check Preview.

11   Using the single arrows to the right of Surface, click to navigate through the different faces of the box. Choose the surface 1 of 16, and click on the Symbol drop-down menu. Select your saved symbol named Superstar.

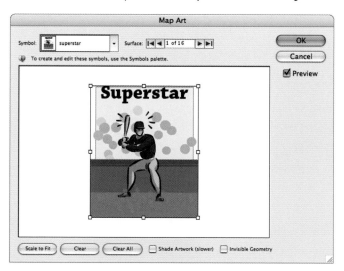

12   Click Scale to Fit to resize the artwork automatically.

13 Click on the right single arrow (▶) in the Surface text field, or type in **11** to get to the 11th surface. Choose the symbol named Cereal.

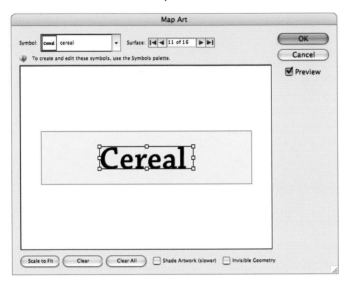

14 Click OK, and OK again. Congratulations! You have completed the lesson.

To map artwork to a 3D object

Following is some helpful information about mapping artwork to 3D objects.

- To move the symbol, position the cursor inside the bounding box and drag; to scale, drag a side or corner handle; to rotate, drag outside and near a bounding box handle.

- To make the mapped artwork fit to the boundaries of the selected surface, click Scale To Fit.

- To remove artwork from a single surface, select the surface using the Surface options, and then either choose None from the Symbol menu or click Clear.

- To remove all maps from all of the 3D object's surfaces, click Clear All.

- To shade and apply the object's lighting to the mapped artwork, select Shade Artwork.

- To show only the artwork map, not the geometry of a 3D object, select Invisible Geometry. This is useful when you want to use the 3D mapping feature as a three-dimensional warping tool. For example, you could use this option to map text to the side of an extruded wavy line, so that the text appears warped as if on a flag.

—From Illustrator Help

Exploring on your own

Symbols do not have to be applied with the Symbol Sprayer. Try to integrate symbols into illustrations with repeated artwork, such as maps that contain repeated icons and road signs, to creative and customized bullets for text. Symbols make it easy to update logos in business cards or name tags, or any artwork created with multiple placements of the same art.

To place multiple symbol instances, do the following:

1   Select the artwork that is to become a symbol.

2   Drag the art using the Selection tool (▶) into the Symbols palette. Delete the original art once it is in the Symbols palette.

3   To use the first instance, drag the symbol from the Symbols palette to a location on your artboard.

4   Drag as many instances of the symbol as you like, or Alt/Option drag the original instance to clone it to other locations.

5   The symbols are now linked to the original symbol in the Symbols palette. If it is updated, all placed instances will be updated.

Note: You can break the link between the placed symbol by right-clicking (Windows) or Control+clicking (Mac OS) and selecting Break Link to Symbol from the contextual menu.

Review

▶ **Review questions**

1   What are three benefits of using a symbol?

2   Name the symbolizer tool that is used for changing tints and shades of a symbol.

3   If you are using a Symbolizer on an area that has two different symbols applied, which one becomes affected?

4   How do you update an existing symbol?

5   What is something that cannot be used as a symbol?

6   How do you access symbols from other documents?

▶ **Review answers**

1   Three benefits of using symbols are:

- Easy application of multiple shapes.

- You can edit one symbol, and all instances will be updated.

- You can map artwork to 3D objects.

2   The Symbol Stainer tool changes the tints and shades of a symbol.

3   If you are using a Symbolizer tool over an area that has two different symbol instances, the symbol active in the Symbols palette will be the only instance affected.

4   To update existing symbol instances, do the following:

   a Use the Place Symbol button.

   b Expand the artwork.

   c Make any changes.

   d Alt/Option drag the new artwork on top of the original symbol in the Symbols palette.

5   Non-embedded images and groups of graphs cannot be used as symbols.

6   You can access symbols from saved documents by choosing Window > Symbol Libraries > Other Libraries or from the Symbols palette menu.

LAKESIDE DESIGNS

The variety of brush types in Adobe Illustrator CS2 lets you create a myriad of effects simply by painting or drawing on paths. You can choose from the provided Art, Calligraphic, Patterns and Scatter brushes, or create new ones from your Illustrator artwork. Use the Paintbrush tool or the drawing tools to apply brushes to artwork, and use the Scribble effect to add some free form scribbles to the image.

10 | Working with Brushes and Scribbles

In this lesson, you'll learn how to do the following:

- Use the four brush types: Art, Calligraphic, Pattern, and Scatter.
- Change brush color and adjust brush settings.
- Create new brushes from Adobe Illustrator artwork.
- Apply brushes to paths created with drawing tools.
- Use the Scribble Effect for artwork and text.

Getting started

Adobe Illustrator brushes let you apply artwork to paths to decorate them with patterns, figures, textures, or angled strokes. You can modify the brushes provided with Illustrator, and you can create your own brushes. Brushes appear in the Brushes palette.

You apply brushes to paths using the Paintbrush tool or the drawing tools. To apply brushes using the Paintbrush tool, you choose a brush from the Brushes palette and draw in the artwork. The brush is applied directly to the paths as you draw. To apply brushes using a drawing tool, you draw in the artwork, select a path in the artwork, and then choose a brush in the Brushes palette. The brush is applied to the selected path.

You can change the color, size, and other features of a brush. You can also edit paths after brushes are applied.

In this lesson, you'll learn to use the four brush types in the Brushes palette, including how to change brush options and how to create your own brushes. Before you begin, you'll need to restore the default preferences for Adobe Illustrator. Then you'll open the finished art file for this lesson to see what you'll create.

1   To ensure that the tools and palettes function exactly as described in this lesson, delete or deactivate (by renaming) the Adobe Illustrator CS2 preferences file. See "Restoring default preferences" on page 3.

2   Start Adobe Illustrator CS2.

3   Choose File > Open, and open the L10end.ai file in the Lesson10 folder, located inside the Lessons folder in the AICIB folder on your hard drive.

4   If you like, choose View > Zoom Out to make the finished artwork smaller, adjust the window size, and leave it on your screen as you work. (Use the Hand tool (✋) to move the artwork where you want it in the window.) If you don't want to leave the image open, choose File > Close.

To begin working, you'll open an existing art file set up with guides to draw the artwork.

5   Choose File > Open to open the L10start.ai file in the Lesson10 folder inside the AICIB folder on your hard drive.

6   Choose File > Save As, name the file **Brushes.ai,** and save in the Lesson10 folder. Leave the type of format set to Adobe Illustrator Document (.AI), and click Save. In the Illustrator Options dialog box, accept the defaults settings and click OK.

Using Art brushes

Art brushes stretch artwork evenly along a path. Art brushes include strokes resembling various graphic media, such as the Charcoal-Feather and Marker-Rough brushes. Art brushes also include images, such as the Arrow brush, and text, such as the Type brush, which paints the characters *A-R-T* along a path. In this section, you'll use the Charcoal-Feather brush to draw the trunk and limbs of a tree.

The start file has been created with guides that you can use to create and align your artwork for the lesson. Guides are paths that have been converted using the View > Make Guides command. The guides are locked and cannot be selected, moved, modified, or printed (unless they are unlocked).

Drawing with the Paintbrush tool

Now you'll use the Paintbrush tool to apply a brush to the artwork.

1 In the toolbox, click the Paintbrush tool (✎) to select it.

You select a brush in the Brushes palette to be applied to the artwork.

2 Choose Window > Brushes to open the Brushes palette.

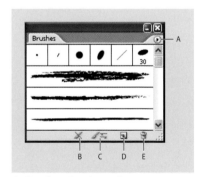

A. Displays Brushes palette menu.
B. Remove Brush Stroke.
C. Options of Selected Object.
D. New Brush. E. Delete Brush.

By default, brushes appear as icons. You can also view brushes by name. When viewed by name, a small icon to the right of the brush name indicates the brush type.

3　In the Brushes palette, position the mouse button over the triangle in the top right corner of the Brushes palette, press the mouse button to display the palette menu, and choose List View.

You can choose which types of brushes are displayed in the Brushes palette to reduce the palette size and make it easier to find the brushes you want to use. Choose Show Calligraphic Brushes and Show Art Brushes if there is no checkbox to the left.

Showing and hiding brush types.

4　Select the Charcoal-Feather art brush in the Brushes palette.

Brushes are applied to paths as a stroke color. If you have a fill color selected when you apply a brush to a path, the path will be stroked with the brush and filled with the fill color. Use a fill of None when applying brushes to prevent the brushed paths from being filled. Later in this lesson you'll use a fill color with a brush. For more information on stroke and fill color, see Lesson 5, "Color and Painting."

5　In the Control palette, click on the Fill box and choose the None (☑) swatch.

6　Use the Paintbrush tool to draw a long, upward stroke to create the left side of the tree trunk, tracing over the guides as you draw. Don't worry if your stroke doesn't follow the guide exactly. You'll remove the guides at the end of the lesson, so that they won't show through the finished artwork.

7   Draw a second upward stroke to create the right side of the tree trunk, using the guide to place your drawing.

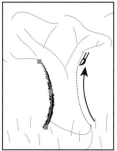
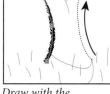

Draw with the Paintbrush tool.

Last path drawn remains selected.

Each path remains selected after you draw it, until you draw another path.

8   Choose File > Save to save your work.

Editing paths with the Paintbrush tool

When you draw with the Paintbrush tool, the last path you draw remains selected by default. This feature makes it easy to edit paths as you draw. If you draw over the selected path with the Paintbrush tool, the part of the selected path that you drew over is edited. You can disable or set a tolerance for path editing in the Paintbrush tool Preferences dialog box.

Now you'll use the Paintbrush tool to edit the selected path.

1   Place the Paintbrush tool ( ) near the top of the selected path (the right side of the tree trunk) and draw upward.

The selected path is edited from the point where you began drawing over it. The new path is added to the selected path (instead of becoming a separate path).

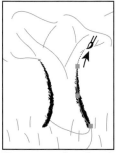

Draw over selected path to edit it.   *Selected path is edited.*

When drawing with the Paintbrush tool, you may want paths to remain unselected so that you can draw over paths without altering them, and create layered or overlapping strokes. You can change the Paintbrush tool preferences to keep paths unselected as you draw.

2   Choose Select > Deselect.

3   In the toolbox, double-click the Paintbrush tool to display the Paintbrush tool Preferences dialog box. You use this dialog box to change the way the Paintbrush tool functions.

4   Click the Keep Selected option to deselect it, and click OK. Now paths will remain unselected as you draw, and you can draw overlapping paths without altering the earlier paths.

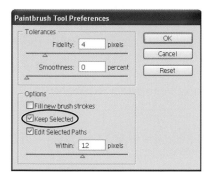

Now you'll draw the limbs of the tree.

5   Draw shorter strokes to create the limbs of the tree.

When the Keep Selected option is turned off, you can edit a path with the Paintbrush tool by selecting the path with the Selection tool (▶) or by selecting a segment or point on the path with the Direct Selection tool (▷) and then redrawing the path with the Paintbrush tool.

6   Press Ctrl (Windows) or Command (Mac OS) to toggle to the Selection tool, and select from the artwork a limb that you want to redraw.

Pressing Ctrl/Command temporarily selects the Selection tool (or the Direct Selection or Group Selection tool, whichever was used last) when another tool is selected.

Draw with the   *Path remains unselected.*   *Select path to edit it.*
Paintbrush tool.

7   Use the Paintbrush tool to draw over the selected path.

You can also edit paths using the Smooth tool (✐) and the Erase tool (✐) (located under the Pencil tool (✐) in the toolbox) to redraw or remove parts of a path drawn with the Paintbrush tool.

After you apply a brush to an object, it's easy to apply another brush to the paths to change the appearance of the object.

8   Choose the Selection tool (▶) and drag a marquee to select the tree trunk and branches.

9   In the Brushes palette, click the Marker-Rough brush. The new brush is applied to the selected paths in the artwork.

Charcoal-Feather strokes selected.   *Selecting Marker-Rough brush.*   *Marker brush-Rough applied.*

10   Click outside the artwork to deselect it and view the tree without selection highlights.

11   Drag a selection marquee to select the tree again.

12   Click several other brushes in the Brushes palette to see the effects of those brushes in the artwork. When you have finished, click the Charcoal-Feather brush again to reapply that brush.

13   Click outside the artwork to deselect it.

14   Choose File > Save to save your work.

As you complete the rest of this lesson, use the methods you learned in this section to edit paths as you draw with the Paintbrush tool. You can use the brushes, editing paths with the Keep Selected option, if you want strokes to remain selected as you draw, or you can use the Selection tool to select strokes to be edited.

Using Scatter brushes

Scatter brushes randomly spread an object, such as a leaf, a ladybug, or a strawberry, along a path. In this section, you'll use the Fall Leaf Scatter brush to create leaves on the tree. You'll start by adjusting options for the brush to change its appearance in the artwork.

Changing brush options

You change the appearance of a brush by adjusting its settings in the Brush Options dialog box, either before or after brushes have been applied to artwork. The changes you make appear when you apply the brush to artwork, but do not appear in the brush icon in the Brushes palette.

1   In the Brushes palette, choose Show Scatter Brushes from the palette menu to select that option. Then choose Show Art Brushes to deselect that option.

Note: *If the Brush type is already checked, selecting it again hides the type in the Brushes palette.*

2   Double-click the Fall Leaf brush to open the Scatter Brush Options dialog box.

Brush options vary according to the type of brush. For Scatter brushes, you can set either fixed values or a (random) range of values for the brush size, spacing, scatter, and rotation. If you have a pressure-sensitive drawing tablet attached to your computer, you can also set the pressure of the stylus using the Pressure option.

3   Set the following values, either dragging the slider or entering values, and pressing the Tab key to move between the text fields:

•   For Size, set the size of the brush object relative to the default (100%) by choosing Random and entering **40%** and **60%**.

•   For Spacing, set the distance between brush objects on a path relative to 100% (objects touching but not overlapping) by choosing Random and entering **10%** and **30%**.

•   For Scatter, indicate how far objects will deviate from either side of the path, where 0% is aligned on the path, by choosing Random and entering **–40%** and **40%**.

•   For Rotation relative to the page or path, enter **–180°** and **180°**, then choose Rotation Relative to Page.

Select Fall Leaf brush.

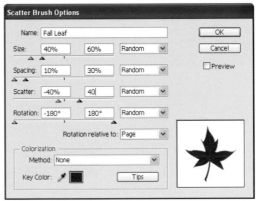

Set brush options.

4   Click OK.

In addition to the features you adjusted in this section, you can change the color of a brush. You'll change the color of the Fall Leaf brush and another brush later in this lesson.

Applying a Scatter brush to paths

Now you'll use the Fall Leaf brush with its adjusted settings to draw leaves on the tree in the artwork. First you'll select and lock the tree. Locking an object prevents it from being altered while you work on other objects in the artwork.

1   Use the Selection tool (▶) to drag a marquee around all parts of the tree to select them.

2   Choose Object > Lock > Selection.

The bounding box around the tree disappears, and the tree is locked.

3   Select the Fall Leaf Scatter brush.

4   Use the Paintbrush tool (✎) to draw strokes with the Fall Leaf brush above the tree branches, using the guides to help place your paths. Remember that if you want to edit paths as you draw, you can use the Keep Selected option for the Paintbrush tool or select paths with the Selection tool.

Drawing with Paintbrush tool.   *Fall Leaf brush applied to artwork.*

5   Choose File > Save.

Changing the color attributes of brushes

You'll change the color of the Fall Leaf brush in the artwork.

Before you change the brush color, it's helpful to understand how Illustrator applies color to brushes.

To change the color of Art, Pattern, and Scatter brushes, you use one of three colorization methods—models for applying color to the artwork in a brush. To change the color of Calligraphic brushes, you simply select the brush and choose a stroke color. (See Lesson 5, "Color and Painting," for information on choosing a stroke color.) You can change the color attributes of a brush before and after you apply the brush to artwork.

When you apply a brush to artwork, Illustrator uses the current stroke color for the brush only if a colorization method is chosen. Selecting brush strokes and choosing a new stroke color applies that new color to the brush. If no colorization method is set, Illustrator uses the brush's default color. For example, the Fall Leaf brush was applied with its default color of red (not the current stroke of black) because its colorization method was set to None.

To colorize Art, Pattern, and Scatter brushes, you choose from three colorization methods—Tints, Tints and Shades, and Hue Shift:

• **Tints** displays the brush stroke in tints of the stroke color. Portions of the art that are black become the stroke color, portions that aren't black become tints of the stroke color, and white remains white. If you use a spot color as the stroke, Tints generates tints of the spot color. Choose Tints for brushes that are in black and white, or when you want to paint a brush stroke with a spot color.

• **Tints and Shades** displays the brush stroke in tints and shades of the stroke color. Tints and Shades maintains black and white, and everything between becomes a blend from black to white through the stroke color. Because black is added, you may not be able to print to a single plate when using Tints and Shades with a spot color. Choose Tints and Shades for brushes that are in grayscale.

- **Hue Shift** uses the key color in the brush artwork, by default the most prominent color in the art. Everything in the brush artwork that is the key color becomes the stroke color. Other colors in the brush artwork become colors related to the stroke color (the complement on the color wheel). Hue Shift maintains black, white, and gray. Choose Hue Shift for brushes that use multiple colors. You can change the key color. (If the original brush has only one color, the Hue Shift colorized brush also will contain only one color.)

Note: Brushes colorized with a stroke color of white may appear entirely white. Brushes colorized with a stroke color of black may appear entirely black. Results depend on the original brush colors.

Changing the brush color using Hue Shift colorization

Now you'll change the color of the Fall Leaf brush using the Hue Shift colorization method.

1 Choose the Selection tool (➤), and drag a selection marquee to select the Fall Leaf strokes in the artwork.

2 Hold down the Shift key and click on the Stroke color box to the right of Stroke in the Control palette. This links to the Color palette. If you prefer to not use the Control palette, choose Window > Color instead.

3 Click in the color bar to select a color for the Fall Leaf brush. (We chose a lavender color.)

4 In the Brushes palette, double-click the Fall Leaf brush to view the Scatter Brush Options dialog box for the brush. Move the dialog box off to the side so that you can see your artwork as you work.

You'll select a colorization method for the brush. For brushes set to a default colorization method of None, you must choose a colorization method before you can change the brush color. Brushes set to the Tints, Tints and Shades, or Hue Shift colorization method, by default, automatically apply the current stroke color to the brush when you use it in the artwork.

Note: To find a brush's default colorization setting, double-click the brush in the Brushes palette to view the Scatter Brush Options dialog box, and then select the setting in the Method drop-down menu in the Colorization section.

5   In the Colorization section in the dialog box, choose Hue Shift from the Method drop-down menu.

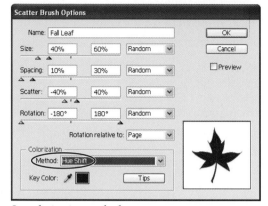

Select brush color.   *Set colorization method.*

The Key Color swatch in the Colorization section indicates the brush color that will shift to the new stroke color. The Key Color box displays the default key color (in this case, the leaf's red color) or the key color you select. For this lesson, you'll use the default key color.

It can be useful to select a new key color if a brush contains several colors and you want to shift different colors in the brush. To select a different key color, you click the Key Color Eyedropper (✐) in the dialog box and position the Eyedropper on the desired color in the preview (such as one of the black veins in the leaf), and click. The new key color shifts to the stroke color when you use the brush in the artwork (and other colors in the brush will shift correspondingly).

6   Click Preview to preview the color to be applied by the colorization method.

The selected Fall Leaf strokes are colorized with the current stroke color (the color you selected in step 3). This color will appear when you apply the Hue Shift colorization method.

7   If desired, choose the Tints, or Tints and Shades, colorization method from the drop-down menu to preview the change. Then return to the Hue Shift method.

8   Click OK. At the alert message, click Apply To Strokes to apply the colorization change to the strokes in the artwork. You can also choose to change only subsequent brush strokes and leave existing strokes unchanged.

Once you select a colorization method for a brush, the new stroke color applies to selected brush strokes and to new paths painted with the brush.

9   Choose Window > Color and select Show Options from the Color palette menu. Click on Stroke to bring it forward and then click the color bar in several different places to try other stroke colors for the selected brush strokes.

10   When you are satisfied with the color of the Fall Leaf brush strokes, click away from the artwork to deselect it.

11   Choose File > Save.

Changing the brush color using Tints colorization

Now you'll apply a new color to the Marker-Rough brush in the Art Brushes section of the Brushes palette, and use the brush to draw blades of grass in the artwork.

You'll begin by selecting the brush in the Brushes palette.

1   In the Brushes palette menu, choose Show Art Brushes, if it is not already checked. If Show Scatter Brushes is checked, then choose it to hide those brushes.

You'll display the Brush Options dialog box for the Marker-Rough brush to see the default colorization settings for the brush and change the brush size.

2   In the Brushes palette, double-click the Marker-Rough brush. The brush's original color is black.

3   In the Art Brush Options dialog box, note that the Marker-Rough brush is set by default to the Tints colorization method.

The Tints colorization method replaces black with the stroke color. Neither the Tints and Shades nor the Hue Shift colorization method works with black brushes. Both methods replace the original black color with black, leaving the brush unchanged.

4   In the Size section of the dialog box, enter **50%** for Width to change the size to a more appropriate scale for drawing in the artwork.

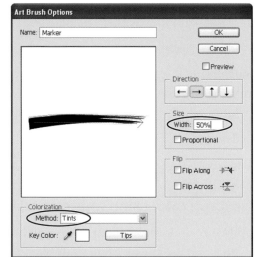

Marker-Rough brush selected.   *Marker-Rough brush with default Tints colorization method.*

5   Click OK to accept the settings and close the dialog box.

Now you'll select a color for the grass, and draw the grass with the Marker-Rough brush.

6   In the Color palette, click in the color bar to select a color for the grass. (We chose a bright green.)

7   Use the Paintbrush tool ( ) to draw short, upward strokes around the base of the tree, applying the stroke color you selected in step 6. Use the guides to place your drawing. Don't paint the grass around the canoe; you'll paint this later in the lesson. Click off the page to deselect all items.

Note: *If you find strokes disappearing as you create new ones, uncheck Keep Selected from the Paintbrush options.*

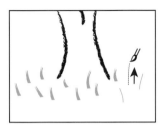

Because the Marker-Rough brush is all one color, the Tints colorization method applies the new stroke color as one color (rather than varied tints of the color). When the original brush contains several colors, the Tints colorization method applies a different tint for each color in the brush.

Using a fill color with brushes

When you apply a brush to an object's stroke, you can also apply a fill color to paint the interior of the object with a color. When you use a fill color with a brush, the brush objects appear on top of the fill color in places where the fill and the brush objects overlap.

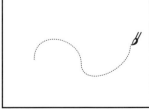
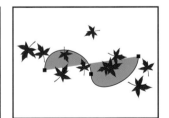

Choose fill color.   *Draw with paintbrush.*   *Brush objects appear on top of fill.*

Now you'll use the Paintbrush tool to draw a canoe at the edge of the grass with an Art brush. You'll begin by selecting the brush in the Brushes palette.

1 In the Brushes palette, select the Tapered Stroke brush.

The Tapered Stroke brush uses the Tints colorization method by default. To change the color of the Tapered Stroke brush, you'll simply select a stroke color.

2 In the Color palette, make sure that the Stroke box is selected. Then click in the color bar to select a color for the edges of the canoe. (We chose a dark orange.)

Now you'll use the Paintbrush tool to draw the edges of the canoe. Use the guides to align your drawing.

3 Use the Paintbrush tool (✐) to draw a crescent shape to make the side and bottom of the canoe:

• Draw a long stroke from left to right to make the side edge of the canoe. Do not release the mouse button.

• While still holding down the mouse button, draw a second long stroke beneath the first, from right to left, connecting the two strokes at the right endpoint of the object, to make a crescent shape. When you have drawn the second stroke, release the mouse button.

You may have to draw the crescent shape more than once to create a shape with a single path. Remember that you can edit paths as you draw. Use the Direct Selection tool (▹) to select a segment of the path that you want to redraw.

Don't worry if your drawing doesn't match the guides exactly. What's important is drawing the shape as one path, without releasing the mouse button, so that you can fill the object correctly. (If a shape is made of separate paths, the fill color is applied to each path separately, yielding unpredictable results.)

4   Draw a third long stroke for the top side of the canoe. Then draw two shorter strokes for the crossbars. (Draw the top side and crossbars as separate paths, releasing the mouse button after each one.)

Draw crescent as one path.   *Add top.*   *Add crossbars.*

Now you'll fill the side of the canoe with a color.

5   Choose the Selection tool (↖), and select the crescent shape you drew for the lower side and bottom of the canoe.

6   Select the Fill color box in the Control palette, when the Swatch palette appears, choose to select a fill color for the canoe. (We chose the Sunshine swatch.)

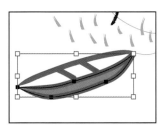

Selected shape is filled.

7   Click outside the artwork to deselect it.

8   Choose File > Save.

Using Calligraphic brushes

Calligraphic brushes resemble strokes drawn with the angled point of a calligraphic pen Calligraphic brushes are defined by an elliptical shape whose center follows the path. Use these brushes to create the appearance of hand-drawn strokes made with a flat, angled pen tip.

You'll use a Calligraphic pen to draw water in front of the canoe. You'll begin by selecting the brush, and then choose a color for the brush.

1   If not already selected, in the Brushes palette, choose Show Calligraphic Brushes from the palette menu. Then choose Show Art Brushes from the menu to deselect that option.

2   In the Brushes palette, select the 15 pt Oval brush.

3   In the Color palette, click the Stroke box. Then click in the color bar to select a new color for the water. (We chose a light blue.)

Calligraphic brushes use the current stroke color when you apply the brushes to artwork. You do not use colorization methods with Calligraphic brushes.

4   In the Color palette, click the Fill box and then click the None box (⊠). A fill of None with brushes prevents paths from being filled when you apply the brush.

5   Select the Paintbrush tool (✐), and draw wavy lines for the water surface. The paths you draw use the stroke color you selected in step 3.

Now you'll change the shape of the 15 pt Oval brush in the Brush Options dialog box to change the appearance of the strokes made with the brush.

6   In the Brushes palette, double-click the 15 pt Oval brush to display the Calligraphic Brush Options dialog box.

You can change the angle of the brush (relative to a horizontal line), the roundness (from a flat line to a full circle), and the diameter (from 0 to 1296 points) to change the shape that defines the brush's tip, and change the appearance of the stroke that the brush makes. Now you'll change the diameter of the brush.

7   Enter **8 pt** for Diameter. In the Name text field, enter **8 pt Oval**. Notice that the weight of the Calligraphic brush strokes in the artwork decreases.

The Preview window in the dialog box shows changes you make to the brush.

8   Click OK. At the alert message, click Apply To Strokes to apply the change to the strokes in the artwork.

12 pt Oval brush.

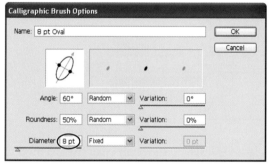
Selecting 8 pt Oval brush.

Result.

9   Ctrl/Command+click outside the artwork or choose Select > Deselect to deselect it.

10   Choose File > Save.

Using Pattern brushes

Pattern brushes paint a pattern made up of separate sections, or tiles, for the sides (middle sections), ends, and corners of the path. When you apply a Pattern brush to artwork, the brush applies different tiles from the pattern to different sections of the path, depending on where the section falls on the path (at an end, in the middle, or at a corner). You'll open an existing Pattern Brush library and choose a Dashed Circle pattern to represent a chain. There are hundreds of interesting pattern brushes you can choose from when creating your own projects—from dog tracks to teacups.

1   In the Brushes palette, choose Open Brush Library, a choice of brushes appears. Choose Borders_Dashed; a separate palette appears with various dashed borders that are ready to use.

2   Choose List View from the Borders_Dashed palette menu.

3   Choose Select > Deselect and then click the Dashed Circles 1.4 brush to add it to the Brushes palette. Close the Borders_Dashed palette.

4   Double-click on the Dashed Circle pattern brush you just added to the Brushes palette. This displays the Pattern Brush Options dialog box for the brush.

The Pattern Brush Options dialog box displays the tiles in the Dashed Circle brush. The first tile on the left is the Side tile, used to paint the middle sections of a path. The second tile is the Outer Corner tile. The third tile is the Inner Corner tile.

Pattern brushes can have up to five tiles—the Side, Start, and End tiles, plus an Outer Corner tile and an Inner Corner tile to paint sharp corners on a path. Some brushes have no corner tiles because the brush is designed for curved paths, not sharp corners. In the next part of this lesson, you'll create your own Pattern brush that uses corner tiles.

Now you'll change the scale of the Pattern brush so that the brush is in scale with the rest of the artwork when you apply it.

5 In the Pattern Brush Options dialog box, enter **20%** in the Scale text field, and click OK.

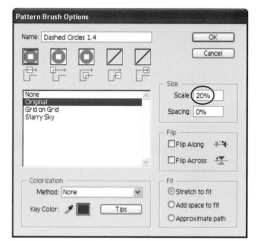

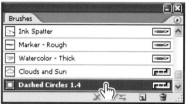

Dashed Circles 1.4 brush.

Dashed Circles with tiles scaled 20%.

6 Select the Paintbrush tool (), and draw a path that loops around the base of the tree. Then draw a second path that leads from the loop around the tree to the canoe.

Draw the stroke as two separate paths, rather than one path, to avoid creating a path with a sharp angle. (Because the Dashed Circle brush does not include corner tiles, the brush uses Side tiles to paint sharp angles. The Side tiles appear severed at sharp corners, and the rope appears to be cut.)

Apply Rope brush as two separate paths.

Now you'll select a blade of grass you created earlier in the lesson and move it in front of the rope to make the rope appear to lie behind the grass.

7   Choose the Selection tool (↖), and then select a grass blade lying along the path of the chain you created with the Dashed Circle brush. (Be careful not to select the chain along with the grass.)

If you like, you can Shift+click to select additional grass blades along the path of the rope.

8   Choose Object > Arrange > Bring to Front.

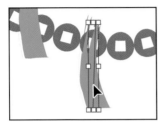

Select grass blade.   *Bring grass to front.*

9   Choose File > Save.

Tips for using brushes

When you work with brushes, keep the following points in mind:

• You can often use Scatter brushes and Pattern brushes to achieve the same effect. However, one way in which they differ is that Pattern brushes follow the path exactly, whereas Scatter brushes do not.

• If you apply a brush to a closed path and want to control the placement of the end of the path, select the Scissors tool (✂) and split the path. To change again, select the endpoints, choose Object > Path > Join, and use the scissors again.

• To select all brushstroke paths in the current artwork, choose Select > Object > Brush Strokes.

• For better performance when creating a brush from art that contains multiple overlapping paths filled with the same color and with no stroke, select the paths and click the Unite button in the Pathfinder palette before you create the brush.

—From Illustrator Help

Creating brushes

You can create new brushes of all four brush types, using artwork in an Illustrator file as the basis for the brush. In this section, you'll use artwork provided with the lesson to create a new Pattern brush with three tiles: a cloud for the Side tile, and a sun for the Outer Corner tile and Inner Corner tile.

Creating swatches for a Pattern brush

You create Pattern brushes by first creating swatches in the Swatches palette with the artwork that will be used for the Pattern brush tiles. In this section, you'll use the cloud and sun drawings included with the artwork file to create swatches.

1 Use the scroll bars, the Hand tool (🖑), or the Navigator palette to display the scratch area to the right of the artboard to view the cloud and sun drawings located there.

🔲 For information on moving to different areas of the document window, see Lesson 1, "Getting to Know the Work Area."

You'll unlock the sun and cloud artwork, and then use the artwork to create swatches. The objects were locked to prevent them from being altered while you completed the earlier sections of the lesson.

2 Choose Object > Unlock All.

Bounding boxes and selection highlights appear around the sun and cloud, indicating that the objects are unlocked and selected. The tree, which you locked earlier in the lesson, is also unlocked and selected. (The tree can be unlocked, because you've finished drawing in the area of the tree.)

3 Using the Selection tool (▶), click outside the artwork to deselect the objects.

4 Click the Swatches palette tab to view the Swatches palette. (If the palette isn't visible on-screen, choose Window > Swatches.)

Now you'll create a pattern swatch.

5   Select the Selection tool, and drag the cloud onto the Swatches palette. The new swatch appears in the pattern swatches group.

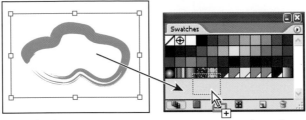 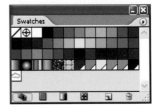

Select cloud.   *Drag it onto Swatches palette.*   *Cloud swatch is added to palette.*

6   Click away from the artwork to deselect the cloud.

7   In the Swatches palette, double-click the cloud swatch. Double-clicking the cloud swatch changes the current fill or stroke box to that swatch and opens the Swatch Options dialog box.

8   Name the swatch **Cloud**, and then click OK.

9   Now repeat steps 5 through 8 to create a pattern swatch of the sun art:

• Use the Selection tool to drag the sun onto the Swatches palette. The new swatch appears in the pattern swatches group.

• Click away from the artwork to deselect the sun.

• In the Swatches palette, double-click the sun swatch.

• Name the swatch **Sun**, and then click OK.

For more information on creating pattern swatches, see "About patterns" in Illustrator Help.

Creating a Pattern brush from swatches

To create a new Pattern brush, you apply swatches from the Swatches palette to tiles in the Brush Options dialog box. Now you'll apply the Cloud and Sun swatches to tiles for a new Pattern brush.

First you'll open a Brush Options dialog box for a new Pattern brush.

1 Click the Brushes palette tab to view the palette.

2 In the Brushes palette, click the New Brush button.

3 Select New Pattern Brush and click OK.

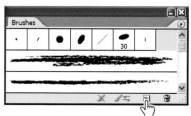

Create new brush.   *Select brush type.*

You'll apply the Cloud swatch to the Side tile for the New Pattern Brush.

4 In the Pattern Brush Options dialog box, select the Side tile box (the far left tile box).

5 In the pattern swatches scroll list, select the Cloud swatch. The Cloud swatch appears in the Side tile box.

Next you'll apply the Sun swatch to the Outer Corner tile and Inner Corner tile for the new Pattern brush.

6 In the Pattern Brush Options dialog box, select the Outer Corner tile box (the second tile box from the left). In the pattern swatches scroll list, select the Sun swatch. The Sun swatch appears in the Outer Corner tile box.

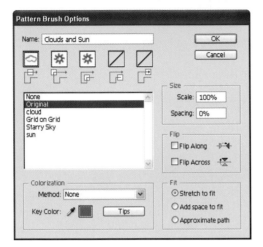

In the Pattern Brush Options dialog box, select the Inner Corner tile box (the middle tile box). In the pattern swatches scroll list, select the Sun swatch. The Sun swatch appears in the Inner Corner tile box.

You won't create a Start tile or End tile for the new brush. (You'll apply the new brush to a closed path in the artwork later in the lesson, so you won't need Start or End tiles at this time. When you want to create a Pattern brush that includes Start and End tiles, you add those tiles the same way as you did the Side and Corner tiles.)

7 In the Name text field, name the brush **Clouds and Sun**. Then click OK.

The Clouds and Sun brush appears in the Pattern brush section in the Brushes palette.

Note: When you create a new brush, the brush appears in the Brushes palette of the current artwork only. If you open another file in Illustrator, the Clouds and Sun brush won't appear in that file's Brushes palette.

To save a brush and reuse it in another file, you can create a brush library with the brushes you want to use. For more information, see "About brush libraries and the Brushes palette" in Illustrator Help.

Painting with the Pattern brush

So far in this lesson, you've used the Paintbrush tool to apply brushes to paths. You can also apply brushes to paths created with any drawing tool—including the Pen, Pencil, Ellipse, and Rectangle tools—and the other basic shape tools. In this section, you'll use the Rectangle tool to apply the Clouds and Sun brush to a rectangular border around the artwork.

When you use drawing tools to apply brushes to artwork, you first draw the path with the tool and then select the brush in the Brushes palette to apply the brush to the path.

First you'll set the fill and stroke color to None.

1 In the toolbox, click Fill and click None (◻). Then click on Stroke and click None.

2 Use the Navigator palette or the Zoom tool (🔍) to reduce the view of the artwork. Now you'll draw a border with the Rectangle tool, and apply the brush to the path.

3 Select the Rectangle tool (▢). Drag to draw a rectangle on the artboard, about 1/2-inch inside the imageable area on each side, as indicated by the guide.

4 In the Brushes palette, click the Clouds and Sun brush.

The rectangle path is painted with the Clouds and Sun brush, with the Cloud tile on the sides and the Sun tile on the corners.

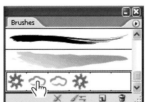

Draw rectangle.   *Select Pattern brush.*   *Brush is applied to rectangle path.*

5   Ctrl+click (Windows) or Command+click (Mac OS) outside the art to deselect it. Now you'll draw a curved path using the Clouds and Sun brush.

6   In the Brushes palette, double-click the Clouds and Sun Pattern brush to view the Pattern Brush Options dialog box for the brush.

You'll change the scale and spacing of the brush for a different look.

7   Under Size, enter **250%** for Scale, and **30%** for Spacing. Click OK.

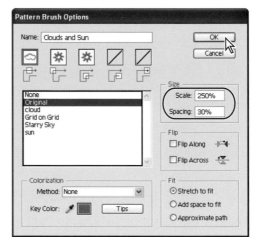

Select Clouds and Sun Pattern   *Change scale and spacing.*
brush.

8   At the Brush Change alert message, click Leave Strokes to keep the border brush strokes as they are.

The Leave Strokes option preserves paths in the artwork that are already painted with the brush. The changes you made to the brush will apply to subsequent uses of the brush. Now you'll use the brush to paint a curved path in the artwork.

9   Select the Paintbrush tool ( ) and draw a smooth curve over the tree. Use the guides for placement.

Apply Pattern brush to   *Result.*
path with paintbrush.

The path is painted with the clouds from the Clouds and Sun brush (the Side tile in the brush). Because the path does not include sharp corners, the Outer Corner tile and Inner Corner tile (the Sun tiles) are not applied to the path.

Applying the Scribble effect

The Scribble effect is a feature in Illustrator CS2 that lets you apply loose or mechanical-like scribbling to fills and strokes. This includes fills of gradients and patterns.

You will create the lake water, grass, and text using the Scribble Effect and its options.

1   Create a rectangle over the tree to create the grass. Fill the rectangle with the Green swatch from the Swatches palette and give it a Stroke of None.

2   Create the rectangle for the lake water by following the guide that is behind the boat. Fill this rectangle with the gradient named water in the Swatches palette.

Create two rectangles using
guides for the grass and lake.

3   Choose the Gradient tool (▣). Change the direction and length of the gradient in the water by clicking in the lower section of the rectangle and dragging upwards. The distance and the direction that you drag determines the length and direction of the gradient. Do this as many times as you like until you are satisfied with the gradient.

> 💡 *You don't have to click and drag with the Gradient tool at the bottom of the rectangle or even in the rectangle. Get different effects by clicking in the middle of the rectangle and dragging up, or even clicking outside the rectangle and dragging up and over the top.*

4   With the water still selected, choose Effect > Stylize > Scribble.

The Scribble effect options appear, giving you choices that range from changing the width of the scribbled stroke to loopiness and tightness.

5   Choose options in the Scribble Options dialog box to make the blue look more like water. (We used the following settings; Angle **30°**, Path Overlap -**2.5 pt**, Variation **5 pt**, Stroke Width **10 pt**. The curviness was set to be more angular with a setting of **0** (zero), but variations were made to make the strokes look less mechanical with a Curviness Variation setting of **21%**. Spacing between the strokes was set to **14 pt** with a variation of **.5 pt**.) Click OK.

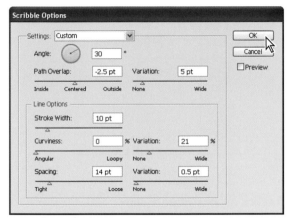

Using the Stroke Options to create water.

Now you create the grass using slightly different settings.

6   Using the Selection tool (▸), select the rectangle forming the grass and choose Effect > Stylize > Scribble. Don't choose the Scribble directly under the Effect menu. That will apply the last used settings of the Scribble effect without opening the options dialog box.

7   Using the options to create a tighter, more mechanical, scribble for the grass. (We used: Angle **90˚**, Path Overlap **0** (zero), Variation **5 pt**, Stroke width **3 pt**, Curviness **5 %**, Variation for Curviness **1%**, Spacing **5 pt**, Variation for Spacing **.5 pt**.) Click OK.

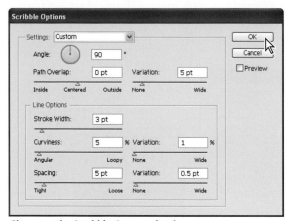

Changing the Scribble Options for the grass.

8   Using the Selection tool, Shift+click on the water to select both the grass and water rectangles simultaneously.

9   Choose Object > Arrange > Send to Back to reveal the boat and ripples in the water again.

Now you will use the Scribble Effect on live text.

10   Select the Type tool (T) and click in the middle of the water rectangle. Before typing, set up your character attributes. Click on Character in the Control palette or choose Window > Type > Character. (We chose Myriad Pro Black, which comes with Adobe Illustrator CS2. For more information about the fonts that come with your software, choose Help > Welcome Menu and click on Browse Cool Extras.) Change the font size and leading to **72 pt**. Click on the Align Center button in the Control palette to Align Center the text.

11 Type **LAKESIDE DESIGNS** in all caps, and press the Return key after the word LAKESIDE.

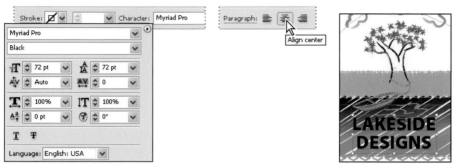

Choose the font style and alignment.

12 Use the Selection tool to select the text, choose Effect > Stylize > Scribble. Using the Scribble Options, make the text look scribbled but readable. We chose to tighten up the scribble with the following settings: Angle **0°** (zero), Path Overlap **0** (zero), Variation **.5 pt**, Stroke Width **2 pt**, Curviness **0** (zero), Curviness Variation **0** (zero), Spacing **3 pt**, Variation for Spacing **0** (zero). Click OK.

The text is still live text. If you were to change the font or size, it would still maintain the scribbled look.

You've completed the artwork for the lesson. Now you'll remove the guides so you can view the artwork in its finished form.

When working with guides, you can temporarily hide guides by choosing View > Guides > Hide Guides. The guides disappear but are preserved in the artwork. You can display hidden guides by choosing View > Guides > Show Guides. You won't need the guides again in this lesson, so you'll delete them using the Clear Guides command.

13 Choose View > Guides > Clear Guides. The guides are deleted from the artwork.

14 Choose File > Save to save your work. Choose File > Close to close the file.

Exploring on your own

Practice applying brushes to paths you create with drawing tools (just as you applied the Clouds and Sun Pattern brush to a path drawn with the Rectangle tool in the final section of the lesson).

1   Choose File > New, to create a document for practice.

2   In the Brushes palette menu, choose Open Brush library, and choose Decorative_ Scatter.

3   Use the drawing tools (the Pen or Pencil tool, and any of the basic shapes tools) to draw objects. Use the default fill and stroke colors when you draw.

4   With one of the objects selected, click a brush in the Decorative Scatter palette to apply the brush to the object's path.

As you select a Scatter brush, it is automatically added to the Brushes palette.

5   Repeat step 4 for each object you drew.

6   Double-click on a used Scatter brush listed in the Brushes palette to display the Scatter Brush Options dialog box for one of the brushes you used in step 4, and change the color, size, or other features of the brush. After you close the dialog box, click Apply To Strokes to apply your changes to the brush in the artwork.

Creating brushes

Use one of the basic shapes tools to create artwork to use as a new Scatter brush.

1 Select a basic Shape tool in the toolbox, and draw an object, keeping it selected.

2 Click the New Brush button at the bottom of the Brushes palette.

Note: You can use more than one object to create the new brush. All selected objects in the artwork will be included in the brush. If you use a brush to create artwork for a new brush, remember to expand the brush strokes before creating the new brush.

3 In the New Brush dialog box, select New Scatter Brush, and click OK.

The Brush Options dialog box for the new brush appears with the selected objects displayed in the brush example. The new brush is named Scatter Brush 1 by default.

4 Enter a new name for the brush. Then click OK to accept the settings for the brush.

5 Select the Paintbrush tool (✐) and draw a path. The new brush is applied to the path.

6 Double-click the new brush to display the Brush Options dialog box. Change the brush settings to try out different versions of the brush. When you have finished, click OK.

Using a brush library

Try out some of the brushes included in the brush libraries in Illustrator.

1 To open a brush library, choose Window > Brush Libraries.

2 Choose a library from the submenu. Illustrator includes 17 brush libraries in addition to the default brush library that appears when you start the program.

⚟ You can also create your own brush libraries. See "About brush libraries and the Brushes palette" in Illustrator Help.

Review

▶ **Review questions**

1   Describe each of the four brush types: Art, Calligraphic, Pattern, and Scatter.

2   What is the difference between applying a brush to artwork using the Paintbrush tool and applying a brush to artwork using one of the drawing tools?

3   Describe how to edit paths with the Paintbrush tool as you draw. How does the Keep Selected option affect the Paintbrush tool?

4   How do you change the colorization method for an Art, Pattern, or Scatter brush? (Remember, you don't use colorization methods with Calligraphic brushes.)

5   How can you make the Scribble effect more mechanical rather than loose and flowing?

▶ **Review answers**

1   The following are the four brush types:

•   Art brushes stretch artwork evenly along a path. Art brushes include strokes that resemble graphic media (such as the Charcoal-Feather brush used to create the tree, or the Marker-Rough brush used to create the grass). Art brushes also include objects, such as the Arrow brush.

•   Calligraphic brushes are defined by an elliptical shape whose center follows the path. They create strokes that resemble hand-drawn lines made with a flat, angled calligraphic pen tip.

•   Pattern brushes paint a pattern made up of separate sections, or tiles, for the sides (middle sections), ends, and corners of the path. When you apply a Pattern brush to artwork, the brush applies different tiles from the pattern to different sections of the path, depending on where the section falls on the path (at an end, in the middle, or at a corner).

•   Scatter brushes scatter an object, such as a leaf, along a path. You can adjust the Size, Spacing, Scatter, and Rotation options for a Scatter brush to change the brush's appearance.

2   To apply brushes using the Paintbrush tool, you select the tool, choose a brush from the Brushes palette, and draw in the artwork. The brush is applied directly to the paths as you draw. To apply brushes using a drawing tool, you select the tool and draw in the artwork; then you select the path in the artwork and choose a brush in the Brushes palette. The brush is applied to the selected path.

3   To edit a path with the Paintbrush tool, simply drag over a selected path to redraw it. The Keep Selected option keeps the last path selected as you draw with the Paintbrush tool. Leave the Keep Selected option turned on (the default setting) when you want to easily edit the previous path as you draw. Turn off the Keep Selected option when you want to draw layered paths with the paintbrush without altering previous paths. When the Keep Selected option is turned off, you can use the Selection tool to select a path and then edit the path.

4   To change the colorization method of a brush, double-click the brush in the Brushes palette to view the Brush Options dialog box. Use the Method drop-down menu in the Colorization section to select another method. If you choose Hue Shift, you can use the default color displayed in the dialog box preview; or you can change the key color (the new color that will appear) by clicking the Key Color Eyedropper, and clicking a color in the preview. Click OK to accept the settings and close the Brush Options dialog box. Click Apply to Strokes at the alert message if you want to apply the changes to existing strokes in the artwork.

Existing brush strokes are colorized with the stroke color that was selected when the strokes were applied to the artwork. New brush strokes are colorized with the current stroke color. To change the color of existing strokes after applying a different colorization method, select the strokes and select a new stroke color.

5   Using the Scribble Option, you can keep the choices for Curviness Variation and Spacing Variation to a minimum to make the scribble more mechanical.

You can alter the look of an object without changing its structure using appearance attributes—fills, strokes, effects, transparency, blending modes, or any combination of these object properties. You can edit or remove appearance attributes at any time. You can also save them as Graphic styles and apply them to other objects. At any time, you can edit an object that has a Graphic style applied to it, plus edit the Graphic style—an enormous time-saver!

11 | Applying Appearance Attributes, Graphic Styles, and Effects

In this lesson, you'll learn how to do the following:

- Create an appearance attribute.

- Reorder appearance attributes and apply them to layers.

- Copy and remove appearance attributes.

- Add an effect to an appearance and edit an effect.

- Save an appearance as a Graphic Style.

- Apply a Graphic Style to a layer.

- Select appropriate resolution settings for printing or exporting files with transparency.

Getting started

In this lesson, you'll enhance the basic design for a Web page by applying appearance attributes and Graphic Styles to the page's type, background, and three buttons. Before you begin, you'll restore the default preferences for Adobe Illustrator CS2. Then you will open the finished art file for this lesson to see what you'll create.

1   To ensure that the tools and palettes function exactly as described in this lesson, delete or deactivate (by renaming) the Adobe Illustrator CS2 preferences file. See "Restoring default preferences" on page 3 in the Introduction.

2   Start Adobe Illustrator CS2.

3   Choose File > Open, and open the L11end.ai file located in the Lesson11 folder inside the Lessons folder within the AICIB folder on your hard drive.

The artwork in this file is a design mock-up of a Web home page. The design for the completed page includes several Graphic Styles and effects, including overlapping gradients, transparent type, Drop Shadows, and texturized and shaded graphics.

4   If you like, choose View > Zoom Out to make the design mock-up smaller, adjust the window size, and leave it on-screen as you work. (Use the Hand tool (✋) to move the artwork where you want it in the window.) If you don't want to leave the artwork open, choose File > Close.

Using appearance attributes

You can apply appearance attributes to any object, group, or layer by using effects and the Appearance and Graphic Styles palettes. An appearance attribute is an aesthetic property—such as a fill, stroke, transparency, or effect—that affects the look of an object, but does not affect its basic structure. An appearance attribute can be changed or removed at any time without changing the underlying object or any other attributes applied to the object.

The advantage to using the Appearance palette to add effects or other attributes is that these effects or other attributes can be selected and edited at any time.

For example, if you apply a Drop Shadow effect to an object, at any time, you can change the drop shadow distance, blur, or color. You can also copy that effect and apply it to other shapes, groups, or layers. You can even save it as a Graphic Style and use it for other objects or other files. In contrast, if you create a drop shadow by applying the Drop Shadow filter to an object, you cannot edit the filter results, copy the filter effect, or apply it to other objects globally.

The Appearance palette contains the following types of editable attributes:

- **Fill** lists all fill attributes (fill type, color, transparency, and effects).

- **Stroke** lists some stroke attributes (stroke type, brush, color transparency, and effects). All other stroke attributes are displayed in the Stroke palette.

- **Transparency** lists opacity and blending mode.

- **Effect** lists commands in the Effect menu.

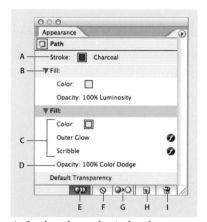

A. Stroke color and paintbrush name.
B. Fill color and opacity.
C. Second fill color and effects.
D. Fill opacity and blending mode.
E. New Art Has Basic Appearance.
F. Clear Appearance.
G. Reduce to Basic Appearance.
H. Duplicate Selected Item.
I. Delete Selected Item.

Note: Later in this lesson, you will learn about flattening artwork using effects that take advantage of transparency. Flattening is an easy and necessary step for files that will be printed. If your artwork is to be printed, make sure that you create files in the CMYK color mode. Flattening is not necessary if your final output is for the Web.

Adding appearance attributes

You'll start by selecting the star shape and adding to its basic appearance using the Appearance palette.

1   Choose File > Open, and open the L11start.ai file, located in the Lesson11 folder inside the Lessons folder within the AICIB folder on your hard drive.

2   Choose File > Save As, name the file **StarArt.ai**, and save it in the Lesson11 folder. Leave the type of file format option set to Adobe Illustrator Document (.AI), and click Save. In the Illustrator Options dialog box, accept the default settings and click OK.

3   Using the Selection tool (▸), select the star shape.

4   In the Layers palette, expand the Star Button layer so that you can see its contents. Notice that the star shape is selected, as indicated by the square to the right of the layer name, and its path is targeted, as indicated by the circle icon (◎) to the right of the path name.

5   Notice the stroke and fill attributes of the star shape listed in the Appearance palette. (If the palette isn't visible on-screen, choose Window > Appearance to display it; a check mark indicates that the palette is open on-screen.)

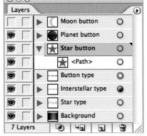
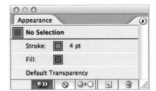

Star selected.   *Expanded Star Button layer.*   *Stroke and fill attributes.*

6   In the Appearance palette, click the Stroke attribute to select it.

Selecting the Stroke attribute lets you change just the stroke in the artwork.

7   In the Transparency palette, choose Multiply from the blending modes drop-down menu.

You can expand and collapse attributes in the Appearance palette by clicking the triangle (▸) to the left of the attribute in the palette list.

8 While remaining on the Selection tool, press and hold the Ctrl+spacebar (Windows) or Command+spacebar (Mac OS) and click the star shape to zoom in to about 200%. Inspect the stroke around the star to see how it has changed. The effect of the Multiply blending mode is similar to drawing on a page with transparent marker pens.

Strokes are centered on a path outline—half of the stroke color overlaps the filled star shape and half of the stroke color overlaps the background gradient.

Star shape with Multiply blending mode applied.

Reordering appearance attributes

Now you'll change the appearance of the Multiply blending mode by rearranging the attributes in the Appearance palette.

1 Resize the Appearance palette so that you can view all its contents. Click the Fill attribute and drag it above the Stroke attribute. (This technique is similar to dragging layers in the Layers palette to adjust their stacking order.)

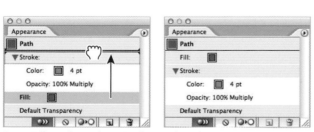

Drag Fill attribute above Stroke attribute.

Result.

Moving the Fill attribute above the Stroke attribute changes the look of the Multiply blending modes on the stroke. Half the stroke has been covered up. Blending modes work only on objects that are beneath them in the stacking order.

You'll now add another stroke to the object using the Appearance palette.

2   With the star shape still selected, choose Add New Stroke from the Appearance palette menu. A stroke is added to the top of the appearance list. It has the same color and stroke weight as the first stroke.

3   In the Color palette, choose RGB from the palette menu, and then use the sliders or text fields to change the color to a dark orange. (We used a color mix of R=255, G= 73, and B=0.)

4   Using the Stroke weight text field in the Control palette, type the value **2 pt**. Press Enter or Return.

You'll rearrange the order of the appearance attributes to prepare for adding live effects in the next part of the lesson.

5   In the Appearance palette, click the triangle to the left of the 4-point Stroke attribute to collapse the attribute, then drag it to the very top of the Appearance attributes list. (It should be directly above the 2-point stroke.)

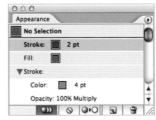

Add new stroke.   Change stroke color.   Rearrange stroke order.

6   Choose Select > Deselect and then File > Save to save the artwork.

Using live effects

The Effect menu commands alter the appearance of an object without changing the underlying object. Many Effect commands also appear in the Filter menu, but only the Effect commands are fully editable. Applying an effect to an object automatically adds the effect to the object's appearance attribute. You can select and edit the effect at any time by double-clicking on the effect in the Appearance palette.

You can apply more than one effect to an object. In this part of the lesson, you'll apply two effects to the star shape—an outer glow to make the star appear radiant, and a texture using a Photoshop effect called Grain.

1   With the Selection tool (▸), select the star, then choose Effect > Stylize > Outer Glow.

Note: Choose the top Stylize command in the Effect menu.

2   Click the Preview option and try different Opacity and Blur amounts until you are satisfied with the result. Leave the blend mode set to Screen. (We used 86% opacity and a 19 pt blur.) Don't click OK yet.

3   Click the color square next to the Mode menu to change the glow color. (We used a color mix of R=255, G=255, and B=51 to get a richer, brighter yellow.) Click OK to exit the Color Picker, and click OK again to apply the effect.

Adding Outer Glow effect.

Now you'll add a second effect to the star shape.

4   Choose Effect > Texture > Grain.

5 Adjust the settings until you are satisfied with the preview in the Grain dialog box. (We used an Intensity of 30, Contrast of 100, and Regular type.)

6 Click OK to see the result. Notice that Grain has been added to the list of attributes in the Appearance palette.

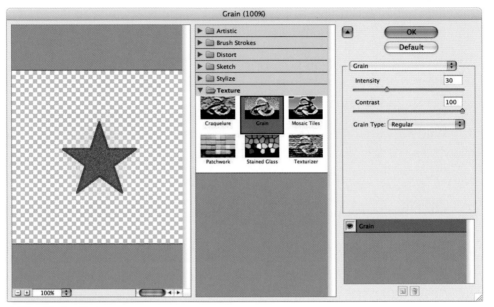

Adding Grain effect.

7 Choose File > Save to save your changes.

Editing an effect

Effects can be edited at any time. To edit an effect, you simply double-click its name in the Appearance palette to display that effect's dialog box. Changes you make will update the artwork.

Next you'll change the texture you applied to the star in the last section.

1 Make sure that the star is still selected.

2 If necessary, resize the Appearance palette to view all its contents. Then double-click the Grain attribute.

3 In the Grain dialog box, change the Type to Soft and click OK.

Now you'll adjust the blending mode of the star's fill to make it glow more.

4   With the star shape still selected, click the Fill attribute in the Appearance palette.

5   In the Transparency palette, choose Luminosity from the blending mode menu.

6   Choose File > Save to save the artwork.

Luminous fill added to effect.

Now you're ready to save the star's appearance as a Graphic Style.

Using Graphic Styles

A Graphic Style is a named set of appearance attributes. By applying different Graphic Styles, you can quickly and globally change the appearance of an object.

For example, you may have a symbol on a map that represents a city, with a Graphic Style applied that paints the symbol green with a drop shadow. You can use that Graphic Style to paint all the cities' symbols on the map. If you change your mind, you can change the fill color of the style to blue. All the symbols painted with that Graphic Style will then be updated automatically.

The Graphic Styles palette lets you create, name, save, and apply various effects and attributes to objects, layers, or groups. Just like attributes and effects, Graphic Styles are completely reversible. For example, you could apply a style to a circle that contains the Zig Zag effect, turning the circle into a starburst. You can revert the object to its original appearance with the Appearance palette, or you can break the link with that Graphic Style and edit one of its attributes without affecting other objects that are painted with the same Graphic Style.

Creating and saving a Graphic Style

Now you'll save and name a new Graphic Style using the appearance attributes you just created for the star button.

1   Click the Graphic Styles tab to bring the palette to the front of its group. (If the Graphic Styles palette isn't visible on-screen, choose Window > Graphic Styles; a check mark indicates that the palette is open on-screen.)

2   Position the Graphic Styles palette and the Appearance palette so that you can see both of them at the same time. Resize the Graphic Styles palette so that all the default styles are visible and there is empty space at the bottom.

3   Make sure that the star shape is still selected so that its appearance attributes are displayed in the Appearance palette.

The appearance attributes are stored in the appearance thumbnail, named Path, in the Appearance palette.

4   In the Appearance palette, drag the Path appearance thumbnail onto the Graphic Styles palette.

5   Release the mouse button when a thick black border appears on the inside of the palette. The border indicates that you are adding a new style to the palette.

The path thumbnail in the Appearance palette will change to "Path: Graphic Style."

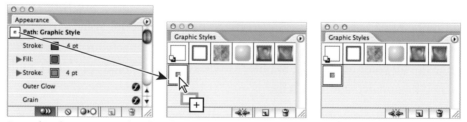

Drag object's appearance thumbnail onto Styles palette to save appearance attributes as new style.

6   In the Graphic Styles palette, choose Graphic Style Options from the palette menu. Name the new style **Grainy Glow**. Click OK.

7   Choose Select > Deselect to deselect the star shape, and then choose File > Save.

Applying a Graphic Style to a layer

Once a Graphic Style is applied to a layer, everything added to that layer will have that same style applied to it. Now you'll create a new Graphic Style, and apply it to a layer. Then you'll create a few new shapes on that layer to see the effect of the style.

1 In the Appearance palette, click the Clear Appearance button at the bottom of the palette. Then select the No Selection appearance name or thumbnail.

2 The Clear Appearance option removes all appearance attributes applied to an object, including any stroke or fill.

3 Choose Effect > Stylize > Drop Shadow.

Use the default settings. If desired, click the radio button to the left of the color swatch in the Drop Shadow dialog box, then click on the color swatch to change the shadow color. (We picked a red color of R=215, G=65, and B=4.) Click OK to exit the Color Picker, and click OK again to apply the effect.

Note: *Because the Drop Shadow appearance has no stroke or fill, its thumbnail will be blank. But once attributes are applied to a shape, the drop shadow will appear.*

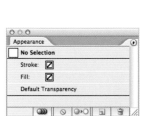 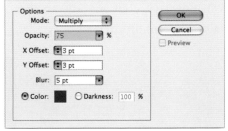 

Choose Drop Shadow effect.   *Result.*

When creating a new style, the Graphic Style palette automatically uses the current appearance attributes displayed in the Appearance palette.

4 In the Graphic Styles palette, Alt+click (Windows) or Option+click (Mac OS) the New Graphic Style button at the bottom of the palette, and type **Drop Shadow** as the name of the new style. Click OK.

Now you'll target the Planet Button layer, to apply a drop shadow to all the shapes on that layer.

5 In the Layers palette, click the triangle to the left of the Planet Button layer to expand the layer. Then click the target indicator (◎) to the right of the Planet Button layer. (Be careful not to target the mesh-filled path, the Planet Button sublayer. If you target the path, only the planet shape will have a drop shadow.)

6 In the Graphic Styles palette, click the Drop Shadow style to apply the style to the layer.

7 Choose Select > Deselect to deselect the planet shape.

Now you'll test the layer effect by adding some shapes to the Planet Button layer.

8 Select the Star tool (☆) in the same group as the Rectangle tool (▦) in the toolbox.

9 Click the Color tab to bring the palette to the front of its group, or choose Window > Color to display it. In the Color palette, choose a fill color (we used R=129, G=23, B=136 for a purple color) and a stroke of None.

10 With the Planet Button layer still selected, in the artwork draw several small stars around the planet shape.

Because the Drop Shadow style contains only an effect, and no stroke or fill, the objects retain their original stroke and fill attributes.

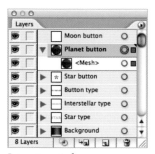

Layer targeted.

Graphic Style applied to layer.

Stylized artwork added to layer.

11 Notice the following icons on the right side of a layer in the Layers palette, indicating whether any appearance attributes are applied to the layer or whether it is targeted:

(◎) indicates that the layer, group, or object is targeted but has no appearance attributes applied to it.

(○) indicates that the layer, group, or object is not targeted and has no appearance attributes applied to it.

(◉) indicates that the layer, group, or object is not targeted but has appearance attributes applied to it.

(◉) indicates that the group is targeted and has appearance attributes applied to it. This icon also designates any targeted object that has appearance attributes more complex than a single fill and stroke applied to it.

12 Choose File > Save to save the artwork.

Applying existing Graphic Styles

Adobe Illustrator comes with a palette of pre-made Graphic Styles that you can apply to your artwork. Now you'll finish the button designs by adding an existing style to the Moon button layer.

A good habit to get into is using the Layers palette to select objects or layers to which you'll apply styles. An effect or style varies, depending on whether you're targeting either a layer or an object, or group within a layer. Now you'll select the Moon button shape, not the layer.

1 In the Layers palette, click the triangle (▷) to expand the Moon button layer.

2 Select the <Path> sublayer to select it. Then click the target indicator (◎) to the right of the <Path> sublayer to target it. Targeting the sublayer selects the path in the artwork.

Note: If you target a layer or sublayer by mistake, Ctrl/Command+click the target indicator to remove it.

3 Click on the Fill box on the Control palette to link to the Swatches palette. In the Swatches palette, select the Moon gradient to fill the selected path.

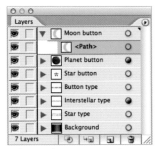
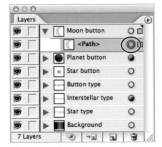
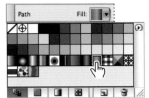

Select path in Layers palette. *Target path in Layers palette.* *Change fill color to Moon gradient.*

Now you'll apply a Graphic Style to the Moon button layer. The style contains a color, which you'll apply to the layer in place of the moon's existing color.

4 In the Layers palette, click the target indicator (◎) for the Moon button layer.

5 Either choose Window > Graphic Styles or click the Graphic Styles tab to bring the palette to the front of its group. In the Graphic Styles palette, click the Green relief style to apply it to the layer.

6 Choose File > Save to save the artwork.

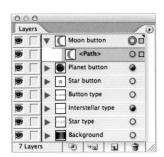

Layer selected. *Graphic Style applied to layer.* *Result.*

Applying an appearance to a layer

You can also apply simple appearance attributes to layers. For example, to make everything on a layer 50% opaque, simply target that layer and change the opacity in the Transparency palette.

Next you'll target a layer and change its blending mode to soften the effect of the type.

1 In the Layers palette, click the downward triangle next to the Moon button layer to collapse the layer.

2 If necessary, scroll to the Star type layer. Then click the target indicator (○) for the Star type layer. This action selects everything on the layer and targets all its objects.

3 In the Transparency palette, choose Soft Light from the blending mode menu.

4 Choose File > Save to save the artwork.

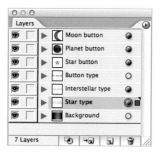
Star Type layer targeted.

Soft Light mode applied.

Result.

Copying, applying, and removing Graphic Styles

Once you've created several Graphic Styles and appearances, you may want to use them on other objects in your artwork. You can use the Graphic Styles palette, the Appearance palette, the Eyedropper tool (✐), or the Paint Bucket tool (⬧) to apply and copy appearance attributes.

Next you'll apply a style to one of the objects using the Appearance palette.

1   Choose Select > Deselect.

2   Select the Selection tool (▸) in the toolbox, and click the star shape to select it.

3   In the Appearance palette, drag the appearance thumbnail (labeled "Path: Grainy Glow") onto the moon shape to apply those attributes to it.

You can apply styles or attributes by dragging them from the Graphic Styles palette or the Appearance palette onto any object. The object doesn't have to be selected.

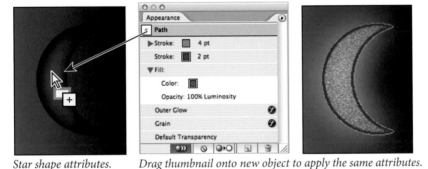

Star shape attributes.   Drag thumbnail onto new object to apply the same attributes.

4   Ctrl+click (Windows) or Command+click (Mac OS) away from the artwork to deselect it.

Next, you'll apply a style by dragging it directly from the Graphic Styles palette onto an object.

5   In the Graphic Styles palette, drag the Green relief style thumbnail onto the moon shape in the artwork.

6   Release the mouse button to apply the style to the shape.

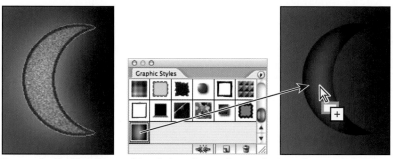

Drag style thumbnail onto object (selected or not) to apply the style.

Now you'll use the Layers palette to copy an attribute from one layer to another.

7   Expand the Layers palette to see all the layers. Then in the Layers palette, Alt+drag (Windows) or Option+drag (Mac OS) the appearance indicator from the Planet button layer onto the appearance indicator of the Button type layer.

Using Alt or Option copies one layer effect onto another, as indicated by the hand cursor with the plus sign. To move an appearance or style just from one layer or object to another, simply drag the appearance indicator.

Alt/Option drag appearance attribute to copy it from one layer to another.

Now you'll remove an appearance from a layer using the Layers palette.

8   In the Layers palette, click the target indicator to the right of the Button type layer.

9   Drag the appearance indicator to the Trash button at the bottom of the Layers palette to remove the appearance attribute.

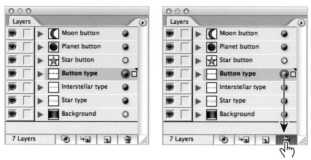

Drag appearance indicator to Trash button to remove attributes.

Another way to remove attributes of a selected object or layer is to use the Appearance palette. Select the object and then click the Reduce to Basic Appearance button at the bottom of the palette to return the object to its original state (including any stroke or fill) before the appearance attribute or style was applied.

10   Choose File > Save, and then File > Close.

Saving and printing files with transparency effects

Now that you have learned to take advantage of Effects and the Appearance palette, you need to learn how to get them to print correctly. Many of the Effects used in this lesson take advantage of Illustrator's ability to create transparency. Transparency is applied to any object that has been modified to affect an underlying object. Illustrator, InDesign and Photoshop work seamlessly together and will maintain transparency from one application to the other if the proper workflow is followed. This simple workflow includes a step at the end necessary for printing, called flattening.

Flattening is a term used to define the process of converting all transparent objects into a collection of opaque objects that retain the appearance of the original transparent objects when printed.

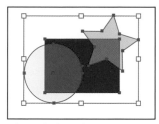

Objects before Flattening.

After Flattening.

Illustrator flattens artwork containing transparency before printing or saving the artwork. During flattening, Illustrator looks for areas where transparent objects overlap other objects and isolates these areas by dividing the artwork into components. Illustrator then analyzes each component to determine if the artwork can be represented using vector data or if the artwork must be rasterized.

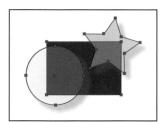

The drop shadow before flattening.

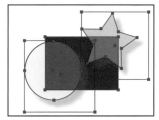

The rasterized drop shadow as a separate object after flattening.

In most cases, the flattening process produces excellent results. However, if your artwork contains complex, overlapping areas and you require high-resolution output, you can control the degree to which artwork is rasterized. To preserve as much of the vector art in your document as possible, use the Raster/Vector Balance slider in the Document Setup dialog box. Illustrator uses these settings to determine the quality, printing speed, or both, for your artwork.

What is rasterization?

Rasterization is the process of changing vector graphics, vector fonts, gradients, and gradient meshes into bitmap images for display and printing, essentially turning vector artwork into pixels. The higher the ppi (pixels per inch), the better the quality. The amount of ppi or dpi (dots per inch) is referred to as the resolution of the artwork.

Vector Object.   *Rasterized at 72 ppi.*   *Rasterized at 300 ppi.*

In Illustrator CS2, you now have the ability to preserve spot color raster in other live effects, including: Rasterize, Feather, Inner/Outer Glow, Gaussian blur, and Radial blur in CMYK and RGB document color spaces.

Specifying the resolution of filters and live effects

For this next exercise, you will create several overlapping shapes with various levels of transparency.

1   Choose File > New, and create a new CMYK document.

If you plan to print your transparent artwork, the document should be in CMYK mode.

2   Using the shape tools, create any three shapes and overlap them.

3   Assign a different color fill to each, and assign None to the stroke.

4   Using the Transparency palette, apply varying levels of transparency to all three shapes. Exact amounts are not important as long as you can see the underlying shapes.

5   With the three shapes selected, choose Effect > Stylize > Drop Shadow. Accept the default settings, and click OK.

6 With the three shapes still selected, choose Effects > Pixelate > Pointilize. Leave at the default settings, and click OK.

Create overlapping shapes with colored fills.   *Apply Transparency.*   *Apply Effect.*

7 Choose File > Save, name the file **shapes.ai**, and select the Lesson11 folder in the Save In menu. Leave the type of file format set to Adobe Illustrator˚ Document (.AI), and click Save. In the Illustrator Options dialog box, leave at the default settings and click OK.

Using Document Raster Effects Settings

1 Select the Zoom tool (🔍) in the toolbox. Position the Zoom tool over any shape's drop shadow and click. Continue clicking on the center of the shapes until you have zoomed in to 300%. You should be able to see the pixelated texture of the drop shadow, and the pointilization effect.

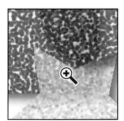

Zoom in to see the details.

Notice the edges of the star shape, with stair-stepping on the angled edges. This is due to the resolution setting for the raster effects. The default setting is 72 ppi.

You will change that setting to improve the quality of the shape's shadow.

2 Choose Effect > Document Raster Effects Settings.

3 Change the Resolution setting to Medium (150 ppi).

4   Leave the other settings as they are, and click OK.

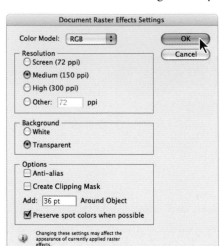

5   Notice that the shadow has become smoother and the pixels have become more precise.

If you were to increase the resolution to 300 ppi, the artwork would be even more well-defined. For this lesson you will leave the setting at 150 ppi.

Now that you have determined the quality of rasteration you want to occur, you will choose your flattening settings using the Flattener Preview palette.

Using the Flattener Preview palette

If you are not sure what objects require flattening, choose Window > Flattener Preview. Use the preview options in the Flattener Preview palette to highlight the areas affected by flattening artwork. Use this information to adjust the flattening options, and save custom flattener presets.

1   On the same shapes.ai file, add another shape. Do not apply transparency or effects to this object.

2   Fill it with a red color from the Swatches palette.

3   Use the Selection tool (▶) to drag the new opaque object on top of any other shape.

4   Choose Window > Attributes and click on the checkbox to Overprint Fill.

5 Choose View > Overprint Preview to show how your overprint will appear when printed.

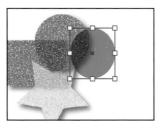 

Check the Overprint fill box.

6 Choose Window > Flattener Preview. The Flattener Preview palette can remain open while you work on your artwork.

7 Click Refresh, and choose Transparent Objects from the Highlight drop-down menu. If necessary, click Refresh again.

All transparent objects are highlighted. Any other objects are gray.

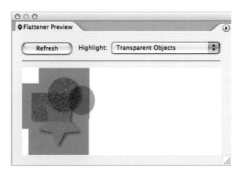

The Flattener Preview palette can show Transparent objects.

8 From the Highlight drop-down menu, choose All Affected Objects. More objects would appear highlighted if you had transparent objects on top of non-transparent objects.

9 Choose Show Options from the Flattener Preview palette menu.

In Options, you can select different settings and preview the result. Note that the Flattening Preview palette does not actually perform the flattening.

Note: *As you change flattening options, click Refresh to update the display in the preview.*

10 From the Overprints drop-down menu, choose Simulate for the type of overprinting to use for the preview. Click Refresh.

- *Preserve* to retain overprinting for devices that support it. In most cases, only separations devices support overprinting.

- *Simulate* to maintain the appearance of overprinting in composite output.

- *Discard* to ignore any overprint settings that are present in your document.

11 From the Preset drop-down window, choose High Resolution from the available presets.

- *Low Resolution* is for quick proofs that will be printed on black-and-white desktop printers, as well as for documents that will be published on the Web, or exported to SVG.

Note: The SVG (Scalable Vector Graphics) format is entirely XML-based and offers many advantages to developers and users alike. With SVG, you can use XML and JavaScript to create web graphics that respond to user actions with sophisticated effects such as highlighting, tool tips, audio, and animation.

- *Medium Resolution* is for desktop proofs and print-on-demand documents that will be printed on PostScript color printers.

- *High Resolution* is for final press output and for high-quality proofs, such as separations-based color proofs. You will now alter the High Resolution setting for your own custom settings.

12 Specify rasterization settings. Drag the Raster/Vector Balance slider to determine the percentage of rasterization. The settings vary from 0 on the left for the greatest rasterization to 100 on the right for the least rasterization on artwork. Select the highest setting to represent as much artwork as possible using vector data, or select the lowest setting to rasterize all the artwork. For this exercise, drag the slider to 90%.

Note: You will not see the rasterization in the Flattener Preview palette.

Understand that rasterizing everything in a file degrades some of vector graphics' crisp edges, but maintaining too much of the vector artwork may make a file difficult to print due to your printer's memory limitations.

13 Specify an output resolution for art and text. In this case, leave the Line Art and Text Resolution at 1200.

If your final output will be separated and printed on a four-color press, you will want to specify a resolution of 1200. If your final output is to be a laser printer or color copier, you can select something lower, such as 600 or 800 dpi. In normal viewing conditions, no difference is visible, but the lower dpi takes less processing time and memory.

14   Set a separate resolution for the Gradients Mesh objects. Generally, these objects require less resolution than solid fill objects. Leave the setting at 300.

15   Leave the Convert All Text to Outlines unchecked. This ensures that the width of text, respectively, remains consistent during flattening.

16   Leave Convert All Strokes to Outlines unchecked. We do not have strokes in this artwork, but if we did, this option would convert all strokes to simple filled paths. This option ensures that the width of strokes stays consistent during flattening, but it will cause thin strokes to appear slightly thicker.

17   Leave the Clip Complex Regions option selected. When selected, this option ensures that the boundaries between vector artwork and rasterized artwork fall along object paths, but it may result in paths that are too complex for the printer to handle.

18   Once you have determined which settings work best for your workflow, choose Save Transparency Flattener Preset... from the palette menu in the upper right of the Flattener Preview.

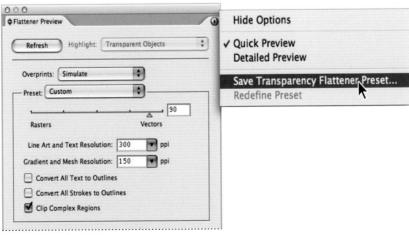

Save your settings as a preset.

19   Name the preset **shapes1** and click OK. You can close the Flattener Preview palette as well.

Note: If you are unsure of which settings to use, contact your printer. A good print provider should be able to discuss the options with you and may even provide a preset that works in their workflow. Learn how to import presets later in this lesson.

Assigning the Flattening preset

Using File > Document Setup, you can either create new flattening settings or assign presets to a document.

1   Choose File > Document Setup.

2   Choose Transparency from the drop-down menu in the Document Setup dialog box.

3   Choose the preset that you created (shapes1) in the Flattener Preview palette.

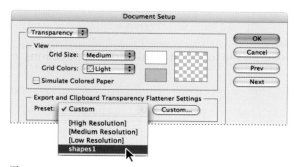

The transparency options in Document Setup.

4   Click OK.

5   Choose File > Save.

Note: You can also create custom flattening settings in the Document Setup window by choosing Custom on the Preset drop-down window and selecting options.

Saving a file with transparency

If you are saving a file that is to be used in other Adobe applications, such as InDesign or Photoshop, keep the transparency live by saving the artwork in the native Adobe Illustrator format. The transparency is supported in the other applications.

In this next exercise, you will save your shape file in two different formats to place into an InDesign or Photoshop document.

1   Choose File > Save As, name the file **shapes1.ai**, and select the Lesson11 folder in the Save In menu. Leave the type of file format set to Adobe Illustrator Document (.AI), and click Save. In the Illustrator Options dialog box, leave at the default settings and click OK.

2   Open Photoshop or InDesign and choose File > New. Create a letter-sized document.

3   Choose File > Place. Locate the file you saved in the Lesson11 folder named shapes1.ai and click Place.

Using Place to import your file allows the artwork to maintain its transparency.

Note: Though you have the ability to drag and drop artwork from one Adobe application to another, transparency will not be supported.

Saving in the EPS format

Save a file as an Encapsulated Postscript file to use in non-Adobe applications, or if you do not need the transparency to remain live.

1   Return to Adobe Illustrator.

2   Choose File > Save As, name the file **shapes2.eps**, and select the Lesson11 folder in the Save In menu. Set the type of file format to Illustrator EPS, and click Save.

3   In the EPS options window, select the preset you created earlier named shapes1. Click OK.

4   Return to the InDesign or Photoshop document.

5   Choose File > Place and select the file you just saved named shapes2.eps and click Place.

Notice that transparency is not supported. The transparent areas of the artwork do not interact with the rest of the document.

Adobe Illustrator format.   EPS format.

6   Return to Illustrator and choose File > Close, or leave the file open to experiment with other flattening options.

Printing transparent artwork

If you have a printer connected, you can experiment with different flattening settings in the Print dialog box.

1   Choose File > Print.

2   Click on Advanced in the options window.

3   From the Preset drop-down menu, choose a transparency preset or click on Custom to create your own.

Exporting and importing flattening settings

Settings that you create can be accessed by using the Document Setup dialog box, but you can import settings that were created in other documents by choosing Edit > Transparency Flattener Presets.

Export from the document in which you created the preset. Use the Import button to make the settings available to any other document. This can be especially useful if you are working with a printer that can supply presets.

You are now finished with the discussion on flattening. More information can be found using Illustrator help or at Adobe.com. Close any files that you have open.

Exploring on your own

Now that you've learned the basic steps to creating and using effects and Graphic Styles, experiment with different combinations of appearance attributes to fashion interesting special effects. Try combining different styles to produce new ones.

For example, here's how to merge two existing styles to create a brand new style:

1   Choose File > New to open a new file.

2   If the Graphic Styles palette isn't visible on-screen, choose Window > Graphic Styles to display it.

3   In the Graphic Styles palette, select Thick Aqua Neon style.

4   Add another style to the selection by Ctrl+clicking (Windows) or Command+ clicking (Mac OS) the style named Chiseled.

5   Choose Merge Graphic Styles from the Graphic Styles palette menu.

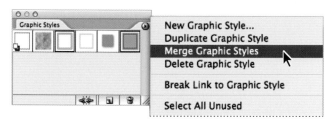

6   Name the new style **merged style** in the Style options dialog box, and click OK.

7   On the artboard, draw a shape or create text. Then apply the new style.

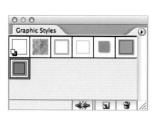 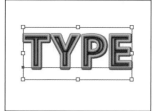

Merged styles.   *Result.*

If you want to edit the style and save it again, do the following:

1   To replace a style, Alt+drag (Windows) or Option+drag (Mac OS) the appearance thumbnail onto the style you are replacing in the Graphic Styles palette.

2   The style being replaced displays a thick black border when you position the cursor over it.

Review

▶ **Review questions**

1   Name two types of Appearance attributes.

2   How do you add a second stroke to an object?

3   What's the difference between a Filter and an Effect?

4   How do you edit an effect that is part of an object's appearance attributes?

5   What's the difference between applying a Graphic Style to a layer versus applying it to an object?

6   How do you remove an appearance using the Layers palette?

7   How do you set the resolution for a file that contains filter effects?

▶ **Review answers**

1   The Appearance palette contains the following types of editable attributes:

- Fill attributes (fill type, color, transparency, and effects).
- Stroke attributes (stroke type, brush, color transparency, and effects).
- Transparency attributes (opacity and blending mode).
- Effects from the Effect menu.

2   From the Appearance palette menu, choose Add New Stroke. A stroke is added to the top of the appearance list. It has the same color and stroke weight as the original stroke.

3   Many commands in the Effect menu also appear in the Filter menu, but only the Effect menu commands are live and fully editable.

4   To edit an effect, double-click its name in the Appearance palette. This displays the effect's dialog box. You can then make changes. Click OK to update the effect in the artwork.

5 Once a Graphic Style is applied to a layer, everything you add to that layer will have that style applied to it. For example, if you create a circle on Layer 1 and then move it to Layer 2, which has a Drop Shadow effect applied, the circle would adopt that effect. When a style is applied to a single object, nothing else on that object's layer is affected by the object's style. For example, if a triangle has a Roughen effect applied to its path, and you move it to another layer, it will still retain the Roughen effect.

6 In the Layers palette, click the target indicator of a layer. Drag the appearance indicator down to the Trash icon in the Layers palette to remove the appearance. You can also remove the appearance of a selected object or layer by using the Appearance palette. Select the object and click the Reduce to Basic Appearance button to return the object to its original state before the appearance attribute or style was applied.

7 You change the resolution in the Rasterize Effects Settings dialog box. Choose Effect > Document Raster Effects Settings. Change the Resolution setting to Low (72 ppi), Medium (150 ppi), High (300 ppi), or Other. Click OK.

It's easy to turn two-dimensional artwork into three-dimensional shapes using the new 3D effect. The new 3D effect also includes features that makes it easy to map artwork to all the surfaces, to control lighting, and apply bevels.

12 | Using the 3D Effect

In this lesson, you'll learn how to do the following:

- Use Warp Effects to create a banner logotype.

- Use Brush Libraries included with Illustrator CS2.

- Create 3D objects from 2D artwork.

- Map artwork to the faces of the 3D objects.

Getting started

In this lesson, you'll create several three-dimensional objects using the new 3D Effects feature in Illustrator. Before you begin, you'll need to restore the default preferences for Adobe Illustrator. Then you'll open a file containing the finished artwork to see what you'll create.

1   To ensure that the tools and palettes function exactly as described in this lesson, delete or deactivate (by renaming) the Adobe Illustrator CS2 preferences file. See "Restoring default preferences" on page 3.

2   Start Adobe Illustrator.

3   Choose File > Open, and open the L12end.ai file in the Lesson12 folder, located inside the Lessons folder within the AICIB folder on your hard drive.

This file displays a completed illustration of a soap can, soap balls, and a vase.

4   Choose View > Zoom Out to make the finished artwork smaller, adjust the window size, and leave it on your screen as you work. (Use the Hand tool (✋) to move the artwork where you want it in the window.) If you don't want to leave the image open, choose File > Close.

To begin working, you'll open an existing art file to which you will add 3D objects.

5   Choose File > Open, and open the L12strt.ai file in the Lesson12 folder, located inside the Lessons folder within the AICIB folder on your hard drive.

6   Choose File > Save As, name the file Lemon.ai, and select the Lesson12 folder in the Save In menu. Leave the type of file format option set to Adobe Illustrator Document (.AI), and click Save. In the Illustrator Options dialog box, leave the Illustrator options at their default settings, and click OK.

Creating a banner logo with the Warp effect

You will use a Warp effect to create the banner logo. Warp effects distort objects, including paths, text, meshes, blends, and raster images. Because Warp effects are live, you can apply a warp to your artwork, and then continue to modify or remove the effect at any time using the Appearance palette.

Creating the logotype

You can make a warp from objects in your artwork, or you can use a preset warp shape or a mesh object as an envelope.

1   Choose the Selection tool (➤) in the toolbox. Then click to select the Lots O' Lemon type.

2   Choose Effect > Warp > Rise.

3   In the Warp Options dialog box, select Preview to preview the effect of changes.

4   Drag the Warp Options dialog box by its title bar so you can see the dialog box and the selected type in the artwork.

5 Set the Bend amount to **93%** to create a ribbon effect. Click OK.

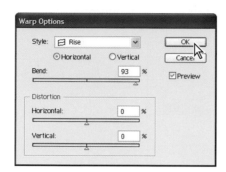

Use the Warp effect to distort the text.

6 Choose File > Save to save your work.

Stylizing the banner and logotype

To complete the banner and logotype, you'll add some sophistication by offsetting a stroke around the text and adding a colored drop shadow.

1 With the Selection tool (↖), click on the logotype if it is not still selected.

2 If the Appearance palette is not visible, choose Window > Appearance.
Notice that the Appearance palette lists the Warp effect that has been applied to the text.

3 From the Appearance palette menu, choose Add New Stroke. Leave the color as black, and set the weight at 1 pt.

You can add multiple strokes to one object, and apply different effects to each one, giving you the opportunity to create unique and interesting artwork.

Add a new stroke.

4 With the Stroke selected in the Appearance palette, choose Effect > Path > Offset Path. Change the Offset to **2 pt**, and click OK. This creates an outline around the text.

Apply the Offset Path effect.

Now you will add a colored drop shadow to the text.

5 In the Appearance palette, click on the word Type. This assures that the drop shadow applies to the text and not to just the offset stroke.

6 Choose Effect > Stylize > Drop Shadow, and check the Preview checkbox. Change the X Offset to 4 pt, the Y Offset to 4 pt, and the Blur to 2 pt. Do not click OK.

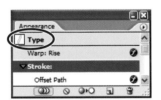

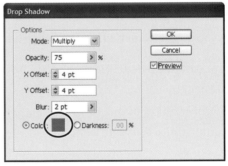

Select Text on the appearance palette.   *Change the Drop Shadow options, including the shadow color.*   *Result.*

7 Click on the color square to the right of the Color radio button. Pick an orange color. (We picked C=10%, M=50%, Y=75%, K=0%.) Click OK.

8 Click OK to the Drop Shadow options window.

9 With the Selection tool, click off the artwork to deselect, or choose Select > Deselect.

10 File > Save. Leave the file open for the next lesson.

Using Brushes for decoration

In this next lesson, you will create a decoration for the side panel using brushes.

You will use a brush included with your exercise file, but understand that you can select brushes from many available brush libraries that come with Illustrator CS2.

If you want to access additional novelty, arrow and artistic brush strokes follow these steps:

1 If your Brushes palette is not visible choose Window > Brushes.

2 From the Brushes palette menu choose Open Brush Library.

Illustrator CS2 comes loaded with many additional brush options.

3 Select from a list of brush palettes.

A separate brush palette appears from which you can choose additional brushes.

Creating the brush decoration

Now you will create the brush decoration for the side panel.

1 First, you will create a path for the brush. If necessary, use the Swatches in the toolbox to change the Stroke to Black and your Fill to None.

2   Choose the Pen tool ( ), and click on the left endpoint of the dashed guide under the artwork. Hold down the Shift key and click on the right endpoint.

3   Choose View > Guides > Clear Guides.

4   From the brush palette, scroll down to the Laurel brush.

5   Using the Selection tool ( ), select the path, and click the Laurel brush. The laurel is repeated the length of the path.

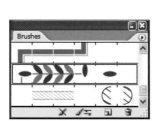
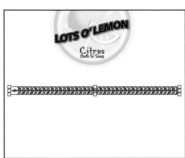

With the path selected, choose the Laurel brush.

Next, you will expand the Laurel brush to change the Fill color of the leaves and stem.

6   Using the path still selected, choose Object > Expand Appearance. This converts the laurel pattern into artwork that can be selected and edited. It is no longer linked to the Brushes palette.

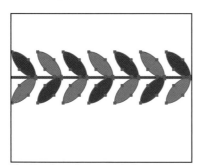

The Brush stroke expanded.

7   With the Selection tool, click off the artwork to deselect it.

8   Using the Direct Selection tool (⬦), click on the dark orange leaf. Choose Select > Same > Fill Color. The Select Same feature is helpful when trying to find items of the same fill stroke or stroke weight.

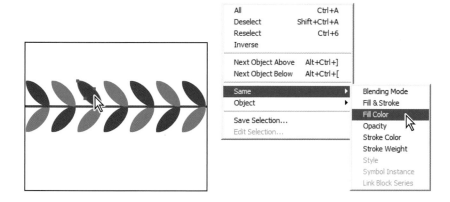

9   With the Fill swatch in the toolbox forward, choose Dark Green color from the Swatches palette. All the dark orange leaves are now filled with the Dark Green color.

10   Choose Select > Deselect.

11   Using the Direct Selection tool, click on the light orange leaf.

12   Choose Select > Same > Fill Color.

13   Change the light orange Fill to the Light green color from the Swatches palette.

14   Choose Select > Deselect.

15   Apply the same steps to change the dark orange stem into a dark green.

Turning the artwork into symbols

You are finished with the artwork for the 3D shape. In order for these designs to be applied to the 3D shape, they must be turned into symbols. The Symbols palette is used for a variety of things, from storing repeatedly used artwork, to creating a library of items that can be mapped to 3D objects. Before starting, choose Window > Symbols if the Symbols palette is not visible.

1   Using the Selection tool (▸), click and drag a marquee surrounding all the leaves.

2   Alt+click (Windows) or Option+click (Mac OS) on the New Symbol button in the lower right of the Symbols palette. Using the Alt/Option key in any palette will allow you to name the item as it is added to the palette.

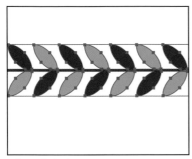

Select all the leaves.

Alt/Option+Click on the New Symbol button.

3   Name the Symbol **Leaves**.

4   With the leaves on the artboard still selected, choose Edit > Clear or press Delete.

5   Unlock Layer 1 by clicking on the padlock to the left of the layer name.

6   Choose Select > All, Control+A (Windows) or Command+A (Mac OS).

7   Alt+click (Windows) or Option+click (Mac OS) on the New Symbol button in the Symbols palette to add the label as a symbol. Name the symbol **Lemon**.

8   With everything still selected on the artboard, choose Edit > Clear or press the Delete key.

There should be nothing on your artboard at this time, and two symbols in the Symbols palette.

The artwork is now symbols.

9   Choose File > Save.

Creating the 3D cylinder

In this part of the lesson, you'll use two-dimensional shapes as the foundation for creating three-dimensional objects. Using the 3D effect, you can control the appearance of 3D objects with lighting, shading, rotation, and other properties.

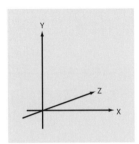

The 3D effect takes advantage of the x, y, and z axes.

There are three ways to create a 3D object:

•   Extrude and Bevel—Uses the Z axis to give a 2D object depth by extruding the object. For example, a circle becomes a cylinder.

•   Revolve—Uses the Y axis to revolve an object around an axis. For example, an arc becomes a circle.

•   Rotate—Uses the Z axis to rotate 2D artwork in 3D space and change the artwork's perspective.

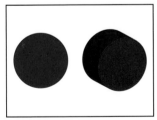 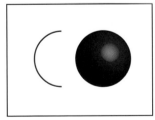 

Extrude and Bevel.   *Revolve.*   *Rotate.*

Using the 3D Extrude effect

In this next lesson, you will create a can to hold the soap for which you have already created a label.

1   Choose the Ellipse tool (○), and click and release on the artboard. In the Ellipse options dialog box, type **285 pt** into the Width text field, and click on the word Height. The values are entered equally, then click OK.

2   Fill the shape with the color Gray from the Swatches palette. Make sure that the Stroke is None.

3   Choose Effect > 3D > Extrude and Bevel, check the Preview checkbox. Click on the title bar of the options window, and drag it to a location that allows you to see your artwork.

The Extrude and Bevel effect has taken the two-dimensional circle and extruded it using the default settings. You will change several options, including the depth and edges.

4   First, click on the Position Cube icon on the left side of the dialog box. Experiment with rotating the object in space by clicking and dragging the cube. When you are finished experimenting, choose Off-Axis Bottom from the Position drop-down menu.

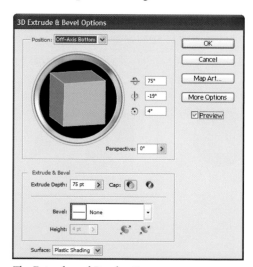

The Extrude and Bevel options.

Result.

5   Make the cylinder taller by using the Extrude Depth slider or typing **75** into the Extrude Depth text field. Check off and on the Preview checkbox to refresh the image.

Cap On or Cap Off?

In the Extrude and Bevel section of the 3D Options window (Extrude and Bevel and Revolve 3D effects) you have a choice to make your object appear solid or hollow.

- Click the Revolve Cap On button to make the object appear solid.
- Click the Revolve Cap Off button to make the object appear hollow.

Cap On.

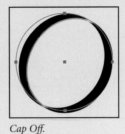

Cap Off.

6   Using the Bevel drop-down menu, experiment with the choice of different bevels to see different variations of edge effects you can easily create.

If you select a bevel from the Bevel drop-down menu, you can add beveling properties to carve away from, or add to the object's surface.

- The Extent Out ( ) button adds the bevel to the object's shape.
- The Extent In ( ) button carves the bevel out of the object's original shape.

7   When you are finished experimenting, return to None.

Note: 3D objects may display anti-aliasing artifacts on screen, but these artifacts disappear when the object is rasterized. Read more about rasterization in the flattening section of Lesson 11, "Applying Appearance Attributes, Graphic Styles, and Effects."

8   Click OK.

9   File > Save. Leave the file open for the next lesson.

Applying the Symbol as mapped artwork

Take any 2D artwork stored as a Symbol in the Symbol's palette, and apply it to selected surfaces on your 3D object.

Every 3D object is composed of several surfaces. For example, the shape that you just created has three external surfaces. It has a top, a bottom, and a side surface that wraps around the shape. In this next lesson, you will take the artwork that you created and map it to the cylinder.

1 Since you are editing the existing Extrude and Bevel effect, locate the Appearance palette, Go to Windows > Appearance if it is not visible, and double-click on 3D Extrude and Bevel. When the Extrude and Bevel options appear, drag the window to the side so that you can see your artwork as you make changes.

Note: Any time that you apply an effect, double-click on the named effect in the Appearance palette to edit it.

2 Press the Map Art button, and check Preview.

When the Map Art window appears, notice the options to select a Symbol and a Surface. A window for positioning the mapped artwork appears below.

3 Click on the single arrow to navigate from one surface to another. Notice that as you rotate through the surfaces, a red highlight appears, indicating what surface you have active in the preview window.

4 Choose 1 of 3. You see the top of the cylinder in the preview palette.

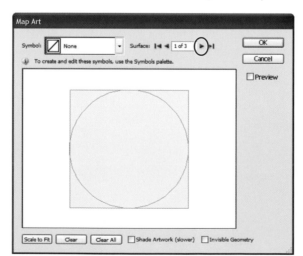

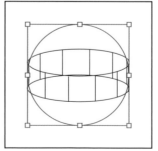

Click on the single arrow to navigate surfaces.   *The highlighted surface.*

5 From the Symbol drop-down menu, choose the Symbol named Lemon.
The Lemon Symbol is placed in the preview palette.

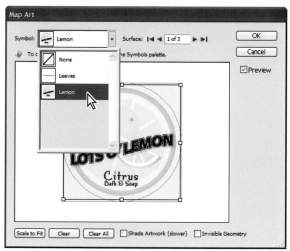

Select the Symbol.

Result.

6 In Surface, click on the single arrow and choose 3 of 3.

7 Choose Leaves from the Symbol drop-down window.

8 Use the preview palette to position the Leaves. In this position, the light gray area is visible. If you like, check Shade Artwork to have the side and top art shaded.

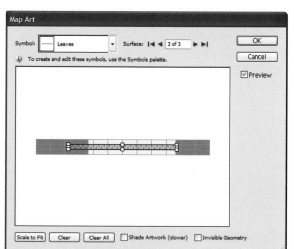

Position the leaves in the light gray area.

9   Click OK, and click OK again.

10   Choose File > Save.

Creating a revolved object

In this next lesson you will create the soap in the shape of a sphere. To begin with, create an arc that will be revolved to create the sphere.

1   Choose the Rectangle tool (▣) and click once on the artboard away from the artwork. When the Rectangle options dialog box appears, type **85 pt** for the Width and **100 pt** for the Height. Click OK.

2   Press D to return the rectangle back to the default colors of black stroke and white fill.

3   Press Ctrl+5 (Windows) or Command+5 (Mac OS) or choose View > Guides > Make Guides, to turn the rectangle into a custom guide.

4   As a default, guides are locked. To verify that guides are locked, choose View > Guides. If there is a check mark to the left of Lock Guides, they are locked. If there is no check mark, choose Lock Guides to lock them.

5   Using the Pen tool (✎), click on the lower right corner of the rectangle guide and drag to the left until the endpoint of the direction line reaches the lower left corner, and release. This creates a directional line.

6   Click on the upper right corner and drag to the right until the endpoint of the directional line reaches the upper left corner and release. You have created an arc.

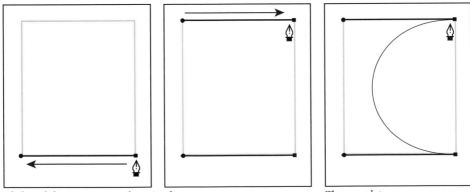

Click and drag to create a direction line.   *The complete arc.*

7   Choose View > Guides > Clear Guides.

8   Using the Selection tool, make sure the arc is selected.

9   Click on the Fill box in the Control palette. When the Swatches palette appears choose None (⬚).

10   Click on the Stroke box in the Control palette. When the Swatches palette appears choose yellow.

11   Choose Effect > 3D > Revolve. Click on Preview to see your changes.

The Revolve option appears. The options appear similar to the Extrude options, but have quite a different effect.

12   Leave the position at the default position of Off-Axis Front.

13   Change the edge from Left Edge to Right Edge. Your arch revolves around the designated edge. The result varies dramatically depending upon the side that you choose. Leave it set to Right Edge. Click OK.

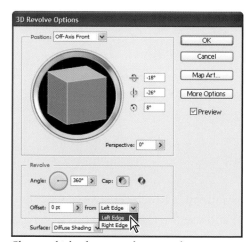

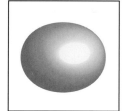

Choose which edge to revolve around.   *Revolve with Left Edge selected.*   *Revolve with Right Edge selected.*

14   File > Save, and keep the file open for the next lesson.

Changing the lighting

In this next lesson, you will use additional options to change the strength and direction of the light source.

1 With the lemon soap shape selected, double-click on 3D Revolve in the Appearance palette. If the Appearance palette is not visible, choose Window > Appearance.

2 Check the Preview checkbox, and press More Options.

Using More Options gives you the opportunity to create custom lighting effects on your 3D object. You will use the preview window in the lower left to reposition the lighting and change the shade color.

3 From the Surface drop-down menu, choose Diffuse Shading.

4 In the preview window, click and drag the white square that represents the light source. This changes the direction of the lighting. For this exercise, drag the light source to the top of the object.

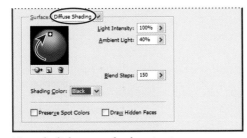

*Move the light source by dragging it
and change the Surface.*

5 Click on the Shading Color drop-down menu, and select Custom. Click on the colored Red square to the right of Custom and use the Color Picker to select a green color, or enter values in the color text fields to the right of the picker window (we used C=90%, M=0%, Y=100%, K=0%), then click OK.

The yellow shape now has green shading applied to it.

6   Change the Ambient Light to **40%**, then click OK.

Ambient light controls the brightness on the surface uniformly.

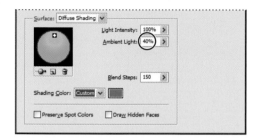

7   Position the soap closer to the soap tin.

8   Choose File > Save.

Mapping a Photoshop image

You can map artwork from Illustrator and also import artwork from other applications, such as Photoshop. In this next part of the lesson, you will place a Photoshop texture into the document, and apply it to the soap.

1   Choose File > Place, and locate the image named Lemonskin.psd in the Lesson12 folder. Make sure that Link is unchecked. Files to be used as symbols must be embedded. Press Place.

2   With the Symbols palette visible, use the Selection tool (k) to drag the image into the Symbols palette. Double-click on the new symbol in the Symbols palette and name it **Texture**.

3   Delete the placed image.

4   Select the soap, and double-click on 3D Revolve in the Appearance palette.

5   Click on Map Art, and then select the outer surface of the lemon. You may have one or more surfaces if the arc edges are not perfectly aligned. Use the Next Surface arrow pointing to right to navigate through the surfaces and choose the one that highlights the outer surface.

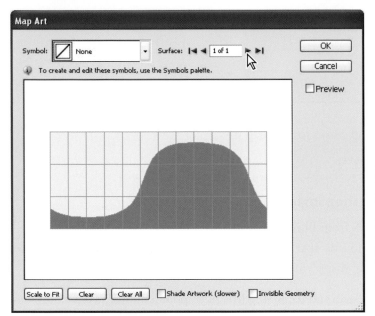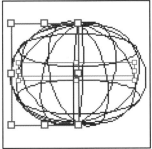

6   Once the surface is located, choose the Texture symbol from the Symbol drop-down menu.

7   Press Scale to Fit, and check Shade Art. Click OK, and OK again.

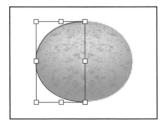

Map a Photoshop image.

The texture now wraps around the soap shape. Next you will clone the 3D objects to add more to the artboard.

8   Using the Selection tool, select the soap shape you just created. Hold down the Alt (Windows) or Option (Mac OS) key, and drag the shape next to itself (left or right), releasing the mouse first. This clones the shape. Clone one more time to have a total of three spheres.

Use Alt/Option to clone the spheres.

Adjusting the lighting

Since 3D objects do not share lighting, you will edit the existing Extrude and Bevel applied to the ellipse you used to create the soap tin.

1   Using the Selection tool (➤), click on the Lemon soap tin.

2   Double-click on 3D Extrude and Bevel to open the 3D options window.

3   In the lighting preview pane, drag the light to the top of the shape. This makes the lighting more consistent with the soap shapes. Click OK.

4   Choose File > Save. Leave the file open for the next lesson.

What are Blend Steps?

In More Options is a textbox for Blend Steps. As a default, this amount is low in order to quickly generate the blend and provide the optimum number of steps for artwork that is viewed on your computer monitor or on the Internet. This low number may cause banding (large, visible shifts of value from one tone to the next) when printing. To learn more about techniques used to avoid banding in gradients, read "To calculate the maximum blend length for gradients" in Illustrator Help.

Creating your own revolved artwork

This is when you have the opportunity to create your own 3D shape. In this next lesson you will create a path and adjust the offset to create a vase. An example of the path that we use is in the file named paths.ai in the Lesson12 folder, but it can be much more worthwhile to apply your own path and see the interesting results you can achieve.

1   Choose View Show Rulers, or Ctrl+R (Windows) or Command+R (Mac OS).

2   Create a vertical guide by clicking on the vertical ruler and dragging it out to a blank area on your artboard.

3   Choose the Pen tool (✎) and create a vertical path with several curves, representing the curves that will be replicated in the 3D shape. If it is easier, use the Pencil tool (✐) to draw a path. The size of the path is not important at this time, it can be scaled later.

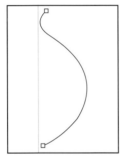

Create a path to revolve.

4   Using the Fill box in the Control panel, select a color for the fill, and choose None in the Stroke fill box.

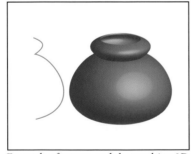 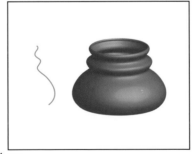

Example of curves and the resulting 3D shape.

5   Choose Effect > 3D > Revolve, and check the Preview checkbox.

6   Depending upon the effect you want to achieve, you can change the axis from the Left Edge to the Right Edge.

7   To make the 3D object wider, choose an offset. The slider moves rather quickly, so type **50** into the Offset text field. If necessary, uncheck and recheck Preview to see the results.

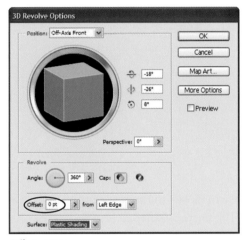

Offset at 0 pt.

Result.

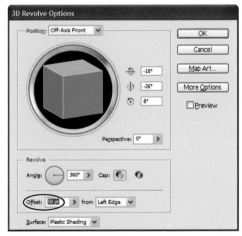

Offset at 50 pt.

Result.

If the lighting options are not visible, click on the More Options button to add an additional light source to the vase.

8   In the lighting preview window, click on the New button (⊡) to add another light source. Position the lights so that one is on the lower left and the other is in the upper right of the preview object.

9   Change the Ambient Light to **25%**.

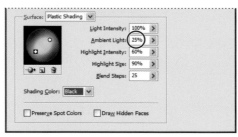

Click the new button to add additional light sources.

10   Click OK.

11   Using the Selection tool, move the vase in closer to the rest of the artwork and choose Object > Arrange > Send to back.

12   Use the Scale tool (⊡) if you feel it is necessary to make your vase larger or smaller.

Move the vase to the back.

13   File > Save. Leave this file open for the next lesson.

Using the 3D Rotate effect

Next you will create the place mat upon which the objects are sitting. For this example you will create a rectangle, fill it with a pattern and use the Rotate effect to make it look as though it is lying down on a flat surface.

1   Create a rectangle that encompasses the entire artwork.

2   Making sure that the Fill swatch is forward in the toolbox, select the pattern Stripes from the Swatches palette.

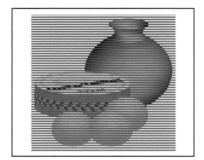

3   Give the rectangle a stroke of None.

4   With the rectangle still selected choose Effect > 3D > Rotate, and check Preview.

5   Using the text fields, enter **70%** for the rotation around the X axis. For the rotation around the Y axis, specify **0%**. Specify **0%** for the rotation around the Z axis.

6   Enter **75%** for the amount of perspective. Click OK.

The rectangle now looks like a place mat sitting on a table. Notice how the pattern also has the perspective applied to it.

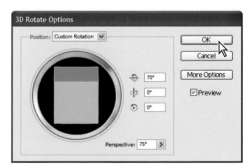

The Rotate Options window.   *Result.*

7   With the rectangle still selected, choose Object > Arrange > Send to Back. Using the Selection tool, position in place.

The completed illustration.

💡 *Once you have applied the 3D effect to an object, it remains a live effect. In other words, you can change the scale of the object or change the color, and the 3D effect remains.*

Note: *Do not rotate objects with the 3D effects applied to them; you will get unexpected results. To rotate a 3D object, double-click on the Appearance palette 3D effect, and rotate the item in space using the Position preview window.*

8   Once you have rearranged objects as you like, you have completed the lesson. Choose File > Save, then choose File > Close.

Exploring on your own

On your own, try to create an additional item for the artwork in this lesson. Choose File > Open, and locate the file in the Lesson12 folder named L12strt2.ai.

1   Choose the Selection tool, and then Select > All.

2   Drag the artwork into the Symbols palette.

3   Double-click on the Symbol in the Symbols palette and name it **Soap**.

4   With the artwork still selected, choose Edit > Clear, or press the Delete key.

5   Choose the Rectangle tool, and click once on the artboard. Enter the values of **325 pt** for the width and **220 pt** for the height; click OK.

6   Choose Effect > 3D > Extrude and Bevel, and experiment with different positions and settings.

7   Choose Map Art, and map the Symbol that you created (Soap) to the top of the box.

8   Click OK and then click OK again when you are finished.

Take the illustration further by creating your own symbols and applying them to the other faces of the box.

Review

▶ Review questions

1   What are the three types of 3D effects that are available? Give a good example of why you would use each one.

2   How can you control lighting on a 3D object? Does one 3D object's lighting affect other 3D objects.

3   What are the steps to mapping artwork to an object?

4   Once a 3D object is created, what is the best way to rotate it?

▶ Review answers

1   Using the 3D effect, you can choose from Extrude and Bevel, Revolve, and Rotate.

•   Extrude and Bevel—Uses the Z axis to give a 2D object depth by extruding the object. For example, a circle becomes a cylinder.

•   Revolve—Uses the Y axis to revolve an object around an axis. For example, an arc becomes a circle.

•   Rotate—Uses the Z axis to rotate 2D artwork in 3D space and change the artwork's perspective.

2   By clicking the More Options button in the 3D options window, you can change the light, the direction of the light, and the shade color. Options for one 3D object's lighting do not affect other 3D objects.

3 Map an artwork to an object by following these steps:

a Select the artwork and hold down the Alt/Option key and click on the New Symbol icon in the Symbols palette.

b Select the object that is to be 3D and choose Effects > 3D > Extrude and Bevel or Revolve.

c Click on Map Art.

d Select the surface using the arrows.

e From the Symbol drop-down menu, select the symbol.

f Click OK, and then click OK again.

4 Once you have created a 3D object, it is best to double-click on the 3D effect in the Appearance palette and use the Position preview window to position it in space. Using the Rotate tool will lead to unexpected results.

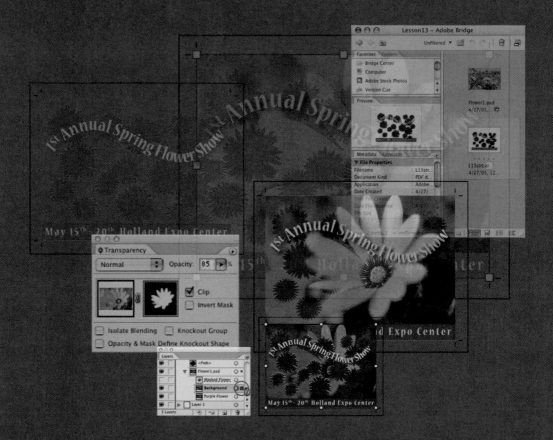

You can easily add an image created
in an image-editing program to an
Adobe Illustrator file. This is an
effective method for seeing how a
photograph looks incorporated with
a line drawing, or for trying out
Illustrator special effects on bitmap
images.

13 | Combining Illustrator CS2 Graphics with the Creative Suite

In this lesson, you'll learn how to do the following:

- Differentiate between vector and bitmap graphics.
- Place embedded Adobe Photoshop graphics in an Adobe Illustrator file.
- Create a clipping mask from compound paths.
- Make an opacity mask to display part of the image.
- Sample color in a placed image.
- Replace a placed image with another, and update the document.
- Export a layered file to Adobe Photoshop and edit the type.

Combining artwork

You can combine Illustrator artwork with images from other graphics applications in a variety of ways for a wide range of creative results. Sharing artwork between applications lets you combine continuous-tone paintings and photographs with line art. Even though Illustrator lets you create certain types of raster images, Photoshop excels at many image-editing tasks; once done, the images can then be placed in Illustrator.

To illustrate how you can combine bitmap images with vector art, and work between applications, this lesson steps you through the process of creating a composite image. In this lesson, you will add photographic images created in Adobe Photoshop to a postcard created in Adobe Illustrator. Then you'll adjust the color in the photo, mask the photo, and sample color from the photo to use in the Illustrator artwork. You'll update a placed image and then export your postcard to Photoshop to complete the type treatment.

Vector versus bitmap graphics

Adobe Illustrator creates vector graphics, also called draw graphics, which are made up of shapes based on mathematical expressions. These graphics consist of clear, smooth lines that retain their crispness when scaled. They are appropriate for illustrations, type, and graphics, such as logos, that may be scaled to different sizes.

Bitmap images, also called raster images, are based on a grid of pixels and are created by image-editing applications such as Adobe Photoshop. In working with bitmap images, you edit groups of pixels rather than objects or shapes. Because bitmap graphics can represent subtle gradations of shade and color, they are appropriate for continuous-tone images such as photographs or artwork created in painting programs. A disadvantage of bitmap graphics is that they lose definition and appear jagged when scaled up.

Logo drawn as vector art.

 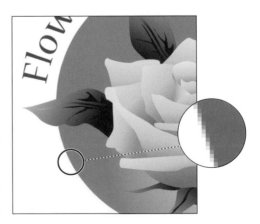

Logo rasterized as bitmap art.

In deciding whether to use Illustrator or a bitmap image program such as Photoshop for creating and combining graphics, consider both the elements of the image and how the image will be used. In general, use Illustrator if you need to create art or type with clean lines that will look good at any magnification. In most cases, you will also want to use Illustrator for laying out a design, because Illustrator offers more flexibility in working with type and with reselecting, moving, and altering images. You can create raster images in Illustrator but its pixel-editing tools are limited. Use Photoshop for images that need pixel-editing, color correcting, painting, and other special effects. Use InDesign for laying out anything from a postcard to a multiple chapter book such as this *Classroom in a Book*.

Getting started

Before you begin, you'll need to restore the default preferences for Adobe Illustrator. Then you'll open the finished art file for this lesson to see what you'll create.

1   To ensure that the tools and palettes function exactly as described in this lesson, delete or deactivate (by renaming) the Adobe Illustrator CS2 preferences file. See "Restoring default preferences" on page 3.

2   Start Adobe Illustrator.

3   Choose File > Open, and open the L13end.ai file in the Lesson13 folder, located inside the Lessons folder within the AICIB folder on your hard drive.

4   Choose View > Zoom Out to make the finished artwork smaller, adjust the window size, and leave it on-screen as you work. (Use the Hand tool (✋) to move the artwork where you want it in the window.) If you don't want to leave the image open, choose File > Close.

Now you'll open the start file to begin the lesson.

5 Choose File > Browse to open the Adobe Bridge, and Navigate to the L13strt.ai file (in the Lesson13 folder, inside the Lessons folder in the AICIB folder, on your hard drive), and choose Open.

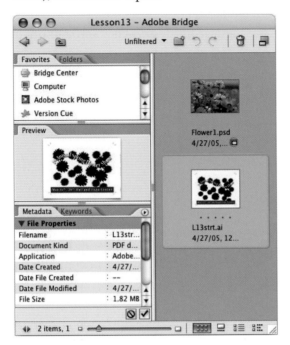

The file has been prepared with three layers: the Text layer, and two additional layers, Flowers and Layer 1, on which you'll place images. Flowers also contains objects that you'll make into a mask.

6   Choose File > Save As, name the file **Postcard.ai**, and select the Lesson13 folder. Leave the type of format set to Adobe Illustrator CS2 Document, and click Save. In the Illustrator Options dialog box leave at the default settings and click OK.

Placing an Adobe Photoshop file

You'll begin by placing a Photoshop file that contains two layer comps in the Illustrator document as an embedded file. Placed files can be embedded or linked. Embedded files are added to the Illustrator file, and the Illustrator file size increases to reflect the addition of the placed file. Linked files remain separate, external files, with a link to the placed file in the Illustrator file. (The linked file must always accompany the Illustrator file, or the link will break and the placed file will not appear in the Illustrator artwork.)

About layer comps

Designers often create multiple compositions, or comps, of a page layout to show clients. Using layer comps, you can create, manage, and view multiple versions of a layout in a single Photoshop or ImageReady file. Layer comps are fully interchangeable between Photoshop and ImageReady if the image color mode is RGB.

A layer comp is a snapshot of a state of the Layers palette. Layer comps record three types of layer options:

• Layer visibility—whether a layer is showing or hidden.

• Layer position in the document.

• Layer appearance—whether a layer style is applied to the layer and the layer's blending mode.

You create a comp by making changes to the layers in your document and updating the comp in the Layer Comps palette. You view comps by applying them in the document. You can export layer comps to separate files, to a single PDF, or to a web photo gallery.

1   Resize the Layers palette so you can see all the layers.

2   In the Layers palette, select the Flowers layer.

When you place an image, it is added to the selected layer. You'll use the Flowers layer for the placed image. The layer includes artwork for a mask for the image that you'll create later in the lesson.

3   Choose File > Place.

4   Navigate to the Flower1.psd file (in the Lesson13 folder inside the Lessons folder, in the AICIB folder, on your hard drive), and select it. Do not double-click the file or click Place yet.

5   If Link is checked, uncheck the Link option.

6   Click Place.

7   In the Photoshop Import dialog box, select Background 2 in the Layer Comp drop-down menu, then check the Show Preview option to view the comps.

8   Select the Convert Photoshop layers to objects option. Click OK.

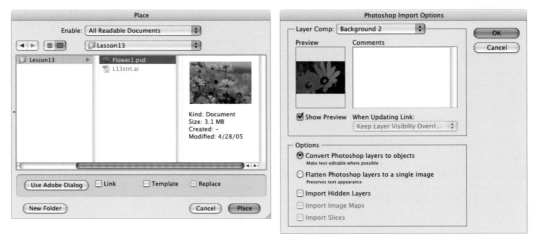

Rather than flatten the file, you want to convert the Photoshop layers to objects. This is because the Flower1.psd file contains two layers and one layer mask. You will use them later in the lesson.

Now you'll move the placed image, using the guides in the artwork to place the image precisely.

9   Choose the Selection tool (▸) in the toolbox. Click on the edge of the placed image (don't select a bounding box handle as it will resize the image), and drag the image onto the guides provided in the artwork. Release the mouse button when you have aligned the image with the guides.

By pressing the arrow keys you can nudge the selection into place.

The placed image covers up the black flowers in the Flowers layer. The placed image was added as a sublayer to the Flowers layer because it was selected when you chose the Place command.

10   Choose File > Save

Now you will move the image below the black flowers and duplicate it.

Duplicating a placed image

You can duplicate placed images just as you do other objects in an Illustrator file. The copy of the image can then be modified independently of the original.

Now you'll reposition and duplicate the Flower1.psd image in the Layers palette.

1   Click the Expand triangle (▶) to the left of the Flowers layer to expand it. Enlarge the Layers palette so that you can see all the contents of the Flowers layer.

2   Drag the Flower1.psd layer down the list until it is at the bottom of the Flowers layer. Release the mouse button when the indicator bar appears between the last <Path> layer and Layer 1.

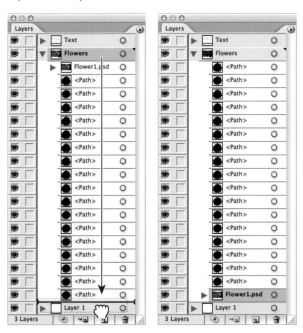

Indicator bar.   *Flower1.psd layer moved.*

3 Click the triangle to the left of the Flower1.psd layer to expand it. Notice that the Flower1.psd layer has two sublayers, Masked Flower and Background. You will now duplicate the Background layer.

4 To duplicate the Background layer, click on the named layer and drag its thumbnail onto the New Layer button at the bottom of the Layers palette. Another layer called Background is created.

5 Double-click the lower Background layer and rename it **Pink Flower**. Click OK. You will change the color of this image later in the lesson.

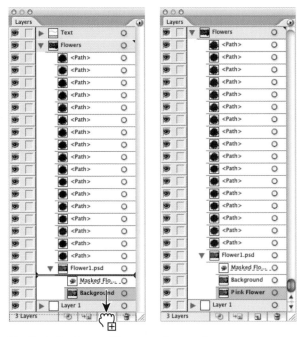

Duplicate Background layer.   *Rename layer.*

6 Choose File > Save.

Adjusting color in a placed image

Use filters to modify colors in placed images in a variety of ways. You can use filters to convert to a different color mode (such as RGB, CMYK, or grayscale) or to adjust individual color values. You can also use filters to saturate or desaturate (darken or lighten) colors, or invert colors (create a color negative).

For information on color modes and modifying colors with filters, see "About Color models and color modes" and "Applying filters and effects" in Illustrator Help.

In this section, you'll adjust colors in the Background layer. Later in the lesson, you'll apply a mask to this image and then adjust colors in the Pink Flower layer so that the two layers appear in contrasting colors through the mask.

1 In the Layers palette, select the Background sublayer.

2 Click the eye icon (👁) to the far left of the Masked Flower layer to hide it.

When you hide a layer, all objects on that layer are deselected, hidden, and locked.

3 In the Layers palette, click the selection column to the far right of the Background layer to select its contents quickly.

Masked Flower layer hidden and contents of Background layer selected.

4 Choose Filter > Colors > Adjust Colors.

5   In the Adjust Colors dialog box, select Preview so that you can see the color changes. Drag the sliders or enter values for the CMYK percentages to change the colors in the image. You can press Tab to move between the text fields. (We used the following values to create a blue/purple cast: C=54, M=20, Y=−59, and K=0.)

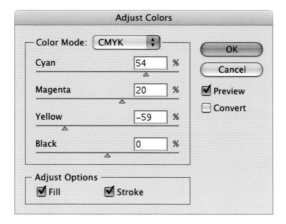

6   When you are satisfied with the color in the image, click OK.

7   Click outside the artwork to deselect the Background image, and then choose File > Save.

You can also use filters to apply special effects to images, distort images, produce a hand-drawn appearance, and create other interesting effects. See "Changing the appearance of bitmap images with filters and effects" in Illustrator Help.

Masking an image

Masks crop part of an image so that only a portion of the image appears through the shape of the mask. You can make a mask from a single path or a compound path. You can also import masks made in Photoshop files.

Creating compound paths and opacity masks

In this section, you'll create a compound path from the flower pattern on the Flower layer and create an opacity mask from the compound path, so that the Background layer appears through the mask. Then you'll adjust the colors in Pink Flower to contrast with the Background layer. You'll also use an opacity mask that was created in Photoshop and saved as a layer mask.

1   Select the Magic Wand tool (✻) in the toolbox.

2   Using the Magic Wand tool, click the upper left black flower in the flower pattern to select all the black flowers. This action selects the flowers and deselects the background.

🔲 You can use the Magic Wand tool to select all objects in a document with the same or similar fill color, stroke weight, stroke color, opacity, or blending mode. See "Using the Magic Wand tool and palette" in Illustrator Help.

3   Choose Object > Compound Path > Make.

Notice how all the flowers have been placed onto one layer, called <Compound Path>, in the Layers palette.

The Compound Path command creates a single compound object from two or more objects. Compound paths act as grouped objects. The Compound Path command lets you create complex objects more easily than if you used the drawing tools or the Pathfinder commands.

4   With the compound path selected, in the Layers palette Shift+click the selection column to the far right of the Background layer. This selects it and adds it to the <Compound Path> selection. (The Selection indicator (■) appears and the Background layer is added to the selection.)

Note: Both the masking object and the object to be masked must be selected in order to create a mask.

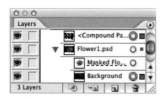

Background and
<Compound Path> selected.

5   Click the Transparency palette tab to bring it to the front of its group. (If the Transparency palette isn't visible on-screen, choose Window > Transparency.)

6   From the Transparency palette menu, choose Show Options.

Now you'll mask the Background layer with an opacity mask. This allows you to use the change in luminosity in the overlying flower pattern to affect the background. Similar to a clipping mask, an opacity mask lets you make color and other fine adjustments that you can't make with a clipping mask.

7   From the Transparency palette menu, choose Make Opacity Mask. Select both the Clip and Invert Mask options to see the effect.

Dotted line indicates mask.

Preview includes opacity mask.

The Background layer is now masked with the flower pattern, as indicated by the dotted underline beneath the layer name. The Pink Flower layer appears through the masked sections of the Background layer.

Now you'll apply the Adjust Colors filter to the Pink Flower layer to create a stronger contrast between the two images.

8   In the Layers palette, click to the right of the target indicator (○) of the Pink Flower layer to turn on the selection indicator (■). This selects only the Pink Flower layer's contents.

9   Choose Filter > Colors > Adjust Colors.

The most recently used filter (in this case, Adjust Colors) appears at the top of the Filter menu, letting you easily reapply the filter. (Choosing Filter > Apply Adjust Colors would apply the filter with the same settings used on the Background layer.)

10   Click Preview to preview changes in the artwork.

11   Drag the sliders for the CMYK values to change the colors in the image. (We used the following values to create a blue cast: C=–10, M=–17, Y=–91, and K=0.) Note that some of these numbers are negative. You can compare the color in Pink Flower to that in the Background layer to choose a color that contrasts effectively.

12   When you are satisfied with the color, click OK. With the Selection tool (➤), click outside the artwork to deselect the Pink Flower image.

13   Choose File > Save.

Editing an imported mask

You've made an opacity mask from artwork created in Illustrator. Now you'll use a mask that was created in Photoshop and imported when you placed the Flower1.psd file. You'll experiment with changing the color of the image and then adjusting the transparency of the opacity mask to tone down the effect.

1   In the Layers palette, click the eye column to show the Masked Flower layer.

2   Click the selection indicator (■) for the Masked Flower layer to select its contents. (The dotted line under its layer name indicates that the Masked Flower layer has an opacity mask applied to it.)

3   Choose Filter > Colors > Adjust Colors.

4   In the Adjust Colors dialog box, click Preview to preview changes in the artwork. Drag the sliders for the CMYK values to change the colors in the image. (We used the following values to create a yellow cast: C=–79, M=–35, Y=–22, and K=0.) Note that some of these numbers are negative. Click OK.

5   In the Transparency palette, change the opacity setting, enter **85** for the Masked Flower layer and press Enter.

Mask opacity set to 85%.   *Result.*

6   Choose File > Save.

Sampling colors in placed images

You can sample, or copy, the colors in placed images, to apply the colors to other objects in the artwork. Sampling colors enables you to easily make colors consistent in a file combining Photoshop images and Illustrator artwork.

In this section, you'll use the Eyedropper tool to sample colors from the placed image, and apply the colors to selected type on the Text layer.

1   Use the Selection tool (⬉) to click in the text at the bottom of the artwork to select the entire text block.

2   Click on Fill in the toolbox and use the Swatches palette change the Fill to None.

3   Select the Eyedropper tool (⬈), and Shift+click in the image to sample a color to be applied to the selected text. (We chose a yellow color from the petals of the flower in the middle.)

The color you sample is applied to the selected text.

4   Choose File > Save.

To copy appearance attributes using the Eyedropper tool

You can use the Eyedropper tool to copy appearance attributes from one object to another, including character, paragraph, fill, and stroke attributes between type objects. By default, the Eyedropper tool affects all attributes of a selection. To customize the attributes affected by this tool, use the Eyedropper dialog box.

1. Select the object, type object, or characters whose attributes you want to change.

2. Select the Eyedropper tool ( ).

3. Move the Eyedropper tool onto the object whose attributes you want to sample. (When you're correctly positioned over type, the pointer displays a small T.)

4. Do one of the following:

• Click the Eyedropper tool to sample all appearance attributes and apply them to the selected object.

• Shift-click to sample only the color from a portion of a gradient, pattern, mesh object, or placed image and apply the color to the selected fill or stroke.

• Hold down the Shift key and then the Alt (Windows) or Option (Mac OS) key while clicking to add the appearance attributes of an object to the selected object's appearance attributes. Alternatively, click first, and then hold down Shift and then Alt or Option.

Note: You can also click an unselected object to sample its attributes, and Alt-click (Windows) or Option-click (Mac OS) an unselected object to which you want to apply the attributes.

—From Illustrator Help

Replacing a placed image

You can easily replace a placed image with another image to update a document. The replacement image is positioned exactly where the original image was, so you don't have to align the replacement image. (If you scaled the original images, you may have to resize the replacement image to match the original image.)

Now you'll replace the Pink Flower image with the Flower1.psd image using Layer comp Background 1 to create a new version of the postcard.

1   Choose File > Save As, enter **Postcard2.ai** for the file name, and select the Lesson13 folder in the Save In menu. Leave the type of format set to Adobe Illustrator (.AI), and click Save. In the Illustrator options dialog box, leave at the default settings and click OK.

2   Click the Links tab to bring the Links palette to the front of its group. (If the Links palette isn't visible on-screen, choose Window > Links.)

3   Click the last link in the Links palette to select it. (These links don't have names because we embedded them instead of linking them.)

4   Click the Relink button (⬅) at the bottom of the Links palette.

5   In the Place dialog box, navigate to the Flower1.psd image in the Lesson13 folder and select it. Make sure that the Link option is deselected. Click Place and select Background 1 in the Layer comp drop-down menu to replace the Pink Flower image with the new one.

The replacement image appears in the Flowers layer as a Flowers1.psd sublayer with no color adjustments applied. When you replace an image, color adjustments you made to the original image are not applied to the replacement. However, masks applied to the original image are preserved. Any layer modes and transparency adjustments you've made to other layers also may affect the image's appearance.

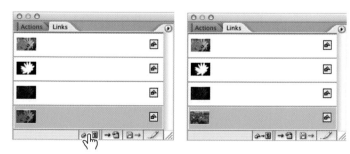

Select image in Links palette.   *Click Replace Link button to replace with new image.*

6   Choose File > Save.

You have completed the lesson. If you want to learn how to open and manipulate a layered Illustrator file in Photoshop, continue. If not, skip to "Exploring on your own".

Exporting a layered file to Photoshop

Not only can you open layered Photoshop files in Illustrator, but you can also save layered Illustrator files and then open them in Photoshop. Working with layered files between Illustrator and Photoshop is very helpful when creating and editing Web graphics. You can preserve the hierarchical relationship of the layers by selecting the Write Layers option when saving your file. You can also open and edit type objects.

1   Choose File > Export.

2   Navigate to the folder where you'll save the file, and name the file **Postcard2.psd**. Changing the file name preserves your original Illustrator file.

3   Choose Photoshop (PSD) from the Save as Type (Windows) or Format (Mac OS) drop-down menu, and click Save (Windows) or Export (Mac OS).

4   In the Photoshop Export Options dialog box, choose CMYK as the Color Model, select Screen (72 ppi) for Resolution, and check Write Layers. Leave Preserve Text Editability and Maximum Editability checked. Check Anti-alias. Click OK.

The Anti-alias option removes jagged edges in the artwork. The Write Layers option lets you export each Illustrator top-level layer as a separate Photoshop layer.

5   Start Adobe Photoshop CS2.

6   Open the Postcard2.psd file that you exported in step 4.

7   If prompted to update text layers, click Update.

8   Select the Type tool (T) in the toolbox.

9   Click the Type tool within the text on the path, and choose Select > All to select all the text.

10   In the control bar, change the text attributes by changing the font and size.

11   Choose File > Save. Choose File > Close to close the file.

Importing Adobe Illustrator graphics in InDesign CS2

How you save and import Illustrator graphics depends on how you want to edit the art once you place it in InDesign.

If you plan to edit a graphic only in Illustrator...

Save the graphic in native Illustrator format (.ai). Some graphics require the extensive drawing tools available in Illustrator or are in their final form and shouldn't be edited. In InDesign, you can place a native Illustrator graphic and transform it as a single object (you can resize or rotate it, for example). Use the Edit > Edit Original command to open the graphic in Illustrator and edit it there.

If you want to adjust layer visibility in InDesign...

Save the Illustrator CS2 file in layered PDF format. For some documents, you want to control the visibility of the layers of a graphic depending on the context. For example, for a multilanguage publication, you can create a single illustration that includes one text layer for each language. Using the layered PDF format, you can transform the illustration as a single object in InDesign but you cannot edit the paths, objects, or text within the illustration.

If you want to edit objects and paths in InDesign...

Copy the art from Illustrator and paste it into an InDesign document. For some graphics, you might want to edit them after they're placed in the InDesign document. For example, in a magazine, you might use the same design element in each issue, but want to change its color every month. If you paste a graphic into InDesign and edit it there, you cannot set layer transparency or edit the text.

Exploring on your own

Now that you know how to place and mask an image in an Illustrator file, you can place other images and apply a variety of modifications to the images. You can also create masks for images from objects you create in Illustrator. For more practice, try the following:

• In addition to adjusting color in images, apply transformation effects (such as shearing or rotating) or filters or effects (such as one of the Artistic or Distort filters/ effects), to create contrast between the two images in the flower pattern.

• Use the basic shapes tools or the drawing tools to draw objects to create a compound path to use as a mask. Then place the Flower1.psd image into the file with the compound path, and apply the compound path as a mask.

• Create large type and use the type as a mask to mask a placed object.

Review

▶ Review questions

1 Describe the difference between linking and embedding a placed file in Illustrator.

2 How do you create an opacity mask for a placed image?

3 What kinds of objects can be used as masks?

4 What color modifications can you apply to a selected object using filters?

5 Describe how to replace a placed image with another image in a document.

▶ Review answers

1 A linked file is a separate, external file connected to the Illustrator file by an electronic link. A linked file does not add significantly to the size of the Illustrator file. The linked file must accompany the Illustrator file to preserve the link and ensure that the placed file appears in the Illustrator file. An embedded file is included in the Illustrator file. The Illustrator file size reflects the addition of the embedded file. Because the embedded file is part of the Illustrator file, no link can be broken. Both linked and embedded files can be updated using the Replace Link button in the Links palette.

2 You create an opacity mask by placing the object to be used as a mask on top of the object to be masked. Then you select the mask and the objects to be masked, and choose Make Opacity Mask from the Transparency palette menu.

3 A mask can be a simple or compound path. You can use type as a mask. You can import opacity masks with placed Photoshop files. You can also create layer clipping masks with any shape that is the topmost object of a group or layer.

4 You can use filters to change the color mode (RGB, CMYK, or grayscale) or adjust individual colors in a selected object. You can also saturate or desaturate colors or invert colors in a selected object. You can apply color modifications to placed images, as well as to artwork created in Illustrator.

5   To replace a placed image, select the placed image in the Links palette. Then click the Replace Link button, and locate and select the image to be used as the replacement. Then click Place. The replacement image appears in the artwork in place of the original image.

The quality and color of your final printed output are determined by the process you follow to prepare an image for print. Whether you're printing a draft of your work on a desktop printer or outputting color separations to be printed on a commercial press, learning fundamental printing concepts helps ensure that your printed results meet your expectations.

14 | Printing Artwork and Producing Color Separations

In this lesson, you'll learn about the following:

- Different types of printing requirements and printing devices.
- Printing concepts and printing terminology.
- Basic color principles.
- How to separate your color artwork for output to print.
- How to use spot colors for two-color printing.
- Special considerations when outputting to print.

Printing: An overview

When you print a document from a computer, data is sent from the document to the printing device, either to be printed on paper or to be converted to a positive or negative image on film. For black-and-white, grayscale, or low quantities of color artwork, many people use desktop printers. However, if you require large quantities of printed output, such as a brochure or magazine ad, you'll need to prepare your artwork for output on a commercial printing press. Printing on a commercial press is an art that requires time and experience to perfect. In addition to close communication with a printing professional, learning basic printing concepts and terminology will help you produce printed results that meet your expectations.

Note: This lesson assumes that you have a desktop printer for use with the exercises. If you don't have a desktop printer available, you can read the sections and skip the step-by-step instructions.

Different printing requirements require different printing processes. To determine your printing requirements, consider the following: What effect do you want the printed piece to have on your audience? Will your artwork be printed in black and white? Color? Does it require special paper? How many printed copies do you need? If you're printing in color, is precise color matching necessary, or will approximate color matching suffice?

Take a moment to consider several types of printing jobs:

- A black-and-white interoffice newsletter, requiring a low quantity of printed copies. For this type of printing job, you can generally use a 300-600 dpi (dots per inch) desktop laser printer to output the original, and then use a copy machine to reproduce the larger quantity.

- A business card using black and one other color. The term two-color printing typically refers to printing with black and one other color, although it may also refer to printing with two colors that are not black. Two-color printing is less expensive than four-color printing and lets you select exact color matches, called spot colors, which can be important for logos. For precise color matching, two-color printing is done on a printing press; if only an approximate color match is required, you might use a desktop color printer.

- A party invitation using two colors and tints of those colors. In addition to printing two solid colors, you can print tints of the colors to add depth to your printed artwork. Two-color printing is often done on colored paper that complements the ink colors and might be done on a desktop color printer or on a printing press, depending on the desired quantity and the degree of color matching required.

- A newspaper. Newspapers are typically printed on a printing press because they are time-sensitive publications printed in large quantities. In addition, newspapers are generally printed on large rolls of newsprint, which are then trimmed and folded to the correct size.

- A fashion magazine or catalog requiring accurate color reproduction. Four-color printing refers to mixing the four process ink colors (cyan, magenta, yellow, and black, or CMYK) for printed output. When accurate color reproduction is required, printing is done on a printing press using CMYK inks. CMYK inks can reproduce a good amount of the visible color spectrum, with the exception of neon or metallic colors. You'll learn more about color models in the next section.

About printing devices

Now that you've looked at several types of publications and different ways to reproduce them, you'll begin learning basic printing concepts and printing terminology.

Halftone screens

To reproduce any type of artwork, a printing device typically breaks down the artwork into a series of dots of various sizes called a halftone screen. Black dots are used to print black-and-white or grayscale artwork. For color artwork, a halftone screen is created for each ink color (cyan, magenta, yellow, and black); these then overlay one another at different angles to produce the full range of printed color. To see a good example of how individual halftone screens overlay each other at different angles on a printed page, look at a color comics page through a magnifying glass.

The size of the dots in a halftone screen determines how light or dark colors appear in print. The smaller the dot, the lighter the color appears; the larger the dot, the darker the color appears.

Enlarged detail showing dots in halftone screen.

Screen frequency

Screen frequency (also called line screen, screen ruling, or halftone frequency) refers to the number of rows or lines of dots used to render an image on film or paper. In addition, the rows of dots are broken down into individual squares, called halftone cells. Screen frequency is measured in lines per inch (lpi) and is a fixed value you can set for your printing device.

As a general rule, higher screen frequencies produce finer detail in printed output. This is because the higher the screen frequency, the smaller the halftone cells, and subsequently, the smaller the halftone dot in the cell.

However, a high screen frequency alone does not guarantee high-quality output. The screen frequency must be appropriate to the paper, the inks, and the printer or printing press used to output the artwork. Your printing professional will help you select the appropriate line screen value for your artwork and output device.

Low-screen ruling (65 lpi) is often used to print newsletters.

High-screen ruling (150–200 lpi) is used for high-quality books.

Output device resolution

The resolution of a printing device describes the number of dots the printing device has available to render, or create, a halftone dot. The higher the output device resolution, the higher the quality of the printed output. For example, the printed quality of an image output at 2400 dots per inch (dpi) is higher than the printed quality of an image output at 300 dpi. Adobe Illustrator is resolution-independent and will always print at the printing device's highest resolution capability.

The quality of printed output depends on the relationship between the resolution of the output device (dpi) and the screen frequency (lpi). As a general rule, high-resolution output devices use higher screen frequency values to produce the highest quality images. For example, an imagesetter with a resolution of 2400 dpi and a screen frequency of 177 lpi produces a higher quality image than a desktop printer with a resolution of 300 to 600 dpi and a screen frequency of 85 lpi.

About color

Color is produced by a computer monitor and printing device using two different color models (methods for displaying and measuring color). The human eye perceives color according to the wavelength of the light it receives. Light containing the full color spectrum is perceived as white; in the absence of light, the eye perceives black.

The gamut of a color model is the range of colors that can be displayed or printed. The largest color gamut is that viewed in nature; all other color gamuts produce a subset of nature's color gamut. The two most common color models are red, green, and blue (RGB), the method by which monitors display color; and cyan, magenta, yellow, and black (CMYK), the method by which images are printed using four process ink colors.

The RGB color model

A large percentage of the visible spectrum of color can be represented by mixing three basic components of colored light in various proportions. These components are known as the additive colors: red, green, and blue (RGB). The RGB color model is called the additive color model because various percentages of each colored light are added to create color. All monitors display color using the RGB color model.

The CMYK color model

If 100% of red, green, or blue is subtracted from white light, the resulting color is cyan, magenta, or yellow. For example, if an object absorbs (subtracts) 100% red light and reflects green and blue, cyan is the perceived color. Cyan, magenta, and yellow are called the subtractive primaries, and they form the basis for printed colors. In addition to cyan, magenta, and yellow, black ink is used to generate true black and to deepen the shadows in images. These four inks (CMYK) are often called process colors because they are the four standard inks used in the printing process.

Spot colors

Whereas process colors are reproduced using cyan, magenta, yellow, and black inks, spot colors are premixed inks used in place of, or in addition to, CMYK colors. Spot colors can be selected from color-matching systems, such as the PANTONE® or TOYO™ color libraries.

Many spot colors can be converted to their process color equivalents when printed; however, some spot colors, such as metallic or iridescent colors, require their own plate on press.

Use spot color in the following situations:

- To save money on one-color and two-color print jobs. (When your printing budget won't allow for four-color printing, you can still print relatively inexpensively using one or two colors.)

- To print logos or other graphic elements that require precise color matching. You want the printer in Boston to use the same color of red as the printer in New York.

- To print special inks, such as metallic, fluorescent, or pearlescent colors.

Getting started

Before you begin, you must restore the default preferences for Adobe Illustrator CS2. Then you'll open the art file for this lesson.

1   To ensure that the tools and palettes function exactly as described in this lesson, delete or deactivate (by renaming) the Adobe Illustrator CS2 preferences file. See "Restoring default preferences" on page 3.

2   Start Adobe Illustrator CS2.

3   Choose File > Open, and open the L14strt1.ai file in the Lesson14 folder, located inside the Lessons folder within the AICIB folder on your hard drive.

4   Choose File > Save As, name the file **Circus.ai**, and select the Lesson14 folder. Leave the Format option set to Adobe Illustrator Document, and click Save. In the Illustrator Options dialog box, leave at the defaults and click OK.

What is color management?

Color-matching problems result from various devices and software using different color spaces. One solution is to have a system that interprets and translates color accurately between devices. A color management system (CMS) compares the color space in which a color was created to the color space in which the same color will be output, and makes the necessary adjustments to represent the color as consistently as possible among different devices.

A color management system translates colors with the help of color profiles. A profile is a mathematical description of a device's color space. This is also referred to as a device's color gamut, the range of color that it can interpret. Obviously, there will be some devices capable of seeing more color (or having a larger color gamut) than others. This is why Adobe applications use ICC profiles, a format defined by the International Color Consortium (ICC) as a cross-platform standard to keeping color within a device's gamut.

In this lesson you will see how to use Color Settings to prepare an Illustrator CS2 file for print output.

Setting up color management in Adobe applications.

The default color settings are sufficient for most users. However, you can change the color settings by doing one of the following:

If you installed Creative Suite 2 and use multiple Adobe applications, use Bridge to choose a standard color management configuration and synchronize color settings across applications before working with documents.

If you use only one Adobe application, or if you want to customize advanced color management options, you can change color settings for a specific application.

For this example, you will choose North America Prepress 2. If you have the entire suite loaded, try using the Synchronized method. If you did not install the entire Creative Suite 2, use the application method.

Synchronizing color using Adobe Bridge

When you set up color management using Adobe Bridge, color settings are automatically synchronized across applications.

1 Open Bridge.

2 To open Bridge from another Creative Suite application, choose File > Browse from the application. To open Bridge directly, either choose Adobe Bridge from the Start menu (Windows) or double-click the Adobe Bridge icon (Mac OS).

3 Choose Edit > Creative Suite Color Settings.

4   Select a North America Prepress 2 from the list, and click Apply.

Note: If none of the default settings were to meet your requirements, you could select Show Expanded List Of Color Setting Files to view additional settings. To install a custom settings file, such as a file you received from a print service provider, click Show Saved Color Settings Files.

Color Settings in Adobe Bridge, prior being Synchronized.

Color Settings after selecting a setting and choosing Apply.

Application color settings

Set up the Color Settings for only Adobe Illustrator CS2.

1   Choose Edit > Color Settings.

2   Select North America Prepress 2 from the Settings menu, and click OK. Your settings may become Unsynchronized, this is OK.

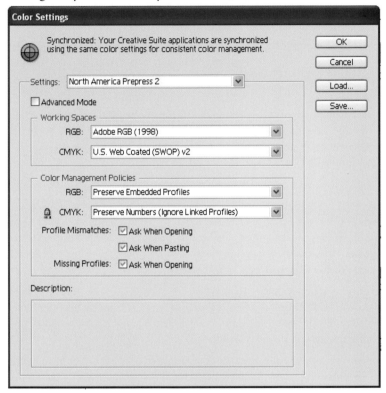

Color Settings in Illustrator CS2.

Note: By selecting the appropriate profile you are not magically guaranteeing perfect color, but you can expect a more realistic on-screen view of how the printed artwork will appear. Essentially, color management enables the RGB monitor to represent consistent color as it appears when printed in CMYK. Talk to your service provider or printer for more specifications that will help you create more accurate color.

About missing and mismatched color profiles

For a newly created document, the color workflow usually operates seamlessly: unless specified otherwise, the document uses the working space profile associated with its color mode for creating and editing colors.

However, some existing documents may not use the working space profile that you have specified, and some existing documents may not be color-managed. It is common to encounter the following exceptions to your color-managed workflow:

You might open a document or import color data (for example, by copying and pasting or dragging and dropping) from a document that is not tagged with a profile. This is often the case when you open a document created in an application that either does not support color management or has color management turned off.

You might open a document or import color data from a document that is tagged with a profile different from the current working space. This may be the case when you open a document that has been created using different color management settings, or a document that has been scanned and tagged with a scanner profile.

In either case, the application uses a color management policy to decide how to handle the color data in the document.

If the profile is missing or does not match the working space, the application may display a warning message, depending on options you set in the Color Settings dialog box. Profile warnings are turned off by default, but you can turn them on to ensure the appropriate color management of documents on a case-by-case basis. The warning messages vary between applications, but in general you have the following options:

- (Recommended) Leave the document or imported color data as it is. For example, you can choose to use the embedded profile (if one exists), leave the document without a color profile (if one doesn't exist), or preserve the numbers in pasted color data.

- Adjust the document or imported color data. For example, when opening a document with a missing color profile, you can choose to assign the current working space profile or a different profile. When opening a document with a mismatched color profile, you can choose to discard the profile or convert the colors to the current working space. When importing color data, you can choose to convert the colors to the current working space in order to preserve their appearance.

—From Illustrator Help

Printing black-and-white proofs

As a general rule, you should print black-and-white proofs of all your documents at different stages of your work to check the layout and to verify the accuracy of text and graphics before preparing the document for final output.

Now you'll print a draft of the Circus.ai file.

1   In the Circus.ai file, notice the crop marks, the pairs of lines at each corner of the artwork. Crop marks define where the artwork is trimmed after it is printed. The crop marks indicate a bleed, the area of artwork that falls outside the crop marks, and which will be removed when the printed artwork is trimmed. The bleed is used to ensure that the artwork prints to the edge of the trimmed page. For more information on bleed, read "Specifying the bleed area" later in this lesson.

You can set crop marks where you want them directly in the artwork. See "To define the crop area" in Illustrator Help.

2   If you're not connected to a black-and-white printer, go on to the next section.

3   Choose File > Print, leave all choices set at the defaults, and click OK (Windows) or Print (Mac OS).

The circus logo is printed in black, white, and shades of gray. Next, you'll soft-proof the color on your monitor screen.

Soft-proofing colors

In a color-managed work flow, you can use the precision of color profiles to soft-proof your document directly on the monitor. Soft-proofing lets you preview on-screen how your document's colors will look when reproduced on a particular output device.

The reliability of soft-proofing completely depends, however, on the quality of your monitor, your monitor profile, and the ambient lighting conditions of your workstation area. In other words, if you are working in an inconsistent environment with varying light throughout the day, you might not get reliable results. For information on creating a monitor profile, see "To calibrate and profile your monitor" in Illustrator Help.

1   Choose View > Proof Setup > Customize. The profile is set to U.S. Web Coated (SWOP) v2. Leave it set to this profile, and click OK.

The View > Proof Colors option is selected by default (indicated by a check mark) so that you can view the artwork as it will look when printed to the selected standard, U.S. Web Coated (SWOP) v2.

Next, you'll change the profile to see what the image will look like if printed on a different output device.

2   Choose View > Proof Setup > Customize.

3   Use the Proof Setup menu to select Euroscale Uncoated v2, and click OK. Because the view is still set to Proof Colors, the image preview automatically shifts colors to display what it would look like were it printed according to the Euroscale Uncoated profile.

Use Proof Setup to change the color preview.

You'll now return the settings to the SWOP settings.

4   Choose View > Proof Setup > Customize. Set the profile to U.S. Web Coated (SWOP) v2, and click OK.

5   Choose View > Proof Colors to turn off the soft-proofing preview.

Next, you'll work with printing color artwork.

Using the Document Info command

Before you take your color artwork to a prepress professional or begin the process of creating color separations on your own, use the Document Info command to generate and save a list of information about all the elements of your artwork file. The Document Info command displays a palette of information on the objects, linked or placed files, colors, gradients, patterns, and fonts in your document.

If you're working with prepress professionals, be sure to provide them with the Document Info list before delivering your files; they can help you determine what you'll need to include with your artwork. For example, if your artwork uses a font that the prepress house does not have, you'll need to bring or supply a copy of the font with your artwork.

1   Choose Window > Document Info. The Document Info palette appears.

2   In the Document Info palette, select different subjects about the document from the palette menu in the upper right corner. The list box displays information about each subject you select.

3   If you have an object selected in the artwork, choose Selection Only from the Document Info palette menu to display information only on that selected object. A check mark indicates that the Selection Only option is turned on.

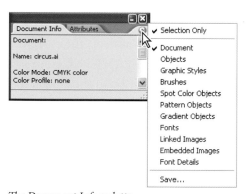

The Document Info palette.

You can also view or print the entire contents of the Document Info palette by saving it, and then opening it in a text editor.

4   To save the Document Info text, choose Save from the palette menu, enter a name for the Document Info file, and click Save. You can open the file in any text editor to review and print the contents of the file.

5   When you have looked through the information on the file, you can leave the Document Info palette open onscreen or close it.

Creating color separations

To print color artwork on a printing press, you must first separate the composite art into its component colors: cyan, magenta, yellow, and black, and any spot colors, if applicable. The process of breaking composite artwork into its component colors is called color separation.

You set separation options in the Print dialog box. It's important to note that before setting separation options, you need to discuss the specific requirements of your print job with your printing professional. (You cannot separate to a non-PostScript® printer.)

1   Make sure that the Circus.ai artwork is still open.

2   Select the Selection tool (◤) in the toolbox. Then click various objects in the artwork to select them.

3   If the Color palette is not visible, choose Window > Color palette. Choose Show Options from the Color palette menu.

As you select different objects, notice that the Color palette reflects the current color's attributes. For example, if you click the flag atop the tent, a PANTONE color swatch appears in the Color palette; if you click the red or green stripe in the clown, the color is mixed using CMYK values.

Selecting a printer description file

The set-up for separations and other options occurs in the Print dialog box.

Important: To be able to continue with this section, your computer must be connected to a PostScript printer. If you are connected to an ink-jet printer or not connected to a printer, the separation options will be dimmed in the Print dialog window.

1   Choose File > Print. The first drop-down window labeled Print Preset is left alone at this point. You will learn how to take your options and turn them into presets later in this lesson.

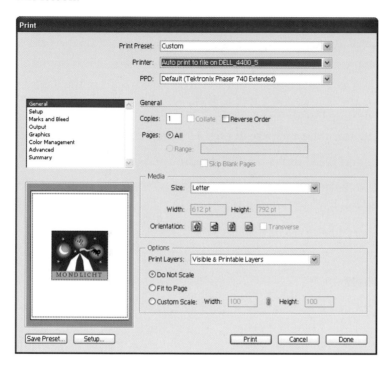

2   First, make sure that you have a printer selected in the Printer drop-down box. If not, select a Postscript printer at this point.

3   Select a PPD.

PostScript Printer Description (PPD) files contain information about the output device, including available page sizes, resolution, available line screen (frequency) values, and the angles of the halftone screens.

Note: *A PostScript Printer Description file with limited selections has been placed in the Lesson14 folder for this exercise. When you install Adobe Illustrator, two PPDs are automatically installed in the Utilities folder within the Adobe Illustrator folder, and additional PPDs are provided on the Adobe Illustrator CD.*

4   In the PPD drop-down window, choose Other.

5   Navigate to the General.ppd file, located in the Lesson14 folder, inside the Lessons folder within the AICIB folder on your hard drive. Click Open.

The Print dialog box is updated with general printer parameters, and a preview of your artwork is displayed on the lower left side of the dialog box. (The preview of your artwork depends on the page size selected in the Page Size menu. Each output device has a variety of page sizes available; select the desired page size from the Page Size menu in the Print dialog box.)

6   Choose US Letter for the paper size in the Media section.

7   Click on Marks and Bleed in the options window on the left.

In this window you can choose which printer's marks are visible. Printer's marks help the printer align the color separations on the press, and check the color and density of the inks being used.

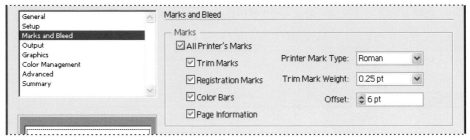

Add all printer's marks, or select just the ones that you want.

8 Click the checkbox to show All Printer's Marks.

The preview shows the crop and other marks in the preview.

Select printer's marks.

A. *Registration mark.* **B.** *Page Information.*
C. *Crop mark.* **D.** *Color bar.*

Specifying the bleed area

Bleed is the amount of artwork that falls outside the printing bounding box or outside the crop marks and trim marks. You can include bleed in your artwork as a margin of error—to ensure that the ink is still printed to the edge of the page after the page is trimmed or to ensure that an image can be stripped into a keyline in a document. Once you create the artwork that extends into the bleed, you can use Illustrator to specify the extent of the bleed.

Changing the bleed moves the crop marks farther from, or closer to, the image; however, the crop marks still define the same size printing bounding box.

Small bleed. *Large bleed.*

1 Specify a bleed of **18 pt** by typing it in the Top bleed text field. If the Link button does not have a square surrounding it, click it now to activate equal bleed settings on all sides.

Add a bleed equal on all sides using the Link button.

This means that the artwork extends 18 points beyond the crop marks on your film. The maximum bleed you can set is 72 points; the minimum bleed is 0 points.

The size of the bleed depends on its purpose. A press bleed (that is, an image that bleeds off the edge of the printed sheet) should be at least 18 points. If the bleed is to ensure that an image fits a keyline, it needs to be no more than 2 or 3 points. Your print shop can advise you on the size of the bleed necessary for your particular job.

For more help, use Illustrator Help "Marks and bleed options for Adobe PDF."

Separating colors

1 Click on Output in the Options window on the left side of the Print dialog window. Choose Separations (Host Based).

The circus artwork is composed of process colors and spot colors, which are displayed in the Document Ink Options window.

To the left of the process color names, a printer icon (🖨) is displayed, indicating that a separation will be generated for each color. To the left of the spot color names, a spot color icon (●) is displayed, indicating that the spot colors will be printed as separate colors.

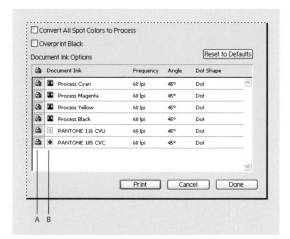

A. Indicates that the color will print.
B. Indicates a spot color.

Illustrator CS2 output mode options

Illustrator CS2 provides three choices for generating color separations:

• Composite—This mode sends all of the color information in your file to your output device. This is the typical setting for everyday printing to a desktop color printer or a color copier.

• Separations (Host Based)—This mode produces the separations on your computer and sends the separated data to your output device.

• In-RIP Separations—This mode performs color separations at the RIP (Raster Image Processor), leaving the host computer free to perform other tasks. When using this mode the output device receiving the data must support In-RIP separations.

If you were to print color separations at this point, all the colors, including the spot colors in the artwork, would be printed into six separations.

Check the box to the left of Convert all Spot colors to Process. Now the spot colors will be broken down into the CMYK builds, and would be printed into four separations.

Composite image.

Cyan separation.

Magenta separation.

Yellow separation.

Black separation.

2   Uncheck the Convert Spot Color To Process, and the spot colors are no longer grayed out, and the process icon to the left returns to a spot icon, indicating that they are going to print.

As you learned earlier, you can print separations using process colors or spot colors, or you can use a combination of both. You'll convert only the first spot color (PANTONE 116) to a process color because a precise color match isn't necessary. The second spot color, PANTONE 185 CVC, will stay a spot color because a precise color match is desired.

3 To convert Pantone 116 to a process color, click the spot color icon to the left of its name in the list of colors.

Document Ink	Frequency	Angle	Dot Shape
Process Cyan	60 lpi	45°	Dot
Process Magenta	60 lpi	45°	Dot
Process Yellow	60 lpi	45°	Dot
Process Black	60 lpi	45°	Dot
PANTONE 116 CVU	60 lpi	45°	Dot
PANTONE 185 CVC	60 lpi	45°	Dot

☐ Convert All Spot Colors to Process
☐ Overprint Black
Document Ink Options   [Reset to Defaults]

[Print]   [Cancel]   [Done]

Click on the color swatch to the left of the color name to change it to process or spot.

If you were to print at this point, five separations would be generated: one each for the cyan, magenta, yellow, and black plates (including the spot color converted to a process color); and a single plate for the PANTONE 185 CVC spot color. (This job would require a more specialized press, capable of printing five colors, or the paper would have to be sent back through the press to print the fifth color.)

Composite image.

Cyan separation.

Magenta separation.

Yellow separation.

Black separation.

Spot separation.

Specifying the screen frequency

At the beginning of this lesson, you learned that the relationship between the output device resolution and the screen frequency determines the quality of the printed output. Depending on the output device you select, more than one screen frequency value may be available. Your printing professional will direct you to select the screen frequency appropriate to your artwork.

1   In the Printer Resolution drop-down menu, choose 60 lpi/300 dpi from the Halftone menu. The first value, 60, represents the screen frequency (lpi), and the second value, 300, represents the output device resolution (dpi).

Additional separation options, such as Emulsion Up/Down, and Positive or Negative film, should be discussed with your printing professional, who can help you determine how these options should be set for your particular job.

Before printing your separations to a high-resolution output device, it's a good idea to print a set of separations, called proofs, on your black-and-white desktop printer. You'll save time and money by making any needed corrections to your files after reviewing the black-and-white proofs.

2   Click on Save Preset button in the lower left of the Print dialog box to name and save this setting for future use. This customer always uses the same settings, so we will name it with their name **Circus**. In the future you can choose this Preset from the Preset drop-down window at the top. Click OK.

Save frequently used print settings as presets.

3   Choose Print to print separations. Five pieces of paper should be printed—one each for cyan, magenta, yellow, and black, and one for the spot color.

Note: *Depending on your chosen printer, you may get a warning message that your PPD doesn't match the current printer. Click Continue to print the proofs.*

4   File > Save and close the Circus.ai file.

Working with two-color illustrations

As you learned earlier, two-color printing generally refers to black and one spot color, but may also refer to two spot colors. In addition to printing the two solid colors, you can print tints, or screens, of the colors. Two-color printing is much less expensive than four-color printing and lets you create a rich range of depth and color when used effectively.

Editing a spot color

In this section, you'll open a two-color version of the circus illustration containing black, a spot color, and tints of the spot color. Before you separate the illustration, you'll replace the current spot color with another from the PANTONE color library. Illustrator lets you make global adjustments to spot colors and tints of spot colors using a keyboard shortcut.

1   Choose File > Open, and open the L14strt2.ai file in the Lesson14 folder, located inside the Lessons folder within the AICIB folder on your hard drive.

Because you have set up Illustrator to work with a color management profile, you may be prompted each time you open a new file if you want to change how that file is color managed.

2   At the prompt, select Assign current working space, and click OK.

Since Color Management is turned on, you will be prompted with this window when opening files.

3   Choose File > Save As, name the file **Twocolor.ai**, and select the Lesson14 folder in the Save As dialog box. Leave the type of file format set to Adobe Illustrator Document, and click Save. In the Illustrator Options dialog box, leave at the defaults and click OK.

4　Make sure that the Color palette and the Swatches palette are open and visible; if they aren't, use the Window menu to display them.

5　From the Color palette's menu (arrow in the upper right of the palette) choose to Show Options.

6　Using the Selection tool (⬏) click any colored part of the circus tent. Notice the PANTONE 116 C swatch in the Color palette.

Next, you'll replace every instance of the spot color (including any tints of the color) with another spot color.

7　The Swatches palette, like most others, has three different views which you can use. In order to see the swatch color name and the swatch, click on the palette menu in the upper right of the Swatch palette, and choose List View. This provides you with information such as a visual of the swatch, its name and whether it is a process, RGB or spot color.

Change the Swatch palette to List View in order to read the swatch names.

8　Choose Select > Deselect or Ctrl+click (Windows) or Command+click (Mac OS), away from the artwork to deselect it.

9   Choose Window > Swatch Libraries > PANTONE Solid Coated. The PANTONE swatch library appears. From the palette menu, change this palette to be in list view.

You can choose new spot colors from the swatch library by typing the number of the color you want to use.

10   Choose Show Find Field from the Pantone solid coated palette menu and then click in the Find text field. Type **193**. PANTONE 193 C is selected in the palette.

Next, you'll replace the current PANTONE color with the new PANTONE color.

11   Drag the title bar of the PANTONE Solid Coated swatch library closer to the Swatches palette.

12   If necessary, scroll down on the Swatches palette until Pantone 116 is visible, then hold down Alt (Windows) or Option (Mac OS), and drag the PANTONE 193 C swatch from the PANTONE Solid Coated swatch library onto the PANTONE 116 swatch in the Swatches palette.

As you Alt/Option+drag the swatch, the cursor changes to a crosshair.

The PANTONE 193 C replaces the PANTONE 116 C swatch in the Swatches palette, and the artwork is updated with the new PANTONE Solid color.

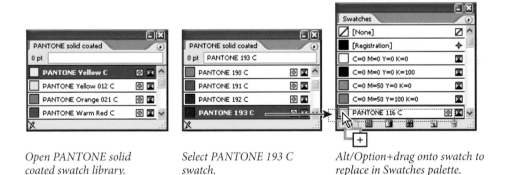

Open PANTONE solid coated swatch library.   *Select PANTONE 193 C swatch.*   *Alt/Option+drag onto swatch to replace in Swatches palette.*

Notice that the updated red swatch still is named PANTONE 116 C. You need to rename the updated swatch to avoid confusion about the spot color when your artwork is printed by a commercial press.

13   In the Swatches palette, double-click the updated swatch (still named PANTONE 116 C), and rename the swatch to match its color, PANTONE 193 C. Click OK.

Note: Certain three-digit Pantone values may require you to add a space before entering the value.

Separating spot colors

As you learned in "Separating colors" earlier in this lesson, you can convert spot colors to their process color equivalents, or you can output them to their own separation. When you're working with a two-color illustration, separating spot colors into their process color equivalents is less cost-effective than outputting the spot color to its own separation (converting to four CMYK plates versus one plate for each individual spot color). You'll deselect the Convert to Process option in the Separation Setup dialog box to output each spot color to its own separation.

Composite image.

Separation 1: Black.

Separation 2: Spot color.

1   Choose File > Print.

2   Click on Output in the Options window on the left.

3   Select Separations (Host-Based) for the Mode.

4   You may notice printer icons (🖶) to the left of multiple colors. Since this is a two-color job, make sure that you leave on only process black and PANTONE 193 C. Click on the printer icon of any unnecessary colors to turn off printing.

	☒	Process Cyan	94.8683 lpi	71.5651°	Dot
	☒	Process Magenta	94.8683 lpi	18.4349°	Dot
	☒	Process Yellow	100 lpi	0°	Dot
🖶	☒	Process Black	106.0660 lpi	45°	Dot
🖶	◉	PANTONE 193 C	106.0660 lpi	45°	Dot

The printer icon indicates that the color will print.

5   Click Save Preset, and name the Preset **Circus 2-color** to save these separation settings.

6   Click Done to save the settings, but do not print at this time.

7 Save and Close the Twocolor.ai file.

Creating a trap

Trapping is used to compensate for any gaps or color shifts that may occur between adjoining or overlapping objects when printing. These gaps or color shifts occur from misregistration, the result of the paper or the printing plates becoming misaligned during printing. Trapping is a technique developed by commercial print shops to slightly overprint the colors along common edges.

Gap created by misregistration. *Gap removed by trapping.*

Although trapping sounds simple enough, it requires a thorough knowledge of color and design and an eye for determining where trapping is necessary. You can create a trap in Adobe Illustrator CS2 using two methods: by applying the Trap filter or Trap effect, for simple artwork whose parts can be selected and trapped individually; and by setting a Stroke value for individual objects you want to trap. Like printing, creating a trap is an art that requires time and experience.

About trapping

Where colors printed from separate plates overlap or adjoin one another, press misregistration can cause gaps between colors on the final output. To compensate for potential gaps between colors in artwork, print shops use a technique called trapping to create a small area of overlap (called a trap) between two adjoining colors. You can use a separate, dedicated trapping program to create traps automatically, or you can use Illustrator to create traps manually.

There are two types of trap: a spread, in which a lighter object overlaps a darker background and seems to expand into the background; and a choke, in which a lighter background overlaps a darker object that falls within the background and seems to squeeze or reduce the object.

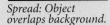

Spread: Object overlaps background.   *Choke: Background overlaps object.*

When overlapping painted objects share a common color, trapping may be unnecessary if the color that is common to both objects creates an automatic trap. For example, if two overlapping objects contain cyan as part of their CMYK values, any gap between them is covered by the cyan content of the object underneath.

Trapping type can present special problems. Avoid applying mixed process colors or tints of process colors to type at small point sizes, because any misregistration can make the text difficult to read. Likewise, trapping type at small point sizes can result in hard-to-read type. As with tint reduction, check with your print shop before trapping such type. For example, if you are printing black type on a colored background, simply overprinting the type onto the background may be enough.

—From Illustrator Help

Overprinting objects

When preparing an image for color separation, you can define how you want overlapping objects of different colors to print. By default, the top object in the Illustrator artwork knocks out, or removes the color of, underlying artwork on the other separations and prints with the color of the top object only. Misregistration may occur when you knock out colors.

Composite image.   *First plate.*   *Second plate.*

You can also specify objects to overprint, or print on top of, any of the artwork under them. Overprinting is the simplest method you can use to prevent misregistration (gaps between colors) on press. The overprinted color automatically traps into the background color.

Composite image.   *First plate.*   *Second plate.*

You'll select an object in the circus illustration and apply the overprint option. Then you will preview the overprint on-screen.

1 Choose File > Open. Locate and open the Circus.ai file, which you saved in the Lesson14 folder, inside the Lessons folder within the AICIB folder on your hard drive.

2   In the Missing Profile dialog box, select Assign Current Working Space: US Web Coated (SWOP) v2, and click OK.

The color version of the circus illustration appears.

3   Choose View > Zoom In to zoom in on the lion. You'll be able to see the overprint lines better if you magnify the view of the image. (We zoomed in to 400%.)

4   Choose the Selection tool (▶) in the toolbox. Then click the lion to select it.

5   Click the Attributes tab to bring the palette to the front of its group. (If the Attributes palette isn't open, choose Window > Attributes.)

6   In the Attributes palette, select Overprint Fill.

Now you'll see an approximation of how overprinting and blending will appear in the color-separated output.

7   Choose View > Overprint Preview to see the effect of the overprinted objects. The effect is subtle; look closely at the tip of the flag to see the overprinting.

If an object has a stroke, you can also select the Overprint Stroke option to make sure that the stroke overprints on the object below it as well. Next you'll add a stroke to an object to create a trap.

8   With the Selection tool, select the yellow flag to the left of the lion.

9   Click the Color tab to bring the palette to the front.

10   In the Color palette, drag the yellow fill swatch onto the Stroke box to stroke the flag with the same color as its fill.

11   Click the Attributes tab to bring the palette to the front of its group. Select the Overprint Stroke option.

Drag the Fill swatch   Result.   Select Overprint Stroke option.
onto the Stroke box.

Depending on what you have discussed with your printing professional, you may want to change the amount of trap specified. You'll try out changing the specified trap now.

12   Select the flag shape with the overprint stroke.

13   Click the Stroke tab to bring the palette to the front of its group. Increase the Stroke weight. In Overprint Preview you can see the results.

No Overprint preview.   Overprint preview.

Strokes are centered over the object's path. This means that if an object is stroked with the same color as its fill, only half the stroke weight actually overprints. For example, if your printing professional wants a 0.5-point trap added to the yellow flag, you would use a 1-point stroke weight to achieve the trap. Half the stroke will appear inside the fill area, and half will appear outside the fill area.

14 Choose File > Save. Choose File > Close to close the file.

You've finished the lesson. In an ordinary workflow situation, you would now be ready to send your artwork to a commercial press to be printed. Include proofs of color separation setups when you send your electronic file to a printer. Also tell your printer about any traps you created in the artwork. Keep in mind that you must remain in close communication with your printing professional for each print job. Each print job has unique requirements that you must consider before you begin the process of color separation.

Review

Review questions

1   How do the RGB and CMYK color gamuts affect the relationship between on-screen colors and printed colors?

2   How can you create a closer match between your on-screen colors and printed colors?

3   What is the benefit of printing interim drafts of your artwork to a black-and-white desktop printer?

4   What does the term color separation mean?

5   What are two ways to output spot colors?

6   What are the advantages of one- or two-color printing?

7   What is trapping?

8   What is a simple method you can use to create trap?

▶ **Review answers**

1   Each color model has a gamut of color that overlaps but does not precisely match the others. Because monitors display color using the RGB color gamut, and printed artwork uses the smaller CMYK color gamut, there may be times when a printed color cannot precisely match an on-screen color.

2   You can select one of Illustrator's built-in color management profiles to better simulate the relationship between on-screen colors and printed colors. You can choose View > Proof Setup and select an output device profile. Then choose View > Proof Colors to get an on-screen version of how the artwork will look when printed to the selected device.

3   It's a good idea to print black-and-white drafts of your artwork on a desktop printer to check the layout and the accuracy of text and graphics in your publication before incurring the expense of printing to a color printer or imagesetter (for separations).

4   Color separation refers to breaking down composite artwork into its component colors—for example, using the four process colors (cyan, magenta, yellow, and black) to reproduce a large portion of the visible color spectrum.

5   You can convert a spot color to its process color equivalents if a precise color match is not required, or you can output a spot color to its own separation.

6   One- or two-color printing is less expensive than four-color printing, and you can use spot colors for precise color matching.

7   Trapping is a technique developed by commercial print shops to slightly overprint the colors along common edges, and it is used to compensate for any gaps or color shifts that may occur between adjoining or overlapping objects when printed.

8   You can specify objects to overprint, or print on top of, any of the artwork under them. Overprinting is the simplest method you can use to create a trap, which compensates for misregistration on press.

Adobe Bridge provides powerful tools for locating, previewing and organizing your files.

If you use Adobe Illustrator as a part of the Adobe Creative Suite 2, you can take advantage of Version Cue to help manage your files.

15 | Working with Adobe Bridge and Version Cue

In this lesson, you'll learn how to do the following:

- Use Adobe Bridge to access and organize files.

- Save files as groups.

- Set up a Version Cue project.

- Create and use file versions.

Note: This lesson is for users who have installed Adobe Illustrator as part of Adobe Creative Suite 2. If you use Adobe Creative Suite 2, you have access to the full set of Version Cue features discussed in this lesson, including Version Cue Administration. If you use only Illustrator CS2, you have access to the features of the Adobe dialog box only. You can use Bridge, rather than the Adobe dialog box, for file browsing. If you don't have Adobe Creative Suite, you can gain access to the full Version Cue feature set by participating in a shared project; that is, if another user on your network installs Adobe Creative Suite 2 and gives you access to a Version Cue project in a Version Cue Workspace.

Getting started

In this lesson, you'll use the Adobe Bridge to locate and access Adobe Illustrator files. You will then create a Version Cue project and create multiple versions using Version Cue.

1 Start Adobe Illustrator CS2.

2 Start Adobe Bridge by doing either one of the following:

- Choose File > Browse from within Adobe Illustrator CS2.

- Click the Go to Bridge button (🖼) in the Control Palette.

The Adobe Bridge application starts, and a new window opens.

Using Adobe Bridge

The new Adobe Bridge provides a convenient, central location for accessing and managing your files and projects. With Adobe Bridge, you can easily locate, preview, and group your project files. Adobe Bridge also provides access to Version Cue's file tracking and organization tools.

Navigating and viewing files

1   Click Bridge Center in the upper left corner of the Bridge window, located under the Favorites tab. The Bridge Center window is displayed.

Use Bridge Center to easily access the Creative Suite 2 documents you've most recently accessed, including those from Illustrator, InDesign, and Photoshop. These are saved in the Recent Folders and Recent Files sections of this window.

2   Click the Folders tab in the upper left corner of the Bridge window, and navigate to locate the Lesson15 folder that you copied to your computer. In the Folders tab, click to select the Lesson15 folder.

All the files in this folder are displayed.

Adobe Bridge provides previews of all Creative Suite 2 documents, including multi-page PDF files.

3   Click once to select the envelope.ai file. Adobe Bridge displays a larger preview of the selected file beneath the Folders tab, along the left side of the Bridge window. Additional information is displayed in the lower left corner of the window.

Keep the envelope.ai file selected.

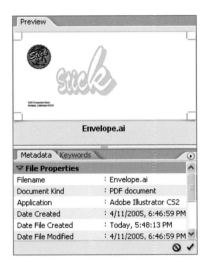

4   Press the Shift key and then click to select the Stationery.ai file. Both the envelope and stationery files should remain selected.

5   Choose File > Open to open both files using Adobe Illustrator CS2.

You can use Adobe Bridge to locate and open your files. Keep the two files open.

Saving File Groups

1   Click Adobe Bridge in your Taskbar (Windows) or Launcher (Mac OS) to return to Adobe Bridge.

2   Click the Favorites Tab in the upper left corner, then click Bridge Center. In Bridge Center, click Save open files into a file group, located under the Saved File Groups section, in the center portion of the window.

In the Adobe Bridge window that opens, enter the name **Surf letterhead and envelope** and click OK. All open files in Creative Suite 2 applications are then saved as a file group. If you were to return to Illustrator, you would see that both of the files you had previously opened are now closed.

3   Click once to select the Surf letterhead and envelope group you created in the previous step, and click Open this file group. All the files in the file group are reopened. In this case, both Illustrator files reopen.

Working with Version Cue

If you own Adobe Creative Suite Standard or Premium, you can take advantage of Adobe Version Cue, an integrated workflow feature designed to help you be more productive by saving you, and others you work with, valuable time.

With Version Cue, you can easily create, manage, and find different versions of your project files. If you collaborate with others, you and your team members can share project files in a multi-user environment that protects content from being accidentally overwritten. You can also maintain descriptive comments with each file version, search embedded file information to quickly locate files, and work with robust file-management features while working directly within each application.

Note: The Version Cue workspace is a feature of Adobe Creative Suite. If you purchased Adobe GoLive CS2, Adobe Illustrator CS2, Adobe InCopy CS2, Adobe InDesign CS2, or Adobe Photoshop CS2 separately, and don't own Adobe Creative Suite, you can use the Version Cue feature in your Adobe CS2 application only if an owner of Adobe Creative Suite gives you network access to their Version Cue workspace.

If you previously installed Version Cue, it must be turned on. Open the Adobe Version Cue preferences from the Control Panel (Windows) or System Preferences (Mac OS), and choose On from the Version Cue drop-down menu.

Creating a new project and adding files

1   In Adobe Illustrator CS2, click the Go to Bridge button (🖼) in the Control palette. In Adobe Bridge choose Tools > Version Cue > New Project.

- For Project Location choose the default workspace on your computer.

- For Project Name enter **Surf Company Identity**.

- For Project Info enter **Create new logo and supporting materials for surf company**.

Click OK

The new project creates a location where you can store and track all the documents for a particular project. You can drag items into the project from your operating system folders, or save directly to the project from within your Creative Suite 2 applications.

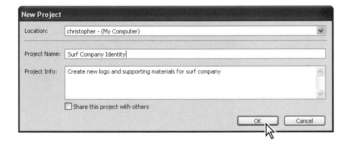

2   Return to Adobe Illustrator. Click to select the envelope and choose File > Save As. In the Save As dialog box, click the Use Adobe Dialog button in the lower left corner.

3   In the Save As dialog box, click Version Cue along the left side and double-click to open the Surf Company identity in the right side of the dialog box. Click the Save As button. In the Illustrator Options window, click OK.

A version of the file is now saved in Version Cue in the Surf Company Identity project.

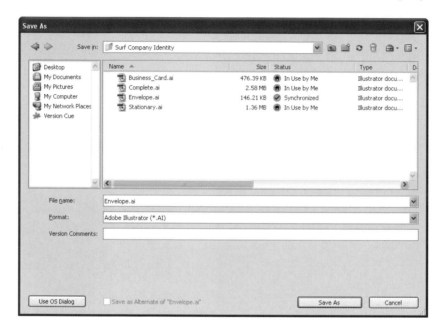

Note: *If Version Cue is not available in your Save As dialog box, you may need to enable the Version Cue preference in Adobe Illustrator CS2. In Illustrator CS2, choose Edit > Preferences > File Handling & Clipboard (Windows) or Illustrator > Preferences > File Handling & Clipboard (Mac OS). Select Enable Version Cue, and click OK.*

4   Close the envelope file by choosing File > Close. Keep Adobe Illustrator CS2 open.

💡 *You can also add files into a Version Cue project by dragging them into the Version Cue window directly from the operating system.*

5   In the Stationery.ai file, repeat the process used in the previous step, using the Save As command to save a copy of this file into the Surf Company Identity project in Version Cue.

6   In the Stationery.ai file, choose the Direct Selection tool. Click to select the background of the logo, positioned in the upper left corner of the stationery.

7 In the Control palette, click the Fill box and choose the color orange, replacing the brown gradient in the logo.

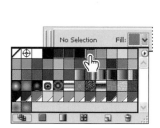 

8 Choose File > Save a Version. The Save a Version dialog box opens. In the dialog box, enter **Changed logo color to orange, per client request**. Click the Save button. An alternate version of the original file is saved.

Working with file versions

File versioning with Version Cue ensures that no one overwrites the work of anyone else in a Version Cue project, but also prevents users from locking out others who need to work on the same file. You can use versioning to seamlessly retain multiple states of a single file as you work on it, in case you need to restore the file to a previous version. You can also use versioning to quickly compare file versions with team members or with a client before selecting a final version.

1   Click the Go to Bridge button (▣) in the Control Palette, then click the Version Cue icon in the Favorites tab on the left side of the window.

2   Double-click to open the Surf Company Identity project folder. Move your cursor over the Stationery file and pause, waiting for the Tool Tip to appear. Note that the Tool Tip indicates that the file has two versions.

3   Right-click (Windows) or Ctrl+click (Mac OS) on the stationery icon, and choose Versions from the context menu. The Versions window opens.

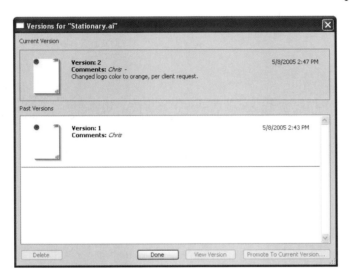

4   Click the icon for Version 1 and click Promote to Current Version. The Save a Version window opens. In the Save a Version window, enter **Client liked original design better** in the comment section, then click Save.

Bridge now displays the current version. Other versions can be viewed at any time by choosing the Versions command.

💡 *You can also view versions of a document by clicking the Versions and alternates view icon in the lower right corner of the document window.*

Version Cue Workspace Administration

By default, you can easily share your Version Cue projects with your peers by choosing the Share this project with others option when creating the project. If your environment requires a more secure workflow, you can set up a controlled environment in which users have to log in before accessing your Version Cue projects. Using the Version Cue Workgroup Administration utility, you can set up user IDs and define their project privileges, remove file locks, edit Version Cue Workspace preferences, and perform other project and workspace maintenance.

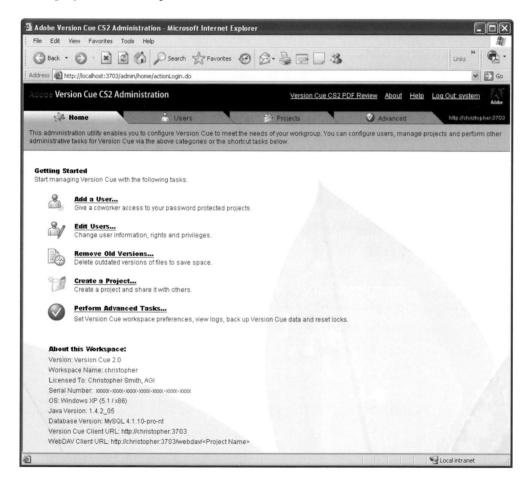

To display the Version Cue Workspace Administration utility log-in page, open the Adobe Version Cue preferences from the Control Panel (Windows) or System Preferences (Mac OS) on the computer where the Version Cue workspace is located, and click Advanced Administration.

For a more complete look at Bridge, Version Cue and all of the Creative Suite 2 features, choose Help > Version Cue Help. The *Adobe Creative Suite 2 Classroom in a Book* also provides a step-by-step guide to using the Creative Suite 2 tools and resources that enhance your ability to collaborate and manage your files and projects.

Organizing and locating files

Adobe Creative Suite 2 applications let you enter a wide variety of information about your documents in the File Info dialog box and in Adobe Bridge. Information added in the File Info dialog box gets embedded into a document as XMP metadata. For example, the metadata might contain a document's title, copyright, keywords, description, properties, author, and origin. Also, any comments you add to each file version when using Version Cue, which is discussed later in this lesson, are included in the file's metadata.

1   Open Adobe Bridge, and click Version Cue under the Favorites tab in the upper left corner of the window.

2   Double-click to open the Surf Company Identity project folder. All the items that are a part of this project are displayed.

3   Locate the Stationery.ai file and right-click (Windows) or Ctrl+click (Mac OS) and from the context menu, choose Label > Red. An Adobe Bridge warning message may appear, indicating that the label information is stored as part of the document metadata. Click OK to close the dialog box. A red label band appears along the bottom of the document. Keep the Stationery.ai file selected.

Note: *If the Stationery.ai file is still open, you will not be able to change the label. If the context menu for the Stationery.ai file does not display the Label option, you can perform this and the next step using the envelope.ai file instead.*

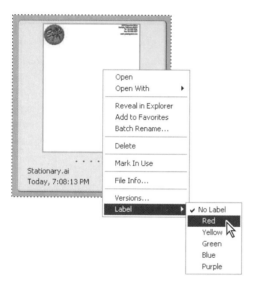

4   Choose Label > ✱✱✱. An Adobe Bridge warning message may appear, indicating that the label information is stored as part of the document metadata. Click OK to close the dialog box. Three stars appear inside of the red label band along the bottom of the document.

You can use color and star labels to help identify and locate your files.

5 Click the Unfiltered drop-down menu in the upper right corner of the Adobe Bridge window. Choose Show Red Label. Only the item labeled as red is displayed. The drop-down menu in the upper right corner now indicates that the view is being filtered—it is showing only selected items. Click the Filtered drop-down menu and choose Show All Items.

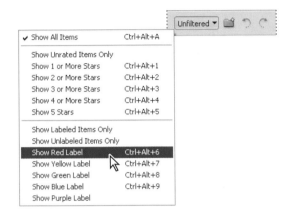

You can also use the Find command available in Adobe Bridge to locate files based upon their name, label, or other metadata. In Adobe Bridge, choose Edit > Find and enter the search criteria you wish to use.

Congratulations! You have finished the lesson.

Exploring on your own

Create your own Version Cue project. Add files to the project, create multiple versions and alternates of the files in the project.

Open Adobe Bridge, then add files to the Favorites section. Label additional files using colors and stars.

Review

▶ **Review questions**

1   What type of files can be accessed using Adobe Bridge?

2   What are the advantages of using Version Cue?

3   Do all participants in a Version Cue workflow need to have Adobe Creative Suite 2?

▶ **Review answers**

1   Adobe Bridge allows you to access all the files that you can normally access through your computer, including files stored on other computers or servers. Additionally, you can use Adobe Bridge to access files that are part of Version Cue projects that are either on your computer or on other computers if the project has been shared.

2   Version Cue provides immediate access to multiple variations of files. When files are part of a Version Cue project, the original design remains safe, as each subsequent revision does not overwrite the original file. Version Cue projects can easily be set up for sharing among other users of Adobe Creative Suite 2 applications.

3   Users of individual Adobe Creative Suite 2 applications can still participate in Version Cue projects, provided that the project has been set up for sharing. This applies to users of Photoshop, Illustrator, InDesign, GoLive, and Acrobat.

Index

A

Actual Size command 41
Actions 109-111, 124, 338
Add-anchor-point tool 39
Adobe Bridge 378, 403-404, 432-435, 437, 440, 442-445
Adjust Colors filter 387
Adobe GoLive 436
Adobe Illustrator
  compared to Adobe Photoshop, 375, 377, 379, 391, 436
Adobe Photoshop
  compared to Adobe Illustrator 375, 379, 392, 436
  exporting editable type to 375, 392
aligning
  objects 19
anchor points 60-61, 64, 76, 91, 103, 116-120, 123-125, 130, 132-133, 139, 218, 231, 247, 253
Anti-alias option 392
appearance attributes
  adding 131, 318, 320, 324, 327
  applying 26-27, 90, 131, 172, 225, 227, 316, 323, 325, 327, 329-330
  changing globally 314
  copying 330
  editable 344
  editing 200
  rearranging 319
  removing 330
Appearance palette 26-27, 90, 154, 159, 164-165, 169, 226-227, 316-325, 330, 332, 348-350, 358

Apply Add Arrowhead command 131
Apply To Strokes command 289, 295, 310, 313
Arc tool 74
Area Type tool 183
arrowheads
  adding 134
Art brushes 277-278, 283, 289, 294, 312
artboard 36
artwork
  printable and nonprintable 36
  scrolling 44
  viewing 33, 37, 41, 153, 216, 218, 339
Assign Current Working Space option 419, 426
Attributes palette 35, 69, 91, 426

B

batch processing 108, 110
bitmap images 101, 334, 374-376, 384
black color box 155
bleeds 414
Blend Options dialog box 245-246, 249
Blend tool 17, 232-233, 246, 249, 253
blending colors 17, 235
blending objects
  creating a new blend 235
  modifying blend 239, 244
  specifying number of steps 249
bounding box
  displaying / hiding 58, 71
  rotating 58, 113
  scaling with 100

Bring To Front command 141, 298
brushes
  brush libraries 302, 311, 351
  changing color 286-289
  changing options 51, 283-289, 295-297, 301-304, 351
  creating 51, 145, 296, 298-299, 301, 311, 351
  custom 299-302
  editing paths with 282
  hiding and showing 278
  Scatter Brush 311
  pattern 171, 275, 286, 296, 298-299, 301-304, 310, 312, 352
  types 274-275, 278, 299, 312
  using 71, 277, 282-283, 291, 294, 296, 311-313, 351-352
  using fill color with 286-290
  using with the Paintbrush tool 280-282, 285, 291
Brushes palette
  menu 277-278, 283, 287, 289, 294, 296, 310, 313, 351
  New Brush button 301, 311
  View By Name command 279

C

Calligraphic brushes 278, 286, 294, 312
center point 69-70, 73, 85, 87, 91, 97, 112, 239
Character palette 24, 191, 216, 266
choke trap 424
Clear Appearance button 325
Clear Guides command 309
clipping masks 222-223, 394
closed paths 134

Production Notes

The *Adobe Illustrator Classroom in a Book* was created electronically using Adobe InDesign. Art was produced using Adobe InDesign, Adobe Illustrator, and Adobe Photoshop. The Myriad Pro and Minion Pro OpenType families of typefaces were used throughout this book.

References to company names in the lessons are for demonstration purposes only and are not intended to refer to any actual organization or person.

A special thank you to istockphoto.com for supplying photographic images.

Images

Photographic images and illustrations are intended for use with the tutorials.

Images provided by istockphoto.com: Tour, Lesson 1, Lesson 6, Lesson 13.

Image provided by Clipart.com: Lesson 2 (French fries), Lesson 9 (ballplayer).

Typefaces used

Adobe Chaparral Pro, Adobe Garamond Pro, and Myriad Pro are used throughout the lessons. More information about OpenType and Adobe fonts is located inside the Studio folder on the *Adobe Illustrator Classroom in a Book* CD.

Team credits

The following individuals contributed to the development of new and updated lessons for this edition of the *Adobe Illustrator CS2 Classroom in a Book*:

Project coordinator, technical writer: Jennifer M. Smith

Additional technical writing: Christopher G. Smith, Greg Urbaniak

Production: AGI Training: Elizabeth Chambers

Proofreading: Jay Donahue

Technical Editors: Joda Alian, Cathy Auclair, Eric Rowse, Patti Scully-Lane